THE WAY TO
LORD'S
CRICKETING LETTERS
TO THE TIMES

THE WAY TO LORD'S

CRICKETING LETTERS TO THE TIMES

SELECTED AND INTRODUCED BY
MARCUS WILLIAMS

WILLOW BOOKS
Collins
8 Grafton Street, London W1
1983

Willow Books
William Collins Sons & Co. Ltd
London · Glasgow · Sydney · Auckland
Toronto · Johannesburg

First published 1983
Introduction, notes and selection
© Marcus Williams 1983
Williams, Marcus
Cricketing letters to The Times
1. Cricket – History – Sources
I. Title
796.358′09′33   GV913

ISBN   0 00 218010 3

Photoset in Linotron Times by
Rowland Phototypesetting Ltd.
Bury St Edmunds, Suffolk
Made and printed in Great Britain by
Robert Hartnoll Ltd, Bodmin

——CONTENTS——

THE WAY TO LORD'S

From Mr D. M. Brittain, 25 June 1968

Sir, Now I know that this country is finished. On Saturday, with Australia playing, I asked a London cabby to take me to Lord's, and had to show him the way.

Your obedient servant,

D. M. BRITTAIN

—ACKNOWLEDGEMENTS—

I must place on record my indebtedness to Gordon Phillips, cricket fanatic, former Archivist of *The Times*, and still, after all my unreasonable demands, a good friend. Without his tireless research and devotion to duty, always conducted with good humour, *The Way to Lord's* would have proved all but impassable. I must also thank all those who have, so readily, met our requests for information and assistance, particularly: John Woodcock; Richard Streeton; James Coldham; David Frith; Leon Pilpel, Letters Editor of *The Times*; Colin Wilson, Librarian of *The Times*, and his staff; Anne Piggott, Archivist and Records Manager of *The Times*; and Stephen Green, Jack Bailey and Jim Fairbrother of MCC; as well as Tim Jollands, of Collins Willow, for remembering me. I must additionally thank D. M. Brittain, and the now forgotten sub-editor who wrote the heading, for the letter which gives this book its title. Reference has been made to a multitude of cricket and other reference books, most extensively to *Wisden Cricketers' Almanack* (almost every edition) and *Barclays World of Cricket*.

Every effort has been made by myself and the publishers to trace the writers of the letters or their heirs and executors. Inevitably we have not always met with success in tracking down the correspondents. To those whom it has been impossible to trace we would express the hope that they will find pleasure in the reproduction of their letters in these pages. To the many who have given permission for their letters to be reproduced, special thanks are due. Regrettably the letters of some of those contacted have had to be omitted for reasons of space.

————FOREWORD————

While writing about a match at the Oval in 1968 I was approached by Ken Barrington, who had decided, rather to his surprise, that there were certain things he wanted to say about 'the modern game'. It should be realized, by the way, that the term 'the modern game', used disparagingly or to evoke memories of days gone by, is almost as old as the game itself. Having discussed the matter with Geoffrey Howard, the then Secretary of Surrey, Ken had come to the conclusion that his best platform would be the correspondence columns of *The Times*. Could that be arranged?

Well, the letter was duly sent and, happily, published, and it is now, with some 360 others, republished. It was a nice compliment to Ken that he should have been 'put in first', at the top of the page. But, as will be seen from this fascinating book, he is only one of a remarkable collection of famous players who have written to *The Times*.

I thought, until I tried, that I would choose an eleven from them. It is 'impossible'. 'W.G.' (The Law of Leg-Before-Wicket, 1901) would, of course, be captain. But who would he want to take in with him? He could have:
A. C. MacLaren (The Fourth Test Match, 1919), P. F. Warner (Over the Pavilion at Lord's, 1935, and others), F. S. Jackson (MCC and the Australian Team, 1908), C. B. Fry (Failure to Score, 1954), R. H. Spooner (Rugby v Marlborough, 1955), G. L. Jessop (MCC and the Australian Team, 1908), F. Mitchell (A Plea for Better Play, 1930), D. R. Jardine (Keeping Cricket Alive, 1947), D. S. Sheppard (Risks of Going Ahead, 1970, and others), R. Subba Row (The Real Test, 1980), G. Boycott (A Cricketer's Plans, 1978) or J. M. Brearley (Racial Bias and Test Cricket, 1969), all of whom, in their day, opened an England innings. Of England's first five batsmen in 'W.G.'s' last Test Match, against Australia at Trent Bridge in 1899, K. S. Ranjitsinhji (Ranjitsinhji's American Cricket Team, 1899, and another), as well as Jackson, Fry and 'W.G.' himself, were, at some time or other, moved to do as Barrington did.

There are no fewer than 16 England captains, and as many others,

ix

most of them among the great names of the game, who won England caps. Learie Constantine (Risks of Going Ahead, 1970) is here, representing West Indies; Australia are represented by Richie Benaud (Not Cricket?, 1967) and J. W. Trumble (Cricket Reform, 1926). What a galaxy! And what a splendid idea to make a collection of their letters. Although those who bat outnumber those who bowl (the reason for this could make the subject for further correspondence) there are plenty of bowlers to go round. A. G. Steel (Present-day Cricket, 1909), A. O. Jones (The Duties of Umpires, 1909), Sammy Woods (Test Match Critics, 1921), B. J. T. Bosanquet (The Leg-Trap Theory, 1933), F. H. Tyson (Racial Bias and Test Cricket, 1969), F. S. Trueman (Yorkshire's Cricket Troubles, 1978), besides Constantine and Benaud: speed, spin, brute force and guile – they are all there.

In 29 years as Cricket Correspondent of *The Times* I have been put off my breakfast more often than I care to remember by the slips and errors either of one's own making or someone else's. How easily, for example, a 'dutiful spell of bowling' can sound, over the telephone, like a 'beautiful spell of bowling' or 'Qadir really spun the ball' can appear as 'Qadir rarely spun the ball'. Because he knows his cricket so well, Marcus Williams, when he is in the office, has a genius for spotting the 'wrong 'un'. Now countless others can be grateful to him, too, for having opened, I promise you, a treasure chest. As a history of cricket, *The Way to Lord's* is unique.

JOHN WOODCOCK
April 1983

———INTRODUCTION———

One recent Editor of *The Times* told me that an irate reader had written complaining of the decline in the standard of the letters' page since he had assumed office. Everyone is, of course, entitled to an opinion and since 2 January 1785 people have been inflicting theirs upon the conductor of the letters' column which certainly has the most prestige and probably the greatest influence. Letters to the Editor number about 200 daily – at times of national or international crisis the total may treble – but only some 15 of those letters appear in print, although all correspondents receive a polite and often personal reply. Just as the Abdication of Edward VIII, the Suez affair, and the Pope and the pill have in the last 50 years provoked readers of *The Times* to put pen to paper or paper to typewriter, so have Bodyline, the lbw law and Kerry Packer. Cricket has inspired more letters to *The Times* than all other sports put together – hence this collection of the best of them.

Cricket has always mattered to *The Times*, since, in its infancy as the *Daily Universal Register*, it proffered the following advice to cricketers on 22 June 1785:

'It is recommended to the Lordling Cricketers who amuse themselves in White Conduit Fields, to procure an Act of Parliament for inclosing their play ground, which will not only prevent their being incommoded, but protect themselves from a repetition of the severe rebuke which they justly merit, and received on Saturday evening from some spirited citizens whom they insulted and attempted *vi et armis* to drive from the foot path, pretending it was within their bounds.'

Twelve days later it reported, with thankfully shorter sentences, that in a 'grand match' those same gentlemen of the White Conduit Club, their innings opened and their team captained by Lord Winchelsea, had beaten Kent 'by a majority of 306', Kent being dismissed in their second innings for a mere 28. Two years later the White Conduit Club moved from Islington to Lord's and subsequently merged with the Marylebone Cricket Club. The rest is history, not a little of which is reflected in the following pages by many eminent correspondents. Although the earliest letter included is

1

dated August 1874, aged correspondents writing to the Editor in the early years of the twentieth century reminisce about the 1840s and 1850s with memories of Wisden, Lillywhite, Caffyn and Clarke.

When MCC celebrated its 150th anniversary in 1937, *The Times* published a magnificent supplement in honour of the occasion. The MCC President at the time was Major the Hon. J. J. Astor (Eton and Buckinghamshire), later Colonel Lord Astor of Hever, a useful opening batsman and a rackets player good enough to win the Public Schools and Army championships. He was also proprietor of *The Times*, so in the President of MCC's message in the supplement he had to thank himself. *The Times* later published a Special Report on Cricket on 21 June 1973. It was of a more general scope than the MCC Number but was just as comprehensive.

I would imagine that some originals of the MCC Number, with their portrait of Thomas Lord on the front page enclosed within a decorative cricketing border, have been lovingly preserved. They were offered gratis with the newspaper of 25 May 1937, which cost 2½d (1p). For 1s (5p) *The Times* additionally offered the supplement reprinted in book form, bound in stout, dark blue boards and bearing the MCC's familiar colours. It is profusely illustrated and covers the game from Test matches to village green, as well as containing chapters on umpiring (by Frank Chester), scoring (Herbert Strudwick) and cricket books (Edmund Blunden).

The section dealing with Lord's and its Founder was written by Lieutenant-Colonel R. S. Rait-Kerr, MCC Secretary from 1936 to 1952, who in a formal letter, published on 15 July 1937, thanked the Editor for the MCC Number:

Sir, I am instructed by the MCC Committee to convey to you the grateful thanks of the committee and members of the Marylebone Cricket Club for the great care and trouble that *The Times* has devoted to the production of the special number dealing with the MCC.

This publication has been acclaimed in cricket circles as one of great interest, and provides a permanent record for which there has been a long-felt want.

The republication of the supplement in book form has added to the debt of gratitude due to *The Times*, and it is hoped that its reception has been as good as it deserves.

Yours faithfully,
R. S. RAIT-KERR, Secretary, MCC

Among the other contributors were Sir John Squire (cricket fanatic and founder of the Invalids CC), Alfred Cochrane (cricket versifier and author), P. G. H. Fender (outstanding captain of Surrey, though never of England) and Sir Home Gordon (cricket writer and spectator from 1878 to 1956); all have letters reproduced in this book. Fender, soon after his ninetieth birthday in 1982, wrote to the Editor of *The Times* about the modern world. The letter was not published, but a thoughtful, cricket-loving sub-editor sent a personal reply, with best wishes for 'one more hundred'.

I have hinted at the range of the cast list and in his foreword John Woodcock has given an idea of the cricketing talent represented among the letters. He is, incidentally, the latest (since 1954) in a distinguished line of cricket correspondents of *The Times*. Remarkably for a newspaper with such a sense of history, particularly its own, the archives possess no precise record of those correspondents; the researcher's task is made no easier by the fact that until 20 January 1967 they were concealed behind the anonymous signature of 'Our Cricket Correspondent'. John Woodcock was the first of the specialist staff correspondents to be named in the paper.

A likely list of his predecessors on the staff would be: Charles Box (*c*.1867–80), G. H. West (1880–96), Sydney H. Pardon (1896–1910), A. C. M. Croome (1910–30), R. B. Vincent (1930–51), Geoffrey Green (1951–54). Like Woodcock now, West and Pardon were also editors of *Wisden*. Regular contributions on cricket to *The Times* have come in the past from such renowned names as P. F. Warner, H. S. Altham, E. B. Noel, C. F. Pardon (also an editor of *Wisden*), F. B. Wilson, H. D. G. Leveson Gower, the Hon G. W. and R. H. Lyttelton, R. C. Robertson-Glasgow, A. A. Thomson, Denzil Batchelor, Charles Bray, Dudley Carew, C. L. R. James, Jack Fingleton and Neville Cardus. William Denison (1801–56), described as the father of daily newspaper cricket reporting, was another and there have been many more. One anecdote about them: 'Beau' Vincent, of *The Times*, and Raymond Robertson-Glasgow, of the *Morning Post*, walking in Manchester in the 1930s, espied two placards displayed adjacently. 'Read R. C. Robertson-Glasgow in the *Morning Post*,' urged one; 'Read *The Times* and see what really happened,' proclaimed the other. By a strange twist of fate, when Vincent was taken ill on the 1950–51 MCC tour of Australia, Robertson-Glasgow stood in for him as *The Times*' special correspondent; moreover, his reports of the Test matches were published in book form.

3

When I was first asked to compile this anthology neither the publishers nor I were aware just how many letters had been published by *The Times* on cricket. The fruits of the correspondence columns have been culled several times but never on a specialized topic. Initial reaction from colleagues within the paper was welcoming though sceptical about the number of letters that had been published about cricket. Hundreds of letters and hours of delight later I can assure them that there have been many; I lost count with the total in the region of the world record first-class score (1107) and still a long way to go. It soon became a matter of not what to include but of what to leave out.

As a starting point one knew that writers of letters to *The Times* had had their say in recent years on issues like the D'Oliveira affair, South Africa, Packer, the Yorkshire turmoils, umpiring and the Centenary Test flop, probably also clergymen had inveighed against Sunday cricket. Further back there was Bodyline and Harry Furniss's famous letter of 1900 encouraging 'arson' at Lord's. With the enlistment of Gordon Phillips, whose many years' experience as Archivist of *The Times* (and equally important, a passion for cricket) was invaluable, the real search began.

A trawl of the letter cuttings in *The Times* Intelligence Department (the library, not a school for Smileys or assessment centre for the gifted) produced the first stitches of a rich seam. The brief, witty gems, such as the letter which gives this book its title, were accompanied by offerings from the likes of Sir Alan Herbert, Sir Pelham Warner, C. B. Fry and B. J. T. Bosanquet (and many of his relatives), not to mention the Hon. R. H. Lyttelton and F. G. J. Ford campaigning vigorously for reform of the lbw law. You would think it hard to enliven such a dry topic, but Ford – 'six feet two of don't care' they called him for his carefree approach to batting – at various times described the pad-play which necessitated the change as: 'the evil microbe'; 'the *fons et origo mali*'; 'this curse of modern cricket which has eaten into the very soul of the game and cast a slur upon the moral value of the very word "cricket" '. He demanded that it be stamped out 'like an earwig under the boot'.

Wisden, as ever, was a mine of information – and a constant diversion – with letters to *The Times* sometimes reprinted and with helpful references such as 'the now famous letter' of F. S. Jackson on the abortive 1909 Triangular Tournament; 'lengthy correspondence in *The Times*' on manifold issues which have long since slipped from memory, and to Lord Harris's eightieth birthday message (sent at the invitation of the then Editor of *The Times*, Geoffrey Dawson). At the same time began the laborious search through the Index to *The Times*, where every reference to cricket in the paper would be found – or so it was believed. In the early days what was indicated with the letter L might be a letter to the Editor or a leading article or what would now be termed a report from a special correspondent. Even in more sophisticated modern days, letters which came to light from other sources were found not to have been indexed. But enough of technicalities.

We were still, if not in the dark, at least in twilight about the number of cricketing letters; but when, gradually, the signatures of cricket's Golden Age giants like Ranjitsinhji, W. G. Grace (much surprise here because one gathered that he read only *The Sportsman*), Lord Harris (often), A. G. Steel, A. C. MacLaren and G. L. Jessop emerged, it was clear that bad light would not stop play. I also derived much pleasure from finding a letter by Professor Thomas Case, President of my old college, Corpus Christi, long-time official of Oxford University CC and once a player for Oxford University and Middlesex; he suggested, perhaps with a touch of donnish humour, that umpires should call 'nears' as well as wides to combat pad-play.

Not only cricketers, of course, have written to *The Times* about the game; the fields of politics, literature and journalism, as well as Academe, are strongly represented. The presence of men of the cloth, traditional devotees of the game, goes without saying. John Woodcock has already mentioned the difficulties of picking an eleven from the Test cricketers, but, following the schoolboy pastime of choosing elevens of Greeks to play Romans, the World to play Mars, or those whose names begin with B and were born in a month with a Y; I offer these teams of letter writers which are in alphabetical order and not necessarily based on their cricketing abilities. I leave it to braver readers to work out the batting order and to decide whether Sir James Barrie (Allahakbarries) or Sir John Squire (Invalids) should captain the literary team, Lord Harris or Field-Marshal Montgomery the Lords and Commons, and the Hon. R. H. Lyttelton or Sir Neville Cardus the cricket writers:

LORDS AND COMMONS: the Lords Buckmaster, Chalfont, Chelmsford, Cobham, Cornwallis, Darling, Harris and Montgomery, the Hon. F. S. Jackson, Major G. Lloyd-George, A. M. Crawley.

AUTHORS AND PUBLISHERS: Sir James Barrie, John Galsworthy,

Richard Gordon, Sir Alan Herbert, E. V. Lucas, A. A. Milne, Sir John Murray, Ned Sherrin, Sir John Squire, Ben Travers, Alec Waugh.

CRICKET WRITERS: John Arlott, Sir Neville Cardus, Dudley Carew, Alfred Cochrane, Frederick Gale, Alan Gibson, Sir Home Gordon, the Hon. R. H. Lyttelton, Robin Marlar, R. C. Robertson-Glasgow, Alan Ross.

One could also get up a pretty useful team of cricketing epistolarians who did not play Test cricket, starting with C. I. (Buns) Thornton, consistently the longest hitter the game has known, and the Hon. Edward Lyttelton, good enough to score the only hundred against the 1878 Australians and later Headmaster of Eton, and taking in Leonard Crawley, who devoted much of his attention to golf but was such a highly considered batsman that he was asked about his availability for the Bodyline tour. He was a forthright man and his letter on the subject allows us to speculate that he might have acted as a restraining influence on Jardine – but perhaps Jardine in 1932–33 was unfetterable!

All those so far mentioned were, of course, amateur players. Cricket dropped the distinction between amateurs and professionals in 1962 and the first full-time professional cricketer to have a letter published in *The Times* was the late Ken Barrington. He has since been followed into print by Fred Trueman and Geoffrey Boycott; no doubt there will be others.

What strikes one most about the letters themselves is that there is no new thing under the sun or any other of the climatic conditions which beset cricket. That the game is dying, or dead, was a popular theory in the last century, but years ahead of their time correspondents to *The Times* were recommending the cancellation of a tour by South Africa (1901); Sunday play in Test matches (1926); a 100-over limit on the first innings in county cricket (1928); or denouncing overseas players in the English game (1909) and the readiness of players to leave the field for bad light (1913).

The letters inevitably reflect the periods during which they were written. Thus Latin and even Greek quotations are quite common up to the Second World War and, in the more verbose days before the First World War, Ranji could write more than a column on the state of the game and say at the end that he had written 'as briefly as possible'. Nowadays he would have received a polite telephone call from the letters' department requesting some cuts.

Until the takeover by Lord Thomson in 1966 and the regular

appearance of news instead of classified advertisements on the front page, *The Times* was a mostly serious, heavy newspaper, seeming often to be written by specialists for specialists. Humour did, however, peep through in the fourth leaders and in letters: thus, in 1896 a correspondent represented the county championship points system as an algebraic formula, perhaps blinding by apparent science, although I am sure he had his tongue in his cheek; in 1926 when debate was raging on cricket reform, a letter in best yokel English from an imaginary village was published.

Wit is frequently an element in modern letters and it is for their entertainment value that many have been selected to take their place alongside letters which make serious cricketing points, some of which have a seminal position in the game's history. A letter published in *The Times* about cricket assuredly finds its way to Lord's and readers will observe how many suggestions have been followed, directly or indirectly, immediately or some time later, by the desired action at headquarters. It was also commonplace for lobbyists to fire off a letter to *The Times* shortly before the MCC annual general meeting or special general meeting at which changes in the laws were to be debated. The response that a letter generates is illustrated by a correspondent in 1930 who wrote a second time to say that he had received 46 replies to a query about a particular big hit at Lord's.

Because there are so many recurrent themes in cricket history the letters have been grouped thematically rather than chronologically They are, however, arranged chronologically (by dates of publication) within their sections, except to emphasize a point, to point a contrast, or to unfold, for example, the story of England v Australia.

In order that the letters should enjoy the widest appreciation notes have been added to put them in their historical context and to show what, if anything, happened as a consequence. I trust that the notes will enhance enjoyment of the letters; cricket historians will probably not need them, although they may, I hope, discover topics which are new or, at least, long dormant.

The letter writers' biographies presented a problem, not least in that some of the personalities warrant, or have been favoured by, a book to themselves. An attempt has been made to illustrate their standing not only in cricket, by the briefest details of their careers at the top level (with dates in brackets), but also in the wider world, by an outline of their fields of activity and major achievements. No claim is made to comprehensiveness; the biographies, which as a rule appear on a correspondent's first letter in the collection, are intended only as a guide and for brevity's sake, in the case of letters with many signatories, only those with major cricketing connections are identified. Those without biographies are in no way intended to be considered lesser mortals or letter writers: far from it. The old myth that one *had* to be an MP or a member of the Athenaeum (or other West End club) or a QC or an Oxford don or a Bishop to have a letter published in *The Times* has long been debunked. Readers will also notice several anonymous letters, signed either with noms de plume – A Student of Cricket History, Senior, Forty Years On – or with initials, even as late as 1950 (they would not be accepted for publication now). Identification, except in a few instances, is all but impossible.

The text of the letters is, with a very few exceptions, as it appeared in *The Times*. The policy of the newspaper is that published letters should be in the writers' own words and any amendments are made only with their approval. However, to avoid irrelevant matter or superfluous notes to explain minor errors of fact, small liberties have been taken; I trust that no one will be offended. In a few cases, too, the headings of the letters have been altered where the originals proved to be inappropriate.

Since statistics play a considerable part in cricket the following may be of interest: the longest cricket letter, as already stated, was Ranji's one and a bit colums (the longest letter published is seven and a half columns on the Dreyfus case in 1898); the shortest Dr Birts's four words – plus sign-off – on the George Davis affair in 1975. The most frequent writers, at least in terms of letters published, have all been closely associated with the game – Lord Harris, the Hon. R. H. Lyttelton, P. F. (later Sir Pelham) Warner and F. G. J. Ford.

The largest correspondence on a cricketing matter was provoked by the abortive 1970 South African tour with well over a hundred letters published in a period of several months; it is a sign of the times that this – and many of the other recent burning issues – had mainly political tones. Bodyline, also political in view of the threatened rift between Australia and England, had more than 40 in a little over a month. Cricket reform has for a hundred years encouraged the picking-up of the pen: 'High Scores and Drawn Matches', a series of articles by 'An Old Blue' (Sir Courtenay Boyle) in 1899, encouraged a weighty correspondence; but this was nothing compared to the response to a speech by Lord Harris (who else?) in 1926 on the need for further measures to help the bowler, who was still on the wrong end of the high scores. Letters were published on the topic daily for more than three weeks, nine (a record) appearing on one day. Among the dottier ideas were that batsmen should discard their pads; the ball should have two criss-cross seams; a batsman who plays out a maiden over should automatically be out; and pitching, baseball-style, should be permitted.

Correspondence on subjects like Old Cricket Customs, A Cricket Curiosity or Women at Cricket might also rumble on for weeks, usually to be found in 'Points from Letters', between the wars a useful depository whose title is self-explanatory. Those letters in the book which appear to have been concluded without the usual courtesies originally, almost without exception, appeared there. Talking of the courtesies, members of staff (who are now barred from the letters' column) signed often 'obediently' or 'obedient servant'; Lord Harris 'faithfully'; Field-Marshal Montgomery 'sincerely'; and W. G. Grace 'W. G. Grace'. The letters can now speak for themselves and I sign myself 'hopefully'

MARCUS WILLIAMS
April 1983

1

SOFT BALLS, GOOGLIES AND SOSTENEUTERS

KENT v SURREY

From Lord Harris, 3 August 1906

George Robert Canning, fourth Lord Harris. Captained Oxford University, Kent and England (1870–1911). Cricket's most influential administrator. President and Secretary of Kent CCC. President (1895), Trustee and Treasurer of MCC. Under-Secretary for India, Under-Secretary for War and Governor of Bombay.

Sir, We who sit on the benches like to theorize about remarkable events at cricket; so I venture to send my theory as to one cause which influenced the collapse of the Surrey eleven yesterday. I believe it was due to a factor of which sufficient consideration is frequently not taken – viz., the wind.

I inquired about the wicket directly I got on to the ground yesterday morning, and was assured that it was as good as the previous evening, when Kent could make 300, and certainly the first 45 minutes' play bore out that description; although the first two batsmen [Hayward and Hobbs] scored but slowly and had to play very carefully, they did not appear to be in difficulties, and I certainly anticipated that, when we got to the best batsmen and the bowlers were getting tired, runs would come more easily.

I was sitting nearly opposite the pavilion and noticed that the wind was blowing at first almost directly in my face, but during that 45 minutes it was constantly freshening and backing against the sun, so that by the end of that time it was blowing almost directly against the sweep of Blythe's arm.

All credit belongs to Mr Mason for his admirable management of the bowling and his personal success, but I am sure he would admit that it was Blythe who won the match, so far as the Surrey second innings was concerned.

My theory is that the wind caused Blythe's ball to hang in its flight and break back from the pitch, and that this was the important influence in making Blythe as unplayable as he was. He is, of course, one of the best bowlers of his type that we have seen, but none of them – Jimmy Shaw, the Woottons, George and Jim, Martin, Rhodes, or any, however good they be – have ever met with such remarkable success on a good fast wicket unless there was some other influence assisting them; to entirely beat Hayward twice in a quarter of an hour is a remarkable performance, for we can say as truly of him as was written 50 years ago of his relative:–

'You may bowl your best at Hayward, and whatever style
   you try
Will be vanquished by the master's steady hand and certain
   eye.'

Some years ago at Canterbury, in a match against the Australians, Mr Burnup and an Australian bowler met with very remarkable success when bowling from the pavilion end against the wind, which was coming directly against the sweep of their arms; an extraordinary number of catches in the slips were made on that occasion; this was, again, I think, largely due to the ball hanging in the wind and then going away; at any rate, these two very similar incidents seem to me to give some justification for the theory I venture to propound.

Yours faithfully,

HARRIS

Blythe's figures were 20–12–25–5, Mason's 2.5–0–8–3 and Kent went on to win the championship.

KEEPING CRICKET ALIVE

From Mr D. R. Jardine, 5 July 1947
Oxford University and captain of Surrey and England (1920–34). Led MCC on the infamous Bodyline tour of Australia in 1932–33.

Sir, People say that they used 'to go and see Lohmann and Richardson bowl'. The same may be said of Barnes, McDonald, Larwood, Verity, and many others. Today, does anyone go to see anyone bowl?

No live game can expect to be static. Three comparatively recent changes covering the size of the wickets, the lbw rule, and the preparation of wickets all indicate that the authorities are aware that balance between bat and ball in first-class cricket needs periodic adjustment. All these recent changes, however, have one thing in common. All are only palliatives aimed at penalizing the bat and thereby only indirectly helping the bowler.

What I hope would command general agreement would be something to raise the morale of the bowler by directly increasing his ability to beat the bat by his own artistry on all wickets. Sticky wicket cricket is the cream of cricket for precisely this reason.

For a long time in conversation I have urged that there is an easy solution which would achieve the object. This is the substitution of the small cricket ball commonly in use at preparatory schools for the present full-sized ball.

In a man's hands this small ball, from the additional swerve and spin which can be imparted to it, should be capable of righting the present maladjustment between bat and ball. Further, it would ensure the production of bowling artists once more, as opposed to the many over-worked and uninspired substitutes doing duty today. I do suggest that it merits a serious consideration and trial.

Exclusive of the last Test match, could it not be tried for the last half of August, 1948, in all first-class matches? If successful when wickets are likely to be fast and true, bowlers weary at the end of a season and batsmen in form, the case for further experiment and gradual adoption would have been made out.

Of course there are cons: there always are. But it is not possible to deal with them adequately in a brief space. I would, however, urge that until the experiment is tried, neither the pros nor the cons can be at all accurately assessed.

I am, Sir, yours faithfully,

D. R. JARDINE

The size of the ball had been reduced in 1927 after the discovery that, two seasons earlier, balls smaller than regulation were in almost general use. The counties experimented with a still smaller ball in 1955, but it found no favour.

SWINGING THE BALL

From Mr A. P. Rossiter, 20 August 1953
Fellow and Tutor in English, Jesus College, Cambridge.

Sir, Permit me to raise a topical hare while examinable evidence is being supplied. Your Cricket Correspondent, writing on the Test match in your issue of 17 August, remarks 'It was overcast, ominous and sultry, so that Bedser, Trueman, and Bailey . . . were able to move the ball about disconcertingly in the air.' The broadcasting commentators have said the same kind of thing, the *Manchester Guardian* endorses it with 'The atmosphere of the morning . . . encouraged the late swinging ball'; but none the less I am of the opinion that these utterances belong to the realms of mythology rather than dynamics.

The very trivial differences in atmospheric density, whether from changes of pressure or humidity, cannot really be supposed to make any marked difference to the behaviour of a ball rotating in those particular ways which distinguish 'seam bowling'. Such is my contention; and as my dynamics are rusty and my bowling swings no more, no matter what the air, I put forward this view for the consideration of the scientifically sporting.

Yours, &c.,

A. P. ROSSITER

From Professor A. Veryan Stephens, 27 August 1953
Professor of Aeronautics, University of Sydney

Sir, Your correspondent Mr Rossiter is trying to blind cricketers with science. It would be better to enlighten commentators with common sense. That the ball swings farthest in damp air may be accepted as a matter of observation. That this is due to abnormally high air density or viscosity is manifestly absurd, but we must not discard evidence because a false explanation has been put forward. Although humidity has little effect upon the relevant properties of air, it does cause significant changes in the geometry of the cricket ball. In damp air the stitches round the seam swell, as your correspondent can verify for himself by holding a ball near the spout of a kettle.

Wind tunnel experiments at this university have shown that spin plays only a secondary part in swing bowling. The vital factor is the orientation of the seam. Spin merely serves to maintain the seam in the correct position. But it is one thing to know the correct position of the seam and quite another matter to put it there.

Yours, &c.,
A. VERYAN STEPHENS

IS IT CRICKET?

From Sir Alan Herbert, 4 September 1959
Author, wit and champion of many causes. Independent MP for Oxford University 1935–50. Knighted 1945. Companion of Honour 1970.

Sir, Mr A. W. Douglas asks in his letter on 1 September if a distinction should not be drawn between trouser-rubbing, intended 'to maintain the original condition of the ball', and rubbing in the dust that 'induces premature old age'.

No, Sir, or not much: for each is an interference with the course of nature not provided for by the laws of cricket. In general the good cricketer must accept the natural hazards which affect the wicket or 'the implements used'. 'Under no circumstances shall a pitch be watered during a match;' nor shall it be mown. The discontented batsmen may not send for a roller, or (it is presumed) pour their lemonades on the pitch. The bowler may not improve the ball with wax or resin, or 'lift the seam'.

But some exceptions are clearly made. After a certain period of wear and tear a new ball may be demanded. 'The batsman may beat the pitch with his bat' (I often wonder why). 'Players may secure their footholds by the use of sawdust'; and 'the bowler may dry the ball when wet on a towel or sawdust.' Nowhere do the laws say that he may rub the ball in the dust when dry to remove the shine or on his abdomen or bosom to preserve or increase the shine.

The first, no doubt, is morally the worse (it is like deliberately damaging the wicket): but the second is unseemly and ridiculous, and if continued may lead to new excesses. If a shirt, why not a brush – or a velvet pad sewn into the trousers? The batsman, too, may wish to keep the shine on the ball, whether to assist in its passage to the boundary or to outwit the bowler who has rubbed it in the dust.

If the umpires and captains have nothing to say, I hope that some aggrieved batsman will bring this question to a head, pick up a dead ball, produce his little polishing set – and see what happens.

Meanwhile, I suggest a simple amendment to law 46: 'The use of resin, wax, &c., by the bowler, *and any attempt by any player to alter the natural condition of the ball when dry, are forbidden*: but a bowler may dry the ball when wet, &c.'

I am, Sir, yours respectfully,
A. P. HERBERT

Polishing of the ball in first-class cricket was banned in 1966, although subsequently reallowed.

EASIER TO SEE

From Mr Alan C. McCallum, 18 August 1964

Sir, It is difficult for spectators at cricket matches to follow the ball from bowler to batsman. It is almost impossible on television to follow the same movement of the ball. When the light is bad, even the batsmen cannot see the ball and play is stopped. Why not use a white ball? It surely must help all to sight the ball easier – from players to spectators alike.

In baseball, where the pitcher throws the ball to the batter, a white ball is used, and I have never heard of 'bad light stopped play' in a baseball match.

Yours truly,
ALAN C. McCALLUM

From Major Rowland Bowen, 25 August 1964

Editor and proprietor, *The Cricket Quarterly*; cricket historian.

Sir, With reference to Mr McCallum's letter in your issue yesterday, there are three reasons why a white ball is unsuitable and a red ball suitable:–

(1) The ball during most of its period of flight is seen against a green background: it is only for a very short period that it is against any other background: if this is a sight-screen, white is manifestly

the wrong colour for the ball, and if it is a crowd, the mottled effect produced also makes a white ball unsuitable.

(2) A white ball, skied in the air, would in many circumstances which obtain, be very difficult to see for a fielder catching it.

(3) Red is the most suitable colour since (*vide* 1) the background is green for the greater part of the time: green and red are at opposite ends of the spectrum and since it is not possible for the human eye to bring both colours into focus simultaneously, it follows that the ball's colour is extremely suitable for the purpose.

The real trouble, of course, is that the ball does not stay red but becomes an ugly shade of dark brown: if balls, even old, were to retain their colour, there would be few sighting problems.

I am, Sir, your obedient servant,
ROWLAND BOWEN

A white ball for floodlit matches – and black sightscreens – was one of many innovations of Kerry Packer's World Series Cricket; it was subsequently used in Australia for all one-day internationals. In Australia in 1983 weight was given to Major Bowen's argument when both fielders and spectators complained of difficulty in sighting the white ball in bright light.

CRICKET WITH SOFT BALLS

From Mr Richard Gordon, 17 July 1971

Dr Gordon Ostlere. Anaesthetist and author. Dedicated supporter of Surrey.

Sir, These columns deplore the tumbling downfall of so many standards that I hesitate to become doomful about cricket balls. A few seasons ago it was unusual for the umpires to inspect the ball and possibly replace it with one of similar wear. Now it is commonplace. At Surrey v Somerset at the Oval last Saturday, for instance, this interrupted play more than once.

Cricketers tell me the modern ball is liable to start losing its shape and hardness after so few as three overs. Though unexpected variation in the state of the pitch is a splendid element of the game, unexpected variation in that of the ball should not be. Law Five regulates the weight and size of the ball, but it would be difficult to legislate for its hardness and durability.

Perhaps your ever-ingenious readers can supply the cause and cure of this degeneration? I don't think it is because modern cricketers hit harder.

I am, etc.
RICHARD GORDON

After years of irritating delays a British Standard (BS 5993) was introduced for cricket balls in 1981. It particularly specified hardness and resistance to wear.

LOBS

An article so titled was published in *The Times* on 21 August 1909

From the writer of 'Lobs', 26 August 1909

E. B. Osborn. Boxing correspondent for *The Times* – he was said to have boxed professionally in Canada – and authoritative critic of cricket and football. Subsequently Literary Editor of the *Morning Post*.

Sir, Mr Cutler's letter interests me much. It is helpful to know that the term 'lob' was used in its present technical sense 60 years ago. I have tried with scant success to find out when the term was first used on the cricket field, and am grateful for any scrap of first-hand information. Mr Cutler's contribution explodes my theory that 'lob' – a word with a somewhat comical look and sound – was invented by the earlier practitioners of over-hand bowling to express a good-natured contempt for old-fangled methods. Also, it pleases me to know that W. Clarke was called a 'pitcher of lobs'; for some years ago, when ordered to take the ball by the captain of a village eleven, the order was a polite request to 'pitch 'em some o' your lobs'. The good old phrases, like the good antique manners, still survive on the few remaining village greens where cricket is still played.

It was from a veteran cricketer – over whom the earth now rests lightly – that much of what I said about the incomparable Clarke was derived. He taught me as a small boy to bowl lobs with a high action, and was of opinion that lob-bowling was unwisely neglected by the cricketers of modern times. It is clear in my memory that he said Clarke did not trouble much about break, though glad to make use of a queer spot on the sporting wickets of his day. The knack of making his balls 'get up' was, so this veteran assured me, the secret of his deadliness.

Curiously enough, I received from an American friend on the day of Mr Cutler's letter appeared an account of an attempt to revive underhand pitching in college baseball. The underhand 'pitcher' got great pace and had a good command of curves, and was very successful for a time. Perhaps this disestablished variant of the baseball pitcher will some day appear once more in the 'batteries' of first-rate teams.

I am, Sir, yours obediently,
THE WRITER OF 'LOBS'

William Clarke founded the Trent Bridge ground, Nottingham, in 1838 and the All-England XI of touring professionals in 1846. At his peak he averaged 340 wickets a season. Mr Cutler had faced Clarke when Clarke coached at Eton in the late 1840s.

UNDERHAND BOWLING

At the Oval in 1884 the Hon. Alfred Lyttelton, England's wicketkeeper, captured four Australian wickets for eight runs with lobs, while W. G. Grace took over the gloves. Declarations were not allowed at the time and Australia, having been 532 for six, were all out for 551.

From Revd the Hon. Edward Lyttelton, 3 September 1937

Cambridge University, Middlesex and Worcestershire (1875–82). Youngest but one – Alfred was the youngest – of eight brothers, seven of whom played for Eton. England football international and later headmaster of Haileybury and Eton.

Sir, Your correspondent alludes to the classic instance of the success of lobs when my brother Alfred secured four Australian wickets in the early eighties for almost no runs. I did not see the achievement, but guessed at the time that the batsmen got out on purpose. On inquiry I learn that two of them were bowlers – Spofforth and Boyle – and one the wicketkeeper, Blackham. If they did not literally get out on purpose they probably cared very little about making runs. The clue to the mystery seems to be that Lord Harris resolved to establish a record by giving every member of the team a chance with the ball; and to make sure of success he put on the wicketkeeper to bowl lobs, who, so far as I know, had never bowled a lob before, and certainly forebore to mar his reputation by bowling in any style again.

Yours faithfully,
E. LYTTELTON

From Sir Nigel Davidson, 6 July 1957

Legal Secretary, Sudan Government 1926–30.

Sir, I believe it was in the 1880s that Alfred Lyttelton, the English wicketkeeper, took off his pads and bowled the Australians out with lobs after all the bowlers had failed to move them. Some 10 years later, when I was a pupil in the great Alfred's chambers, he told me that the feat became an infernal nuisance, because in the succeeding matches, whenever the Australians made a stand of over 30, the crowd would stand up and yell, 'Put on Lyttelton!'

Yours faithfully,

NIGEL DAVIDSON

SHOULD THE MCC BOWL LOBS?

From Mr J. B. Byas, 22 June 1957

Captain of Cricket, Wellington School, Somerset.

Sir, Much discussion has arisen at our school in the past few days over a matter arising from a cricket match against the MCC.

The matter concerns the bowling of lobs by a member (a very distinguished one I may add) of the MCC team. In no way was it meant to be a sneer at the batsmen, and it is only fair to add that the bowler turned the ball a considerable amount in this way. It also brought him a wicket through a mishit off-drive. However, surely one of the objects of an MCC team is to show schoolboys how the game should be played, and the bowling of lobs, though within the letter of the laws in every respect, is carrying gamesmanship rather too far. Please do not think that the school team is offering any grouse, as we feel that any excuses are bound to bring a cry of 'sour grapes' from many people, and we certainly want to avoid this.

Yours faithfully,

JOHN BYAS

The distinguished MCC player was R. J. O. Meyer (Cambridge University and captain of Western India and Somerset, 1924–49), founder and headmaster of Millfield School.

From Mr F. T. Barrett, 25 June 1957

Sir, Why should Wellington feel aggrieved, as appears from the letter from the Captain of Cricket today, at being bowled lobs? I remember, as a schoolboy, seeing Walter Humphreys at Hove (his designedly long shirt sleeve flapping in the breeze) bowling his lobs at W. G. Grace. The great man did not object – he was probably grateful to Walter for giving him practice in how to deal with a turning ball. So should the modern schoolboy.

Yours faithfully,

FREDK. T. BARRETT

Humphreys twice performed the hat-trick for Sussex against the Australians. At the age of 45 he toured Australia with Stoddart's side of 1894–95 but had little success.

SNEAKING RESPECT

In a one-day match at Melbourne, New Zealand needed six runs off the last ball to tie with Australia. Trevor Chappell, on the instructions of his brother and captain, Greg, bowled the ball along the ground to Mc-Kechnie, who blocked it. The incident caused an outcry, up to Prime Ministerial level in both countries, and underarm bowling was thenceforth banned in major one-day competitions throughout the world

From Mr A. D. D. McCallum, 5 February 1981

Sir, Why all this verbosity: 'Bowling under arm along the ground' (cricket report, 3 February)? In the good old days of my youth, in the vocabulary of the real world of cricket played in the garden, or tennis courts, or on the beach, under the umpiring of nannies and governesses, such balls were succinctly and expressively described as 'sneaks' or 'sneakers'.

And what's all this about 'amendment of the laws'? Disputes used to be settled by reasoned debate, with logical arguments such as 'You did – I didn't – you did' or 'It was   it wasn't', and, of course, as these were the pre-pacifist days, there was in extreme cases no shortage of weaponry in the shape of stumps or bat to reinforce one's points. But the laws – mainly unwritten – remained sacrosanct.

Yours faithfully,

A. D. D. McCALLUM

In January 1983 England needed three runs off the last ball to win: Marks was bowled by Snedden. The New Zealand Prime Minister congratulated his countryman for having delivered it overarm.

DOUBTFUL BOWLING ACTIONS

In 1885 Lord Harris persuaded his county, Kent, to cancel their return fixture with Lancashire, who had two 'throwers' in their side. He had written a letter to Lancashire, of which copies were sent to the Press. In July 1901 Arthur Mold, also of Lancashire and identified as a 'thrower' by the county captains, was no-balled 16 times in 10 overs by James Phillips, an Australian umpire who also officiated in England.

From Lord Harris, 23 September 1901

Sir, It is 16 years – June, 1885 – since I addressed a letter to you on the subject of doubtful bowling actions, which you thought worthy of insertion and of editorial notice. History repeats itself, and perhaps you will permit me once more, probably for the last time, to enter the arena; if so I am obliged for the favour.

The position at the moment is as follows:– At their annual meeting last year the county captains condemned the actions of certain bowlers, and expressed a very decided opinion that they should not be played in their county elevens this year. In April, 1901, the committee of the MCC resolved:–

'That this committee approve of the principle and the action taken by the county captains, but are of opinion that it would be expedient to postpone the actual suspension of any bowler during the coming season in the hope that this course may strengthen the hands of the umpires without being unnecessarily drastic.'

Have the umpires regarded the action of the county captains as strengthening their hands? Surely not; the Phillips–Mold incident is, I suggest, merely the exception which proves that as a body they are not more resolute now than they have been for the last 20 years.

Are we likely to expect any more decided action from the umpires in the future? I think not. I look back to the early eighties when I conducted a campaign against doubtful actions; and I cannot forget what Robert Thoms said to me when I asked him to watch an action I thought doubtful – and be it remembered Thoms was a masterful umpire in his day – 'My Lord,' he said, 'we are going to do nothing, it is you gentlemen who have got to do it'; and, therefore, my friends the umpires will excuse me if I express a very strong doubt of their being more determined to suppress doubtful actions in the future than they have been in the past.

If that be so what is to happen? Is this or that county to be able to ignore the umpire's opinion and to put to the test the endurance of the bowler in bowling no-balls and the umpire in calling them, with the risk of the spectators interfering vocally, or even practically, with the match and producing a scene altogether unworthy of the game? If the umpires are not prepared to endorse the opinion expressed by a body so competent to judge, as is one composed of the county captains, then what remedy have those counties which do not include in their teams bowlers condemned by the county captains against those counties which, despite the opinion of the county captains, might deliberately include bowlers so condemned? Is responsibility to be confined solely to the umpire, and not to be distributable? I venture to think it ought to be; and at any rate I can claim that the course I adopted in the early eighties was consistent with that opinion. I declined to play one year for Gentlemen v Players at Lord's because I considered Mr A. H. Evans's action was not above suspicion; I declined to play with and captain England v the Australians at Old Trafford unless Crossland was omitted from the England Eleven for the same reason; and I dropped two bowlers out of the Kent Eleven, C. Collins and Captain Hedley, because doubts were expressed as to the fairness of their deliveries. The remedy I had to resort to in my dispute with the Lancashire committee in 1885, about their bowlers, was a very strong one; and it would be preferable if some remedy – other than exclusion – could be devised.

Now, Sir, let us assume that the umpires are not to be depended upon in this particular matter, and that some counties are not prepared to abide by the expressed opinion of the county captains, unless it be supported by the consideration of some properly constituted body. Can we find some arrangement which will give confidence to the counties? I think so, and I suggest that the body to which the county captains should report is the committee of the MCC. I am not on the committee now, but I have been on it for many years, and I claim for it that it has won and holds allegiance from all the cricketers of the world, and it could not have secured this unless its conduct had been wise. The committee of the MCC, however, is not a body well qualified to decide of its own knowledge questions of this kind – i.e., is this, or that, or the other bowler's action doubtful or above suspicion? – it cannot move about and constantly watch this or that action; it could only, if it accepted such a responsibility, be guided by a sub-committee of experts; and I submit that it would be impossible to find a committee more expert than the captains of first-class counties.

The MCC has always been reluctant to set itself up as a referee on points which, by the laws of the game, are left to the sole judgment of the umpires. But I can conceive the committee consenting to accept the post of arbiter on this particular point, if assisted by such an expert body as the county captains, and if there was a fairly general agreement amongst the county committees that the umpires by their notorious abnegation – for the exception in the Phillips–Mold case proves the rule – of their responsibility in this particular matter should be relieved of it.

The representatives of the first-class counties will meet, as usual, in November or December, to fix the dates for next year's matches; and if they were authorized by their committees to discuss some such suggestion as this, and to vote upon it, it would be possible for the counties, collectively, to approach the MCC before next season.

It is with extreme reluctance that I suggest a remedy which interferes with the legal position of cricket umpires; and I do so only because, after many years' observation of this doubtful action question, I can see none other that would give as much confidence of impartial judgment to the bodies and individuals affected.

I remain yours faithfully,

HARRIS

Throwing was not again a serious problem in English cricket for more than 50 years.

NOT CRICKET

From Dr R. W. Cockshut, 14 July 1966
Chairman of the Cricket Society 1960–65.

Sir, Your Cricket Correspondent's comments (6 July) on bodyline bowling by the West Indians are welcome indeed. For seven years I have tried to organize opposition to dangerous bowling. Perhaps, now, there may be some success. May I make a few points.

1. The latest available Registrar General's reports show 13 men killed at cricket in three years – 12 by head injuries. The best statistical guess I can come by is that probably 100 to 150 suffered irreparable brain injury.

2. Cricket is the only game in the world in which the natural hazards are allowed to be deliberately increased.

3. Such figures for any other game, e.g. boxing, would result in immediate action.

4. Bumpers are aimed at batsmen's heads either to hit their skulls or to make them fear for their skulls. Such bowling is a disgrace to the game.

Yours, &c.,

R. W. COCKSHUT

The fatalities may have occurred to fielders as well as batsmen.

INTIMIDATING BOWLING

From the Editor of The Cricketer, *16 January 1975*

Sir, While being wholeheartedly in agreement with Mr Noel-Baker's condemnation of – for want of a better word – 'bodyline' bowling, I would point out that his call for a law to forbid it is unnecessary, since the Laws of Cricket already cover this matter. Law 46, Note 4 (vi) states: 'The persistent bowling of fast short-pitched balls at the batsman is unfair if, in the opinion of the umpire at the bowler's end, it constitutes a systematic attempt at intimidation.'

The procedure to be adopted by the umpire is then outlined: he should (a) caution the bowler, (b) inform the fielding captain and the other umpire if the first warning proves ineffective, and (c) call 'dead ball' if the intimidatory bowling is continued, and advise the fielding captain, who must take the bowler off forthwith. The offending bowler may not bowl again during the innings – a penalty practically as severe as being sent from the field.

Thus we are talking of two kinds of courage: that of the batsman, who has a bat with which to score runs or defend his wicket *or himself*, and that of the umpire, who is under a different sort of 'pressure'. After Umpire Egar no-balled Meckiff for throwing at Brisbane in 1963–64 he received a number of anonymous threats on his life.

Neutral umpires are not the answer. If anything, this pressure on them would be greater still. Might it not, though, be a solution in such times for the authorities to appoint umpires who are former *batsmen*? Mr Brooks, the senior umpire, used to be a fast bowler (for the same Sydney club side as Keith Miller!).

Yours, etc.,

DAVID FRITH

Editor of *The Cricketer* 1972–78; founding Editor of *Wisden Cricket Monthly* 1979.

CRICKET PITCH DIMENSIONS

From Mr D. E. Fair, 15 July 1976

Sir, Once again we have witnessed the spectacle of a Test umpire admonishing a bowler for dangerous bowling [Alley warned Holding]. It is wrong that an umpire should have to persuade an aggressive and skilful bowler to observe artificial self-restraint and curb his natural talents.

Why don't the cricket authorities acknowledge that we have grown too big for traditional cricket dimensions? When the present 22-yard pitch was first chosen in around 1700, the average man was 5ft 4¾in tall; now he is 5ft 9in. Moreover the speed of bowling has probably grown much more than proportionately; for example the mile is now run 15 per cent faster than a century ago. Some other sports have faced the physical facts of modern life. In the late 1940s for instance, Eton school had finally to enlarge their traditional boats to accommodate the larger bottoms of ever-growing Eton schoolboys.

Is it reasonable to expect an intelligent batsman to face today's giant bowlers from exactly the same distance as his 18th century counterpart? The switch from underarm bowling and developments in cricket ball manufacture only reinforce the need for change.

To allow for the increased stature of the British cricketer the pitch should be lengthened by at least 7 per cent (to 23.5 yards – a metric chain?). Some provision should also be made for the continuing development of the species. On the basis of past experience, the pitch should be extended by 0.17 inches each decade. To compensate slower bowlers the wicket should perhaps be made larger or the bat smaller.

Certainly the dimensions of the traditional cricket pitch are now suitable only for English women cricketers (average height 5ft 4in) and perhaps some Asiatic peoples.

Yours faithfully,

DON FAIR

In 1926, when the bat held sway, a correspondent proposed shortening of the pitch. See page 198.

PENALIZING THE BOUNCER

In the first Test match at Edgbaston the Pakistan night-watchman, Iqbal Qasim, who had been in for 40 minutes, was struck in the face by a bouncer from Bob Willis.

From Professor A. D. Jenkins, FRSChem, 15 June 1978
Professor of Chemistry, University of Sussex.

Sir, Your third leader of 7 June is surely unfair in its rejection of the argument that a night-watchman can be treated by the fielding side as if he were a fully fledged batsman. The captain who sends in a night-watchman is taking a gamble and endeavouring to gain an advantage; it is surely wrong that he should be aided in this by simultaneously depriving the bowler of one of the weapons that he would have been using against the expected recognized batsman. This would be illogical and unfair to the fielding side, and (in my view) justifies the use of the bouncer during the recent Test match, at least within the prevailing practice, which accepts the bouncer as legitimate.

Having said that, may I now suggest that arguments of this kind are much better avoided altogether by banning the bouncer? It seems to me that the true spirit of cricket requires the bowler to aim at or near the stumps, rather than at the batsman's head. Can we not preserve this spirit by outlawing the bouncer or else severely penalizing it – what about 10 runs awarded as extras to the batting side whenever a bouncer is bowled?

Yours,
AUBREY JENKINS

From Mr John Latusek, 17 June 1978

Sir, To eliminate dangerous bowling Mr Frank Richards suggested awarding extra runs when balls are bowled above the batsman's shoulder height. Fine. But to gain advantage from this rule would not selectors choose shorter and shorter players until cricket disappears altogether?

Yours faithfully,
JOHN LATUSEK

From Mrs Alan Robson, 17 June 1978

Sir, In 1860, Lord William Pitt Lennox wrote: 'If the present system of bowling is continued, we should advise that suits of armour from the Tower of London be forwarded to all the members of Lord's and other cricketing clubs. Indeed, the Household Brigade might turn out in jackboots, gauntlets, cuirasses and helmets to contend with the Zingari in chain hauberks, steel head-pieces and iron-armlets.'

Yours, etc,

ELIZABETH ROBSON

From Mr John Boulton, 17 June 1978

Sir, Concerning letters in your columns on means of countering dangerous bowling: the news that a county bowler has had his face broken by a leg-side hit suggests to me that victims have found their own answer – dangerous batting.

Yours sincerely,

JOHN BOULTON

The Test and County Cricket Board 'bitterly regretted' the Qasim incident and reminded the England captain, Mike Brearley, of his responsibilities. Lists of non-recognized batsmen on each side, to be exempt from short-pitched bowling, were exchanged.

DANGEROUS BOWLING

From Mr Windsor Clarke, 23 June 1978
London editor of Westminster Press Limited.

Sir, Controversy over the use by Mr Mike Brearley, or any other batsman, of a safety helmet and face protection seems to be misguided by suggesting that the question of protection is a batsman's problem. It is not.

It is the bowler's problem. The bowling of bumpers today is not in essence different from the leg theory or bodyline bowling of the Larwood era. Mr Justice Sheridan summed up the position neatly at that time when he said:

'Leg-theory bowling is covered by the criminal law, under which it is a serious offence recklessly and wantonly to harm any person, even without malice.'

The fast bowler who delivers bumpers which intimidate a batsman is surely 'recklessly and wantonly' risking doing harm to the batsman – and not always, one fears, without malice.

Perhaps a single criminal prosecution when a batsman is injured would solve the intimidation problem for good, at least in Britain.

Yours sincerely,
WINDSOR CLARKE

CRICKET REMINISCENCES

From Mr C. I. Thornton, 27 August 1919

Cambridge University, Kent and Middlesex (1869–85). One of the game's greatest hitters, six of his blows measuring over 150 yards. For more than 50 years' service to the Scarborough Festival he was made a Freeman of the Borough.

Sir, In all the cricket articles given in your paper regarding selections of the best elevens of past and present generations, not one mentions the best bowler by far, in my opinion, that has ever lived – viz., the late George Freeman, who bowled for Yorkshire in the sixties. In conjunction with Tom Emmett he was a most formidable customer. Taking a very short run, he delivered the ball with great force, and got up off the ground very quickly, with a slight breakback, which often hit the batsman on the leg. I saw the memorable match at Lord's when W. G. Grace and C. E. Green were playing against him for MCC v. Yorkshire [1870. Yorkshire won by one wicket; Freeman took ten – all bowled – for 64 in the match]. They each got 50 or 60 runs, but were simply plastered over with his deliveries on the thighs and ribs. The late Mr I. D. Walker always put him down as the best fast bowler he ever saw, and W. G. also said the same thing. He was a bit faster than Tom Richardson.

I also saw him knock all three stumps down at Lord's, C. R. Filgate being the batsman. The latter feat had been previously done by Harvey Fellows at Canterbury in the sixties, when he knocked G. M. Kelson's three stumps down on a very dry, hard wicket in August. I have asked several people, but no one bar myself can remember seeing it happen. Harvey Fellows was very fast right hand, with a low action.

The curious thing is that George Freeman and Alan Hill both took only three or four steps, and it goes to show that some of these bowlers nowadays that take 20 yards' run up to the wicket do not get any more pace on the ball than Freeman and Hill did, and must get tired much sooner.

Yours truly,
C. I. THORNTON

George Freeman played only five full seasons for Yorkshire, retiring in 1871 to go into business. *Allen* Hill toured Australia in 1876–77 and played in the two matches now classified as the first Tests.

TRUEMAN'S BOWLING

From Mr Austin F. Carris, 28 June 1952

Sir, Trueman's run is at least 28 yards to the bowling crease and is then extended about another eight or 10 yards up the pitch, making a distance, with the return journey, of at least 72 yards, and a quarter of a mile an over of six balls – half of which distance is executed at great strain. At this rate he will have to be very carefully nursed if he is to last many years.

Yours truly,
AUSTIN F. CARRIS

Trueman was nursed until 1969, when he retired with 307 Test wickets and 2304 in all first-class matches.

NOT CRICKET?

From Mr Richard Barry, 16 August 1972

Sir, Commentators assess the run-up of Australian bowler Lillee to be 40 yards. Assuming them right and that Lillee bowls 25 overs to an innings means that in any match 10 fielders, two umpires, two batsmen and countless thousands of spectators wait idly while this fellow runs in excess of 6½ miles.

Would he not be better employed at the White City, leaving the rest of us to get on with the cricket?

Yours faithfully,
RICHARD BARRY

Not to mention the 6½ miles he walks back to his mark.

From Miss Mary Smith, 18 August 1972

Sir, Mr Barry wrote (August 16), as did Jack Fingleton, in your columns criticizing the length of Lillee's run-up. For those of us who do not merely write about cricket or, as Mr Barry, 'idly' listen to commentators, but who actually pay, and support matches in person, the experience of watching Lillee thundering down from the pavilion end is one of the most exciting and thrilling experiences provided by the cricket world for many years.

Yours faithfully,

MARY SMITH

ORIGIN OF THE 'GOOGLIE'

Usually interpreted as an off-break bowled with a leg-break action.

From Mr N. E. T. Bosanquet, 14 October 1936

Sir, As so many inaccurate versions of the origin of the 'googlie' are appearing, it may be of interest to the public to know how it was evolved.

Many years ago – about 1892 – our billiard table at Claysmore was being re-covered, and we used to 'flick' a tennis ball across the bare slates, trying to get the maximum twist on it both ways. My brother, the late B. J. T. Bosanquet, got bitten with the idea of evolving a new sort of 'break' on a cricket ball, and he used to practise hard at a game we played with a solid rubber ball and a broomstick. He never said much about it, and, while he was at Eton, no one had any idea of what was then taking a definite shape. His family had no knowledge of anything beyond this, and the first public appearance of the 'googlie' was as much a surprise to them as to anyone else. He had very exceptionally strong fingers, which, I think, are essential to a successful 'googlie' bowler.

The paralysing effect on the best batsmen of this style of bowling is due, not merely to the off-break with leg-break action, but to the fact that a genuine expert bowls a leg-break, off-break, or no-break ball with the same hand action – or near enough not to be distinguishable. As a matter of fact, I do not think any other bowler has been able to do this efficiently, which would explain why such batsmen as Clem Hill (who was hypnotized by 'Bosies') regarded 'Bos' as the greatest bowler in history. Certainly R. O. Schwarz, a great friend of my brother, could never do it really well, though he made a great reputation on the strength of the 'leg' and 'no' breaks, with an occasional effort at the 'off'. This, in spite of receiving many hours of patient instruction from the inventor, whose only pupil he was.

Unfortunately, my brother certainly developed a form of athlete's heart, which was the main cause of his comparatively early retirement, and which affected him far more than even his friends appreciated, as he never talked about it and would not do anything for it. It was this neglect which undoubtedly caused his untimely death.

Yours faithfully,
NICOLAS BOSANQUET

B. J. T. Bosanquet died in 1936, one day short of his 59th birthday.

From Mr D. R. Dangar, 17 October 1936

Sir, In an account of a cricket tour in which I participated in 1898 or 1899 occurs the following sentence:– X was then tried with his lobs. All that can be said of them is that the best of them was far worse than the worst of Y's 'googlers'. Is this the first mention of the word, allowance being made for the slight difference in the spelling? I may say that the 'X' mentioned is now one of his Majesty's justices.

D. R. DANGAR

From Mr Nigel Dennis, 13 May 1963
Journalist and writer.

Sir, Do you want to be torn to pieces by nettled Bosanquets? That family claims two major innovations: (1) the introduction into Oxford of Hegel and 'German idealism', (2) the introduction into cricket of the 'googly'. It is obvious that (2) was merely the sporting consequence of (1); but just as Bradley must be granted to have helped with the philosophical juggle, so must my dear mother (*née* Louise Bosanquet) be allowed her share in the bowling one.

As a little girl she hero-worshipped her cousin, 'B.J.T.', and paid for it in the 1890s by being made to stand at one end of a lawn for hours, retrieving his experimental googlies. A tennis ball was always used – 'Not a *billiard* ball, a *tennis* ball' were among my mother's last words to me. As she knew nothing about German idealism, I must append the following highly significant dates off my own bat:–

1886. Publication of B. Bosanquet's *The Introduction to Hegel's Philosophy of Fine Art.*

1890. The googly ideal conceived by B. J. T. Bosanquet.

1893. Publication of Bradley's *Appearance & Reality.*

1893–1900. Intensive work, helped by my mother, to hide the reality behind the googly's appearance.

1903. The Ashes regained by the googly – German idealism's first and last sporting victory.

Yours faithfully,
NIGEL DENNIS

Bosanquet's 6 for 51 in fact brought England the Ashes in March 1904.

From Dr R. W. Cockshut, 10 May 1963

Sir, The word 'googly' was first used in a newspaper article in New Zealand in 1903 to describe Bosanquet's new ball. The word means uncanny, weird, ghostly, and is supposed to be of Maori origin. There are many words with the ō or oo vowel sound associated especially with k, j, or g, which express the same quality of fear and wonder. Bogey, boogey-woogey, spook, &c., and Lewis Carroll must have been aware of this when he coined the word Boojum.

A more apt word to describe a leg-break from the off could not be imagined, and we remain indebted to an unknown New Zealand journalist.

Yours faithfully,
R. W. COCKSHUT

Bosanquet toured New Zealand with Lord Hawke's team in 1902–03. Recent research, and Mr Dangar's letter, suggest that 'googly' is of greater antiquity.

From Captain T. G. Usher, 24 May 1963
Aide-de-camp to the Governor-General of New Zealand

Sir, I hope you will be indulgent towards an Antipodean delay in this intervention. Dr Cockshut (10 May) may well be right in claiming that the word 'googly' first appeared in a New Zealand newspaper in 1903; but he is certainly wrong in suggesting that it is of Maori origin. The Maori tongue has neither 'G' nor 'L'.

Hasty telephonic research in cooperation with the office of the Australian High Commissioner here reveals that 'Yooguli!' is Australian aboriginal language for 'I rejoice!' Could Bosanquet have been as multilingual as all that?

T. G. USHER

A 'SOSTENEUTER'

A ball that pitched on the leg stump and hit the off.

From Mr W. A. Marshall, 13 June 1919

Sir, This term, as used by Tom Emmett, must have puzzled many besides your correspondent. A possible explanation of Tom's peculiar terminology is that he had some knowledge of music, as a good Yorkshireman should. If so he would most likely know that in that art the Italian word *sostenuto* is used to indicate when a note of music is to be held in an equal and steady manner to its full length. By analogy he probably adopted this to a ball which he sent down 'full of wickedness to the very end.' *Sostenuto*, I believe, is the past participle of the Italian verb *sostinere* (to sustain). Tom promptly appropriated it and adopted it as a noun, and a very good noun, too, for a ball that could get 'W.G.' first ball.

Yours faithfully,
W. A. MARSHALL

The reply usually given by Emmett, who played for England and was later a popular coach at Rugby School, was: 'What else would you call it'?

2
FROM MULLAGH
TO BOTHAM

WHERE THE GAME IS PLAYED

From Lieutenant-Commander K. A. Sellar, 28 August 1964
Sussex (1928). Toured Canada with MCC 1937. England rugby international.

Sir, What *fun* it would be if we could now burn The Ashes and The Records and scatter the ashes as compost over the village greens of England where the *game* of cricket is still played.

Yours, &c.,

K. A. SELLAR

ABORIGINE TEAM AT LORD'S

From Professor D. J. Mulvaney, FAHA, FSA, 17 March 1977

Commonwealth Visiting Professor, University of Cambridge; Professor of Prehistory, Australian National University. Author of *Cricket Walkabout: the Australian Aboriginal Cricketers on Tour 1867 8.*

Sir, During this nostalgic centenary season of cricketing reminiscence, it is unfortunate that commentators have ignored an earlier centenary landmark in England–Australia fixtures. This is surprising, because their omission concerns the first formal contest between a touring Australian side and the Marylebone Cricket Club, played a decade before the first Test series. It is regrettable, because treating it as a non-event represents a slight to the dignity of Australian Aboriginal people, who merit greater consideration.

On June 12–13, 1868, a team of ten Australian Aborigines was led onto the Lord's field by their captain, Charles Lawrence, a former Surrey player of some merit. The MCC fielded a distinguished team, including its former President, the Earl of Coventry, and Viscount Downe, a future President. MCC trailed on the first innings but won by 55 runs, despite the fact that Eton and Hampshire representative, Lieutenant-Colonel Bathurst, failed to score in both innings.

It is unfortunate that this interesting episode in amicable race relations, in a period not noted for its tolerance, has made so little impact on historians of the game. The tour cannot be dismissed, as some writers have done, as 'not cricket'. The record of their 47 English fixtures, of which they won 14 and lost an equal number, establishes that their playing standards met those of English cricket of that day. No less an authority than W. G. Grace concluded that they 'acquitted themselves very well'. Indeed, the honours for individual performances at Lord's rested with the visitors. Mullagh's first innings score of 75 was the highest of the match, and he also took eight wickets. Cuzens, who bowled true overarm deliveries, then the current rules innovation, finished with 10 wickets from 60 overs, at a cost of 117 runs.

The former Australian Test captain, Ian Johnson, once praised the 'unique' achievement of 'the first of our teams to tour England', and compared the Aboriginal approach to the game to that of latter-day West Indians. It is doubtful whether these 'forgotten men' of Australian cricket were represented at the current Melbourne celebrations by any officially invited representatives of their race.

Yours faithfully,

D. J. MULVANEY

AUSTRALIAN TOUR IN 1873

From Mr E. P. S. Lewin, 2 December 1950

Sir, I have just come across a document which might interest some cricket lovers. It is the draft agreement drawn up by my grandfather for Dr W. G. Grace for members of the cricket team which he was to take to Australia on 22 October, 1873. Among its provisions are the following: (1) Members of the team are engaged to play in 14 matches 'at such times and places as the said William Gilbert Grace shall from time to time direct for a period extending over 100 days and returning on or about the 25th day of March, 1874.' (2) Members of the team shall be paid £150 each, plus £20 'towards expenses for wines, spirits, and other liquors'. (3) Members agree to place themselves 'under the entire disposal and directions of the said William Gilbert Grace and to obey all his orders and to play in each of the aforesaid 14 matches . . .' (4) Members agree 'not to play in any other matches nor engage in any other pursuit without the consent in writing of the said William Gilbert Grace . . .'

(5) Members will be provided with second class return passages and all hotel, travel and other expenses. (6) Payment would be £50 on embarcation at Southampton and a further £50 in instalments during the 100 days already mentioned. The balance is payable after 'the fulfilment of the terms of the agreement'. (7) Any breach of the agreement entails forfeiture of any outstanding payment and the repayment to Dr Grace of sums already received. (8) Members agree 'to the best of their ability to play, perform, and carry out all the matches, arrangements, and engagements which the said William Gilbert Grace shall make for them, and will use their best endeavours to promote the honour and glory of English cricket'.

Pencilled on the back of this draft are the names of the following players: James Lillywhite, James Southerton, Richard Humphrey, Henry Jupp, William Oscroft, Andrew Greenwood, Martin McIntyre, and George Frederick Grace. I wonder whether there is any record of the financial outcome of this tour, and whether the entire expense was borne by the Doctor?

I am, Sir, yours truly,

E. P. S. LEWIN

Grace had been invited by the Melbourne CC, which did not assume financial responsibility, although a syndicate of club members and other cricket devotees 'promoted the interests of the team'. Grace, who brought forward his wedding to the summer, used the tour as a honeymoon. The leading professionals, Emmett and Shaw, had rejected Grace's terms and the party was completed by the amateurs F. H. Boult, James Bush and Walter Gilbert. A hint of the financial success of the tour was that 40,000 spectators paid half-a-crown each to watch the match against Eighteen of Victoria.

THE AUSTRALIAN CRICKET ELEVEN

At Sydney in February 1879 Lord Harris was assaulted after the crowd, incensed by a run out decision against the New South Wales captain, W. L. Murdoch, had invaded the field. Bad feelings lingered and most of the leading counties had completed their fixture lists by the time the Australians decided to tour England in 1880.

From An Old Etonian, 28 June 1880

Sir, While every lover of cricket must be pleased at the notice which has been taken of the team of cricketers from Canada, I would venture to ask you to allow me to say a few words on behalf of the team that has come from Australia, and whose presence, so far as I am aware, has been entirely ignored by almost all our leading clubs; and I must surmise (although unwilling to believe it) that the sole reason for this want of courtesy to our visitors is in a great measure due to the unfortunate dispute with Lord Harris's team when over in Sydney. And, without saying one word *pro* or *con* in connexion with that event, I would ask if it is just to the Australians to make them suffer for what, I would fain hope, has long since been forgiven, if not forgotten. As is well known, the match in which the dispute occurred was with the New South Wales players, three only of whom, Bannerman, Murtock [Murdoch] and Spofforth, are members of the team now in England; and I believe I am correct in saying that, beyond Bannerman being the man who was given out when the *fracas* took place, not one of the three men was in any degree responsible for it.

Surely, Sir, a wish to banish these men from all our chief cricket fields seems somewhat of an un-English spirit, and, too, deprives a vast number of people from witnessing what would doubtless prove a rich cricketing treat. The Australians have not yet been defeated, and the matches which were drawn were greatly in their favour, and as there is so much new blood among them, let us hope that we shall not only have a taste of it, but that our old friend the 'demon bowler' may yet be seen at Lord's and the Oval.

To prevent any misconception as to the purport of this letter, I may state that I am not acquainted with any member of the Australian team. I write simply as a cricketer, a lover of fair play, and

AN OLD ETONIAN

On 5 July the MCC committee agreed to W. G. Grace's proposal for a match at Lord's a fortnight later between Australia and an England team raised by him. The plan fell through because Crystal Palace would not release the Australians from a fixture there on that date. Thanks, however, to the initiative of Surrey CCC and its secretary, Charles Alcock, the first Test match in England was played at the Oval on 6–8 September 1880. Lord Harris captained England; his opposite number was Murdoch, who scored 153 not out in the second innings. Spofforth, the 'demon bowler', missed the match because of a hand injury.

THE CRICKET SCANDAL

Betting on cricket was rife in Australia and in December 1881 two members of Alfred Shaw's all professional touring team were bribed to throw a match against Victoria. The flames were fanned in England when *Cricket: A Weekly Record of the Game*, in best journalistic fashion, included reports of the scandal in its first issue.

From Mr W. R. Wake, 29 May 1882
Yorkshire (1881). Later Registrar of Sheffield County Court.

Sir, My attention has been called to a letter in *The Times* of the 24th on the above subject, bearing the well-known name of Lord Harris. In it the writer asks for a public refutation of the scandal and a statement by the men under oath that no member of the team 'did not do his best'. I, like his lordship, think that some 'authoritative' contradiction should be given, and not only to the accusation of bribery, but to the other items of the rumour, which, in my opinion, are equally disgraceful. Lord Harris's requisition, if complied with, will certainly dispose of the simple question of bribery, but, I venture to suggest to his lordship, and the members of the team (who are all implicated), that any statement they may make should embody answers to certain questions bearing on the whole scandal, and not only the bribery question. The purport of such questions will be better understood when I mention that the rumour as it prevailed here and at Nottingham was as follows:–

'Ulyett and Selby were each to receive £500, and were authorized to offer Scotton £250, to be non-triers. The latter declined the offer, and told Shaw. Selby and Scotton afterwards fought and Scotton was victorious, but was then tackled, with a different result, by Ulyett.'

The questions I would ask the members of the team (or any one else in a position to do so) to answer, are the following:–

39

1. Was there not a fight between Selby and Scotton at Cootamundra (or elsewhere), and were not the stakes £3 a side?

2. What was the cause of the fight?

3. Did not Scotton write home to his father at Nottingham giving particulars of the fight, and also mentioning 'bribery?'

4. Has not Shaw admitted since his arrival in England, that 'something unpleasant' did take place, and have not other members of the team stated that there was more 'carrying on' (I use their own expression) in Shaw's team than any one not present would believe?

5. Was not the 'scandal' one of the principal themes of conversation among the passengers on board the Assam?

I may mention that in framing the above questions I have touched only on matters concerning which I have reliable information, and that I have not brought the matter before the public earlier in the hope that some more competent judge and able writer would have done so. If I have erred in the course I have now adopted, the interest which I now take, and always have taken in our noble game must be my excuse.

I remain, Sir, yours truly,

W. R. WAKE

It being a private tour, there could be no disciplinary action by MCC who were first responsible for a major overseas tour in 1903–04.

THE TEST MATCH OF 1882

England's first defeat on home soil which gave rise to the 'Ashes' obituary notice in the *Sporting Times*.

From Mr N. L. Jackson, 30 July 1931
'Pa' Jackson, founder of the Corinthians FC.

Sir, As a member of the Surrey Club, I was present at the famous Test match at the Oval when the English team had its first defeat. I had a chat with C. T. Studd in the dressing room shortly before he went in, when wickets were falling remarkably fast, and 'C.T.', like most of the other late players, was horribly nervous. [Studd, No. 6 in the first innings, had, by some accounts, begged not to be sent in by his captain in the second innings unless absolutely necessary. He went in No. 10 and did not face a ball.] I remember remarking at the time that most of them were out before they went in. With 'C.T.', however, it is probable that he would have quickly recovered after a few balls and would have averted defeat. He was a fine fellow, mentally and physically. He called on me only two days before he left on his first missionary journey to China and gave me advice, which I much regret I did not follow.

In my long connexion with sport I do not remember anything so extraordinary as the finish of that match. I was in the secretary's office at the Oval when the last English wicket fell. I saw Bonnor throw his 'pork-pie' cap (as were then worn) higher into the air than I thought was possible. On turning round I saw Charlie Alcock (the Surrey Club secretary) sitting inside the iron safe with his head in his hands and apparently oblivious of everything, while one of the committee, Dr Blades, was so overcome that he almost collapsed. Only during the Great War have I ever seen a company so absolutely miserable as that assembled in the secretary's office on that occasion.

To my mind 'Monkey' Hornby lost that match by calling 'W.G.' for a short run, thus getting him run out, when these two looked like getting all the runs required to win. Hornby was an adept at these short runs, but 'W.G.' was a heavy man and could not get into his stride as quickly as the smaller men could.

Yours truly,
N. LANE JACKSON

A spectator at the match was said to have died from excitement.

From Mr E. C. Sewell, 17 August 1926

Sir, In May, 1920, you inserted an inquiry by me regarding the incident in the Test match at the Oval in 1882, when S. P. Jones lost his wicket through the action of W. G. Grace. Several correspondents gave their version of what they recollected, but none tallied. I wrote to Mr Spofforth, who replied after some delay, but said that his letter was not for publication while he was alive. Owing to his recent lamented death, his embargo is removed. The following is his letter:—

'I did not read all the correspondence in *The Times*, but, as far as the Grace incident, it was this. W. L. Murdoch placed a ball from Peate on the leg side and one run was scored, bringing S. P. Jones to the bowling. A. Lyttelton ran after the ball, W. G. Grace going to the wicket, and, on receiving the ball from Lyttelton, he walked up to the bowler, Peate, who was about mid-wickets, but, seeing S. P. Jones come about two yards out of his ground to pat the pitch, Grace walked quietly back and put down the wicket, and appealed to R. Thoms, the umpire. Thoms' reply was: "I am sorry to say the gentleman is out." This is the true account. I might say the worst part was W.G. pretending to give the ball to Peate. I might add this letter is not for publication while I am alive. – FRED R. SPOFFORTH.'

The above confirms in the main Mr F. Ogilvy's account of the incident given in 1920, who added that Grace was 'ever a stickler for the rigour of the game'.

I am, &c.,

E. C. SEWELL

Several accounts of this incident appeared in the correspondence of 1920 and 1926, none of which tally in all details: there was no film or video recording to consult. Charles Pardon says in his book on the 1882 tour that, on inquiry of Thoms at close of play, all the umpire had said was 'Out!' The incident was said to have inspired Spofforth's seven for 44 which gave Australia victory by seven runs.

THE FOURTH TEST MATCH OF 1902

England, needing 124 to win, were beaten by three runs. Australia in their second innings had made 86, of which 37 were scored by Joe Darling; he had been dropped by Fred Tate at deep fine leg early in his innings. The argument that Tate, usually a slip fielder, should not have been in the deep had been revived.

From Mr A. C. MacLaren, 4 July 1919

Lancashire and England (1890–1914), captain of both. Holds record of highest individual first-class score in England, 424 for Lancashire v Somerset in 1895.

Sir, My attention having been drawn to the description of a great Test match at Manchester, 1902, by your correspondent, whose identity to me is apparent, I forward facts which can be corroborated by such as Braund, the bowler, or Lilley, the wicketkeeper, who heard the conversations which took place.

When Darling faced Braund after a single by Gregory, the point and mid-off to him were then the only two men on the on side. With

Darling facing Braund these naturally should fall back on the leg boundary for the left-handed batsman, as no less than five of the seven fieldsmen on the leg side to Gregory had to cross over to the leg side for Darling after a single had been scored. L. C. H. Palairet was moved the whole length of the ground from the leg boundary, when Gregory received the ball, to the leg boundary behind the umpire when Darling faced Braund. The Maharajah Ranjitsinhji was dead lame, and consequently was useless as an outfielder, since he would have made little or no ground to a catch, and for that reason I refused his offer to fall back. As Darling was hitting out at every ball I felt that, with the great amount of what became off break to the left-hand batsman Braund was getting on the ball, the spin would most likely cause Darling's hit to carry behind rather than in front of the square leg boundary, and I accordingly placed L. Palairet in that position with Tate in front. Braund then asked me if he might not have L. C. H. Palairet in front where Tate was fielding, and although I pointed out that the finer long leg was more likely to get the catch, he still preferred to have L. C. H. Palairet in front, and as I never went against any bowler of judgement Tate was allowed to take the fine leg position and Palairet came in front to occupy the position in which he usually fielded for Somerset. Tate got the catch and had the misfortune to drop it. No one was more sorry for Tate than myself, and although I had the greatest respect for Tate as a bowler, it was in my opinion far too late in his career to ask him to play for his first time at so critical a period in the Test games, when we were one down with only two games to play. Your correspondent says that he cannot vouch for it, but the story goes both the Hon. F. S. Jackson and Ranjitsinhji offered to take the long field. The Hon. F. S. Jackson, a fine infield, on the contrary asked to be allowed to retain that position.

Your correspondent says short slip and mid-on were the only two places for Tate. Braund never had a slip and Ranjitsinhji, lame, occupied mid-on. We had no less than four men on the deep leg boundaries for Braund, and if all four moved right across the ground for six singles in one over when a left-handed batsman was in each fieldsman would have covered some 1,200 yards in the over. It is always necessary to save not only your fieldsmen as much as possible but also time. Tate had the very bad luck to do what all of us have done times without number, drop a catch, which, owing to the greatness of the occasion, advertised its costliness. A further piece of bad luck for Tate was having to wait half-an-hour for his innings, when nine runs were wanted, owing to heavy rain falling at the fall of the ninth wicket, the proximity of which rain caused me to jump out to Trumble to win the game quickly, but which proved to be the first and last risk I took in my innings, as Duff made a well-judged running catch on the boundary.

The fielding, catching, and bowling were great on the part of the Australians. Trumble especially bowling according to the positions of his fieldsmen with the greatest accuracy, for although he had but a point and mid-off, his accuracy of length with adoption of pace and spin according to existing conditions was beyond all praise. Darling handled his team with rare judgement, and the manner in which our opponents snatched this victory was electrifying. It was truly a great game if disappointing to us after appearing to have won it.

The Hon. F. S. Jackson played a superb innings of 128 in the first innings, and was well backed up by Braund, 62, who also bowled on the top of his form, as did Lockwood after twice requesting me not to bowl him owing to the very wet state of the wicket in Australia's first innings, and his fear of slipping. Trumper on this wet wicket, with Duff at his best, never did anything better in his life, the century going up in an hour. He cut or drove everything that was sent up to him, and always placed accurately. The wicket in our second innings was nothing like so difficult as made out when once you got the pace of it and you had gauged the bowler's spin without being trapped by Trumble's straight one, delivered as if he was trying to screw the cover off the ball.

The Selection Committee is generally too adversely criticised, for the task of choosing the England Eleven is never an easy one. The Selection Committee always assisted me to the best of its ability, and our relations were friendly enough, even if we could not always see eye to eye where cricketers' merits were discussed, but I was a trifle sore that two of my selections for this match, one of which was Jessop, were struck off my list forwarded to them at their request after I had informed them at a previous meeting that if they would play Jessop in every Test match he would certainly run out Trumper from cover before the last game was played, as he chanced his wicket to this greatest cover in my time on three or four occasions in Australia. He was brought in when too late for the Test game at the Oval (the last one), and Trumper was almost at once run out by him.

Let us hope that in future the England captain will have the chief say in the selection of teams against Australia and South Africa, with the assistance of cricketers of the day rather than of the past. If the Selection Committee is to have power to overrule the captain, then the selection of that Selection Committee, in my opinion, becomes more important than the selection of the team itself. To select a team properly it is absolutely necessary to have a thorough knowledge of your opponents as well of your own players, and yet we have far too often had men on the Selection Committee who had never seen one-half or more of our opponents before arrival in England. The onlooker never did and never will see most of the game, and this fallacy originated probably over a big dinner with plenty of heads, but not cricket ones, the next morning.

Yours faithfully,

A. C. MacLAREN

MCC AND THE AUSTRALIAN TEAM

Sir Abe Bailey, a South African philanthropist, had proposed a triangular contest between England, Australia and South Africa to be held in England in 1909. The Australians were not in favour and on 3 July the Advisory County Cricket Committee asked MCC to withdraw their invitation to the Australians for a tour of England in that season.

From the Hon. F. S. Jackson, 9 July 1908

Cambridge University, Yorkshire and captain of England (1890–1907). Later MP for Howdenshire, Yorkshire; Governor of Bengal; Chairman of the Conservative Party; President of MCC (1921) and Yorkshire; Chairman of England selectors. His fag at Harrow was Winston Churchill. Knighted 1927.

Sir, As one whose good fortune it has been to take some part in international cricket, I should consider it a favour to be allowed to offer, through your columns, a few observations on the recent resolution of the Advisory Board, which it was decided should be sent to Australia subsequent to the intimation from the Board of Control that they were unable to take part in the suggested triangular contest in this country next year.

The resolution, as I read it, seems needlessly curt, not to say ungenerous, though I cannot believe that it is intended to offend. It would really seem as if the Advisory Board had been either misled or unduly hurried to this conclusion, perhaps both. Old friends as well as opponents, the Australians have been coming over here regularly for 30 years, and have, I think, always played the game as it should be played to the advantage of cricket and cricketers here. They would in the ordinary course have received an invitation to send a team here next year, a team which, I believe, would have come to this country under the direction of the new Board of Control, which has been formed largely in deference to our wishes and which has been looking forward to sending a team to play under conditions as regards matches and other details similar to those which have regulated previous tours. The triangular tournament was suggested to this country shortly after the South African tour last year; and I think I am correct when I say that, while received in a kindly spirit, it aroused no great amount of enthusiasm, and that it was, indeed, quietly hinted that its adoption depended entirely on whether or not the Australians would be prepared to take part in the tournament.

We now have Australia's reply. We know that the Australians do not see their way to taking part in such a contest this year. What their reasons may be for refusal I know not. They may think the time inopportune. If they do there are many people in this country who will agree in that view, or they may wish for further time for considering the scheme in detail.

But whatever the reasons which have prompted the action of the Australians, the fact that they have found it necessary to declare themselves unable to take part in the proposed triangular contest is surely no sufficient cause for their being peremptorily told that they must either join in the tournament or stay at home.

Though I hold no brief for the Australians, I do most earnestly plead for that harmony and good feeling which should and must exist between us and them if international cricket is to flourish. That feeling, I fear, will be rudely shattered by the sending of such a message as the decision of the Advisory Board which it is proposed to transmit to Australia. There can be little doubt that a mistake has been made. Why should it not be acknowledged and the resolution withdrawn with no loss of dignity to any one concerned?

I sincerely hope that the counties will see their way to extend to the Australian team on the old lines and with no new conditions a cordial invitation to visit this country next year, and, if this be done, I feel certain that the welcome accorded them will be as hearty and generous as it has always been from all lovers of the game.

Yours &c.,
F. STANLEY JACKSON

From Mr G. L. Jessop, 10 July 1908

Cambridge University, Gloucestershire and England (1894–1914), captaining first two. Legendary hitter and brilliant fielder.

Sir, As one also whose good fortune it has been to take a humble part in international cricket, may I crave a small space in your columns in support of the views of the Hon. Stanley Jackson – and in so doing be it understood I wish to dissociate myself from all things official? As a member of that Advisory Board, I can hardly reveal all the sapient resolutions of that council.

It seems to me that as the MCC were invited to send a team to Australia it was 'up to them', if I may for the once borrow a Yankee colloquialism, to return the invitation. And unless I am mistaken, this was already done – judging from the terms of the meeting of the MCC. That august body passed a resolution something to this effect:– 'That whether the Australians saw fit or not to join in the proposed triangular scheme, it would not interfere with their arranged visit for 1909.' It appears to me there has been a revoke in the game, and to say the least of it I cannot help thinking – in my private capacity of course – that our good friends the Australians have been treated somewhat cavalierly. To hold a pistol to one's head is no slight ordeal to face. I only hope – in my private capacity once again – that our brethren from the Southern Cross will dare the pistol to be snapped.

I am yours sincerely,
GILBERT L. JESSOP

A subsequent letter from W. E. Denison, Nottinghamshire's representative on the Advisory Committee, attributed the controversy to MCC and the counties working at cross purposes, as a result of a misunderstanding of the other's true views. At all events the Advisory Committee was reconvened on 29 July, the earlier decision rescinded, and the invitation to the Australians restored. The credit for getting things put right belonged to the Hon. F. S. Jackson, and the Triangular Tournament eventually came to fruition in 1912 – again beset by difficulties, when six leading Australian players were in dispute with their Board of Control over whether the players or the board should appoint the tour manager.

THE DISPUTE IN AUSTRALIA

From an Australian in London, 2 March 1912

Sir, In view of the report published in your columns today of meetings held in Melbourne to protest against the Board of Control's action, it may be as well to remind British readers that the Board is a representative body elected by the Cricket Associations of five States, the Associations themselves being similarly representative of the great body of cricketers and cricket lovers; that the six players represent no one but themselves; and that the Melbourne Club, which is not a representative body, but a private club, has from the first institution of the Board of Control used Messrs. Noble, Hill, and Co. as a weapon to destroy it, because the club was in pre-Board days the paramount authority in Australian cricket, and desires nothing more than to regain that position.

One may regret that the Board has not used its authority more tactfully; but when that authority is challenged by two small sections of the community on behalf of their private interests lovers of the game as a game must stand by it. And the Melbourne Club's antagonistic demonstration is very considerably discounted by the Victorian Association's practically unanimous support.

Your obedient servant,
AUSTRALIAN IN LONDON

Hill, Trumper, Armstrong, Ransford, Cotter and Carter stayed at home; the South Africans were weak; and it rained – a great deal. England won the tournament, which comprised nine three-day matches, but nothing similar was tried until the World Cup 63 years later.

A REPLY TO MR WARNER

From Mr A. M. Latham, 22 January 1921
Cheshire (1880–93). Recorder of Birkenhead 1912–34.

Sir, May I, as the individual responsible for arranging the Australian fixture list next summer, say one word in self-defence and in reply to Mr P. F. Warner's article this morning? Mr Warner's main objections appear to be three:–

(*a*) There are too many matches.
(*b*) There are too many matches against weak counties.
(*c*) There are no representative matches apart from Test

48

matches, and especially there is no match against the Gentlemen of England.

To deal with (c) first, I feel sure that Mr Warner will be the first to admit that any such representative matches should be played at Lord's, as it is only there that really representative sides can be secured. When the Board of Control honoured me by asking me to undertake the fixture list I immediately asked the authorities at Lord's what dates they wanted; the reply, given, I presume, by the instructions of the committee of the MCC, of which body Mr Warner is, I believe, a member, was that the only date they required apart from the Test match and the Middlesex match was 21, 23 and 24 May against either MCC and Ground or Gentlemen of England, the exact title to be settled later. This was in August. Some considerable time afterwards – I think in October, when the fixture list was practically complete – I was asked for a date so that the Australians might meet the Gentlemen. Unfortunately, none of those dates which I had vacant were suitable, and it was impossible to clear a suitable one.

As to (a), no one knows better than Mr Warner what the expenses of the coming tour are likely to be. It was, therefore, imperative that as many matches as possible should be arranged, with a view to meeting these expenses. Our climate is none too reliable, and three or four matches ruined by rain might make a serious difference to the finances of the tour; and it is not impossible that on the days on which the Australians rested we might have perfect cricket weather, while the rain visited us when they had matches.

As to (b), the weaker counties are mainly those who have a big struggle every year to make both ends meet. A match with the Australians gives these counties a big lift financially, and revives and encourages cricket throughout the length and breadth of these counties. I am sure Mr Warner cannot object to this. I wonder what he would have said if, in the days when Middlesex were not the power in the land they are now, they had been refused a date with the Australians because they were not strong enough. Cricket is a queer game. It is hard to say now what will happen next summer, and it may be that when we get to the end of the 1921 season we shall find a county that was weak in 1920 at the top of the tree, which, though a disappointment, no doubt, to Mr Warner and myself personally, might not be a bad thing for cricket generally.

If a humble person like myself may venture to express an opinion on Mr Warner's article, may I say how cordially I agree with him? I believe we are in for a bumper season. Unless the weather prove a spoil-sport, the public will, I anticipate, patronize cricket as it never has before, and the only trouble will be to accommodate the crowds that want to watch the games, this not only when the Australians are engaged, but at all first-class matches. It makes one wish that one of the big Australian grounds could be set down in the middle of London.

Yours truly,
A. M. LATHAM

TEST MATCH CRITICS

From Mr S. M. J. Woods, 29 June 1921

Secretary of Somerset CCC. Born in New South Wales, he played for Cambridge University, Australia, Somerset and England (1886–1910), captaining Cambridge and Somerset. Also an England rugby international.

Sir, Three great cricketers have been selected to select the English Team.

Having in years gone by played for Australia *versus* England, I am naturally very pleased that we have won two out of the five Test games to be played. The England selectors have a difficult task to pick their side; this is not made any easier by people writing to the papers and giving their ideas of the team that should be picked, and also writing as to how to play fast bowling and how not to.

I am sure if there were less rubbish written on the subject the selected English Eleven would do much better in the future.

Yours,
S. M. J. WOODS

The selectors of 1921 were: J. Daniell (Cambridge University and Somerset), H. K. Foster (Oxford University and Worcestershire) and R. H. Spooner (Lancashire and England). Their decisions – England used a record number of 30 players in the series – and the absence through injury and illness of Hobbs contributed to Australia's 3–0 win in the Tests. The touring side, one of the strongest to visit, won 22 of their 38 matches.

THE LEG-TRAP THEORY

Leg-trap theory or Bodyline – short-pitched fast bowling, aimed at the batsman's body, with an unrestricted ring of close, leg-side fielders – was employed by Douglas Jardine, the England captain, as a means of curbing the prodigious scoring powers of Don Bradman and regaining the Ashes. Although leg theory was no novelty, in the hands of genuinely fast bowlers like Larwood, Voce and Bowes it became a formidable weapon, employed once the shine was off the ball.

From Mr Horace Hill, 4 January 1933

Sir, Until recently stumps were erected on the cricket pitch to be defended by the batsman and hit by the bowler. Endeavours were made by the bowler to make the batsman miss the ball so that he could be bowled. If the batsman made a bad stroke, which was his own fault, he could be caught out. These were among the essentials of cricket. In the leg-trap theory all these are reversed. The stumps are not bowled at, endeavour is made to make the batsman hit the ball either in order to defend himself (not his wicket) or to make a run. He can be caught off a good stroke. The application of the leg-trap theory, therefore, is an artifice, and such a thing, in some opinions, is foreign to 'cricket'.

Although not expressed in the same way, this is probably the basis of Australian criticism, which is not due to ill-feeling, as suggested in some quarters. The method of restricting a batsman to strokes on the on side does away with the possibility of cutting and driving, strokes which the public has paid much money to see.

Your obedient servant,
HORACE HILL

From Mr C. J. F. Gilmore, 13 January 1933

Sir, There seems at present to be much consternation among those who have the best interests of cricket at heart that the success of the leg-trap theory will cause the game to degenerate into a species of baseball. I think there need be little cause for alarm. A critical study of the history of the greatest of all games yields only one certain result – namely, that the game must always rise superior to players or theories of the game. The leg-trap theory will enjoy its successful phase, undoubtedly; just as certainly it will wane from the realm of good tactics.

The Hon. R. H. Lyttelton complained in his chapter on 'Batting' in the Badminton Book (1888) that in any Yorks v. Notts match 'the unhappy batsman would hardly get a single ball outside his legs to hit'. If only a fast bowler were put on (a comparative rarity) the hitting was a joy to behold! *Verb. sap.*

Did not Warwick Armstrong towards the end of that devastating English tour start leg-theory bowling in a mild form? And did not our pundits declare it a confession of weakness? Did not Root, of Worcestershire, play himself into an England team by taking seven Australian wickets for his county in one innings? One remembers the headlines of a provincial paper: 'Seven Cornstalks for one Root'!

The Micawbers of the cricket world are always justified, for something always turns up. The Hegelian dialectic is true to cricket if not to history. The great art of batting must be given a chance to see how it can meet this new Giant Despair. Bradman seems to have had no difficulty in dealing with Bowes and Larwood at Melbourne, and I have myself in a minor match seen the Nawab of Pataudi hit half a dozen boundaries through as many good 'leg-trap' fieldsmen. The only real harm coming from this successful phase of leg bowling is that inevitably next season many of our young hopefuls will bowl at the batsmen's legs instead of aiming at the wicket – a philosophically unsound view of the game. *Hinc illae lacrimae.* Yet the game must always win in the end, and continue flourishing while theories come and go.

Your obedient servant,
CHARLES J. F. GILMORE

The third Test at Adelaide on 13–19 January was one of the angriest and most unpleasant matches ever played. On the second day Woodfull was hit over the heart by the last ball of Larwood's second over. At the start of his next over the leg-trap was positioned and the crowd's anger rose to fury. On the third day Oldfield was put out of the match by a blow on the head from Larwood's bowling – albeit, on the batsman's admission, his own fault.

From Mr A. A. Milne, 20 January 1933
Playwright, essayist and novelist. Creator of Winnie the Pooh and devotee of cricket.

Sir, Now that it is officially announced that the bitter feeling already aroused by the colour of Mr Jardine's cap has been so intensified by the direction of Mr Larwood's bowling as to impair friendly relations between England and Australia, it is necessary that this new 'leg theory', as it is called, should be considered, not only without heat, but also, if possible, with whatever of a sense of humour Test Matches can leave to a cricketer.

It seems funny, then, to one who did not serve his apprenticeship as a writer by playing for Australia that a few years ago we were all agreed that cricket was being 'killed' by 'mammoth scores' and 'Marathon matches', and that as soon as a means is devised of keeping scores down to a reasonable size cricket is 'killed' again. It seems comic to such a one that, after years of outcry against over-prepared wickets, a scream of horror should go up when a bowler proves that even such a wicket has no terrors for him. It is definitely the laugh of the year that, season after season, batsmen should break the hearts of bowlers by protecting their wickets with their persons, and that, when at last the bowler accepts the challenge and bowls at their persons, the outraged batsmen and ex-batsmen should shriek in chorus that he is not playing cricket.

These things seem funny; but there is, of course, a serious side to the Australian Board of Control's protest. This says that the English bowling has made 'protection of the body by the batsman the main consideration', and if this were so there would be legitimate cause of complaint. But let us not forget that Mr McCabe, in his spare moments during the first Test match, managed to collect 180 runs, and Mr Bradman, in the second, 100; each of them scoring (even though scoring was necessarily a minor consideration) four times as quickly as Mr Jardine, whose body (up to the cap) was held as sacred. Let us not forget that, if this new form of bowling is really as startlingly new as is implied, lesser batsmen than these two should at least be given a chance of adapting themselves to it before the white flag is waved. But if modern batsmanship is really so unadventurous and unflexible that after three failures it announces itself beaten and calls for the laws to be altered, why, then, let the laws be altered; let everybody go on making runs, the artisan no less easily than the master; and let us admit frankly that the game is made for the batsmen only, and that it ceases to be cricket as soon as it can no longer be called 'a batsman's paradise'.

Yours, &c.,

A. A. MILNE

From Mr N. Shore, 20 January 1933

Sir, In this part of the world [Clevedon, Somerset] the latest street game is as follows:– Requirements: a rubber ball, a biscuit tin, and a bat. Method of play: the bowler, usually addressed as L . . . . . d, bowls at the batsman, who has to prevent himself from being touched by the ball, either by hitting it with the bat or by dodging. Should the ball touch him the rules of the game insist that he shall lie flat on the ground and then be carried off the field. Next man in.

Yours faithfully,

N. SHORE

Angry words between Woodfull and P. F. Warner, joint-manager of the MCC party, heightened the controversy. The Australian Board of Control cabled: ' . . . unless stopped at once it is likely to upset the friendly relations existing between Australia and England.'

From Viscount Buckmaster, 21 January 1933

Last Liberal Lord Chancellor of England, 1915–16, in Asquith's coalition government.

Sir, The discussion in your paper on 'leg bowling' revives old memories and old desires. Pitches like billiard tables and spectators numbered in thousands make people forget what cricket used to be. Fifty years ago this new danger was a common incident of every match played outside the few places where groundsmen guarded the turf. Fast bowlers – *quorum parvissima pars fui* – were regarded as essential and were often, as I was, most erratic. I have often seen a ball pitch once and then bounce straight into the backstop's hands.

Nor were these bowling eccentricities confined to local grounds. I remember on one occasion the first ball of a match slung with immense violence straight at the big black beard of W. G. Grace. Did he object? Certainly not; he simply hit it out of the ground and waited for the next.

In the country there were some pitches renowned for their fiery qualities. On one of these I recall a game in which Ranjitsinhji took part. Two benches from the village school provided the grand stand and on these were seated the squire, the local doctor – whose patients were long-suffering and few – the publican, and some countrymen.

Ranjitsinhji was clean bowled by the village postman, who wore his official costume, and all the four innings were finished in the day. As for leg balls and head balls and body balls, they formed the feature of the match, which no one seemed more thoroughly to enjoy than Ranjitsinhji himself.

The world has been made smooth for the game and its lords, but is it a better game?

Yours faithfully,
BUCKMASTER

From Mr Reginald Carter, 26 January 1933

Sir, Whether Horace had an instance in mind, or was merely prophetic of the power that games would obtain in the future, I do not know; but here is a remark which agrees with the alarming view taken by the Australian cricket authority of the effect of 'leg-theory' bowling on international relations:–

Horace, Epistle 19 (to Maecenas), last lines:–

> 'Ludus enim genuit trepidum certamen et iram;
> Ira truces inimicitias et funebre bellum!'

Conington being rather diffuse, may I give a plain translation? 'A game may beget dreadful strife and wrath, and from wrath may spring savage enmities and murderous war.'

Yours obediently,
REGINALD CARTER

From Mr L. G. Crawley, 27 January 1933

Cambridge University, Worcestershire and Essex (1922–36). Toured West Indies with MCC 1925–26. Outstanding games player from a famous sporting family, he appeared in four Walker Cup matches and was asked about his availability for this Bodyline tour. Golf correspondent of *The Daily Telegraph* 1947–72.

Sir, May I trespass on your valuable space to discuss the article which appeared in your pages on 19 January with regard to the protest recently received by the MCC from the Australian Board of Control against the employment of a 'leg-theory' in cricket?

In the first place, though McDonald and Gregory did undoubtedly send down an occasional ball at the batsman's body, they cannot be said, anyway while playing for Australia, to have employed a 'leg-theory', in that such balls were exceptional and were bowled to a field with only two men on the leg-side. It is surely unfair to compare these tactics with the policy of delivering six such balls per over to a field so set as to penalize a batsman who is defending not his wicket, but his head.

Your correspondent further suggests that 'so long as a "shock" bowler is not deliberately bumping down short-pitched balls or purposely aiming at the batsman, his bowling is perfectly fair'. Granted; but when six such balls are bowled in each over, either the action is a deliberate one, or else, if the bowler is continuously doing it accidentally, he is a rank bad bowler. You cannot have it both ways. The last thing I wish to do is to bring a charge of malice-aforethought towards the batsman against either our captain or the bowlers he employs. But that our 'shock' bowlers bowl deliberately at the batsman's body cannot honestly be denied.

The real objection of the Australians, your correspondent alleges, is to the 'array of leg-fielders'. I submit that it is to this, in conjunction with body-line bowling, that the Australians, very rightly, in my view, take exception. As long as these tactics are allowed, the batsman will be frightened into giving up his wicket, and if Bradman cannot survive them, I am satisfied that not one of the great players of the past could have fared any better.

It would obviously be impossible for even so august a body as the MCC to dictate to a captain as to how he should place his field. But a short-pitched ball is a bad ball, and one which, without the remotest chance of striking the wicket, stands a considerable chance of doing the batsman bodily harm. And it seems to me that the very least that can be done in the best interests of the game is to empower the umpire to 'no-ball' a bowler for pitching his deliveries short. But to my mind the whole question demands consideration from an entirely different angle. Your correspondent urges the point that 'Cricket is not played with a soft ball, and that a fast ball which hits a batsman on the body is bound to hurt.' Rugby football is also considered by some a fair training ground for manly and courageous virtues. And yet in the event of a player wilfully hacking, tripping, or striking another player, instead of going for the ball, the referee is required by the Laws of Rugby Football to order the offender off the field on the second offence. It seems to me that the analogy between this and the policy of deliberately bowling at a portion of the batsman's body which is not obscuring the wicket is a fairly close one; and the penalty is as well deserved in the one case as the other. In either game enough knocks are given and received in the ordinary course of events to satisfy the most bloodthirsty fire-eater among the spectators. But I would like to see some of the most eloquent supporters of the 'leg-theory' step into the arena against a bowler of Larwood's pace and face it for themselves.

Yours, &c.,

LEONARD CRAWLEY

MCC's reply deplored the tone and content of the Australian cable and left it to the hosts to determine whether the tour should continue. The Australian public, however, were anything but placated

From an Austranglian, 31 January 1933
Described in a leading article the next day as 'a distinguished Australian with friends in the Australian eleven'.

Sir, There are doubtless two sides to the leg-bowling case, but most people are agreed that it has been exaggerated out of all reason. I suggest that the two principal causes for this distortion are: (1) the sensational Press (the responsible Press in Australia, which is of high standard, has preserved a sense of proportion throughout); (2) the atmosphere created by the barrackers.

Nobody wishes to exacerbate the controversy, but it is time the public in England knew some of the facts about barrackers and barracking. My experiences of Anglo-Australian cricket go back 30 years. I know the barrackers well, for I have often sat among them and observed their ways – by choice, for they make an interesting study. They consist, in large part, of larrikins, habitual loafers, and 'dead-beats', or 'grass-chewers' (as they are called in Australia), and irresponsible youths who will always follow the lead of rowdy seniors. They are the worst products of what has been called 'vicarious athleticism': they play no games themselves and therefore understand nothing of the technique of the sports (except racing) which they spend a large part of their lives in watching. They have a lively mother-wit, and when things are going well they are very amusing, in a crude way, and can fairly be described as 'Good-humoured'.

Their intentions are not, in the first instance, hostile, but what they are principally 'out for' is horse-play. Their favourite amusement, for example, is throwing paper bags full of banana-skins and similar ammunition at those who stand up and obstruct the view.

Their horse-play, as usual, degenerates, on the slightest provocation, into brutality. For example: Mr Warner, then captain of England, must remember vividly an occasion (I was present) when the crowd bombarded the empty playing area at Sydney with glass bottles. The only reason was that, after a shower, the umpires took longer than pleased the crowd to resume play. No doubt the person who cast the first bottle did so in coarse fun, but what began in fun ended in scandal. The whims of these onlookers are incalculable, and if they once 'get a down' on a player, often for no reason at all, his life is made a burden to him.

Visitors are not the only victims of these pests. They are equally offensive to some of their own representatives. During the last Australian tour in England I discussed the question with a member of the Australian team, whose name would carry much weight if I were at liberty to mention it. I was surprised at some of the things which he told me, and at the emphasis with which he spoke of them. He said that things had become so bad that the cricketing authorities were considering stern repressive measures; and that it was becoming increasingly difficult to get promising young cricketers to go into 'big' cricket because they did not think it worth the unpleasantness. He referred with unrestrained bitterness to the fickleness of the roughs. 'If you make 100,' he said, 'nothing is good enough for you; and the next moment, if you misfield a ball, they will hoot you.' Another Australian player told me that there had been moments when he 'would willingly have turned a machine-gun on the crowd'.

These facts ought to be known. The hooligans are not representative, but they can and do generate an atmosphere. In that atmosphere is it any wonder if tempers are lost and indiscretions are committed? It is Australia's task to cope with the problem, which has always been bad and is now threatening to kill the game.

Yours faithfully,

AUSTRANGLIAN

The three-week gap between the third and fourth Tests allowed the atmosphere to cool, but not before the Dominions Secretary had summoned MCC officials

From Mr B. J. T. Bosanquet, 6 February 1933

Oxford University, Middlesex and England (1898–1919). Inventor of the googly or 'Bosie'.

Sir, One has tried to avoid being drawn into the so-called 'body-bowling' controversy, but when Cabinet Ministers – well!

Surely the point is generally missed. Any bowler, bowling from the off side of the wicket to a batsman, who pitches a ball without break on it on or outside the leg stump, will miss the leg stump by 1in. to 6in. or more according to length. Such a ball therefore cannot hit the wicket, and so presents no danger to the batsman unless he plays at it. Therefore any batsman who can use his feet has merely to move inwards and let the ball pass him, unless he thinks he can make a scoring stroke off it. If the bowler tires of this game and bowls on the off or middle stump, the batsman has a large unguarded area into which to make his stroke. It is the ball which pitches on the wicket and may hit it which is dangerous, not the ball that must miss it. One would like to see some of the batsmen who object to this type of bowling facing on a bad wicket J. B. King (the Philadelphian) bowling fast 'in-swingers' (*pace* Mr Allom, this was over 35 years ago), or Tom Richardson bowling very fast break-backs, or Cotter at Melbourne with every good-length ball rising shoulder or head high and eight men on the leg side, as many of us had to do. One would also like to see 'W.G.', 'Ranji', MacLaren, Hirst, Trumper, Macartney, and others facing Larwood's long-hops on a good wicket. One can see the scorers being pretty busy.

The Australian Board appear to have forgotten the fact that it does not come within their province or that of the MCC to govern the actual proceedings on the field, which are rightly left to those who represent them and the umpires.

It is not the direction of the ball which is objected to, but the pace. Therefore if any Australians are really aggrieved at having to face fast bowling, let them come over here next year and see our players batting against Constantine (who is really fast). If they hear any squeals, or if the MCC send a cable of protest to the West Indies, then one can only –

> Be jubilant that we have flourished here
> Before the love of cricket overdone
> Had swamped the very players with themselves.
> (With apologies to Tennyson.)
>
> I am yours truly,
> B. J. T. BOSANQUET

England won the series 4–1; Bradman's average, hitherto more than 100, was a mere 56.57

From Mr F. Akenhead, 21 June 1933

Sir, So many adverse comments have appeared in the Australian Press that it may be interesting to read an extract which occurs in a letter which I have received from an old cricketer in Australia who has lived practically all, if not the whole of, his life there:–

'We had a very exciting time of it here during the cricket Test matches, and every one was on tip-toe. The body-bowling of Larwood caused a lot of talk and is still doing so. For my part I welcomed it, and think it will do a tremendous lot of good to big cricket in Western Australia. We were getting swelled-headed and there was far too much "Bradmanitis" in the air.'

Yours, &c.,

F. AKENHEAD

In summer 1933 the West Indians, Constantine and Martindale, at Old Trafford at least, gave England a taste of their own medicine. Hammond was hit in the face; Jardine scored a hundred. Opinion hardened against Bodyline and when assurances were given to the Australians that any form of bowling which was obviously a direct attack on the batsman would be treated as an offence against the spirit of the game, they went ahead with their tour of England in 1934. Although the leg-trap theory died out, intimidation of batsmen continues.

INTIMIDATING BOWLING

From Mrs Fianach Lawry (née Jardine), 18 January 1975

Sir, I agree with Mr Noel-Baker (11 January) that 'bodyline' bowling is highly dangerous. So is fielding close in to the bat – and so are boxing, motor racing, gliding, fox-hunting, rock climbing, aqualung diving and many other sports.

I do not want to discuss the ethics of 'bodyline', but I would like to comment on some of Mr Noel-Baker's remarks about my father, the late Douglas Jardine.

First the suggestion that Jardine hated the Australians is non-sensical to anyone who knew him. He had many friends, and later a company, in Australia.

'Bodyline' bowling was not his exclusive invention (it had been used long before under the term 'leg theory'). It was discussed with and fully approved of by the MCC, as the one way to beat Bradman, before Jardine's team left England in 1932. When the Australians began losing the series and a row blew up, the MCC failed to back Jardine, who took full responsibility and blame. He also showed that, with physical courage, 'bodyline' bowling can be played successfully, and scored centuries off it against the West Indians.

The MCC selectors thought that 'bodyline' was a justifiable weapon with which to win the Ashes in 1932–3, and 43 years later the Australian selectors appear to agree.

Yours, etc,

FIANACH LAWRY

TEST MATCH WICKET

Lancashire had instructed their groundsman to produce pitches which would encourage the bowlers. England beat West Indies by 202 runs, all but three of the wickets falling to spinners.

From Lieutenant Colonel J. W. A. Stephenson, DSO, 16 June 1950
Essex and Worcestershire (1934–47). Played in one 'Victory' Test.

Sir, We have obviously not heard the last of the Test match wicket at Old Trafford. May I, very briefly, before it is too late and before we are subjected to a spate of reasoning as to why this wicket was so 'abominable', 'vile', or 'unfair', plead the cause of the bowler and of the wicket itself? Where a side in Test or country cricket scores 600 to 800 runs and the accredited batsmen have duly recorded their centuries or double centuries, the cry goes up that the wickets are doped and the dice are too heavily loaded against the poor, unfortunate bowlers.

Now we read of a wicket where the bowler is at last on top, and it is the poor batsmen – excluding Evans, of course – who cannot record their hundreds and double hundreds. Judged by the accounts of the match which one has read, the wicket performed not only in a remarkable manner but also possessed a remarkable *repertoire*. If the state of the wicket is always to have the last word in the game then I hope that wicket at Old Trafford will arise in its wrath and soundly rebuke and condemn all those who have criticized it for its unseemly behaviour.

I am, Sir, yours faithfully,

J. W. A. STEPHENSON

FOURTH TEST

From the Rt. Hon. Sir Alan Lascelles, GCB, GCVO, CMG, MC, 2 August 1956

Private Secretary to King George VI 1943–52 and to Queen Elizabeth II 1952–53. Keeper of the Royal Archives. Directorships of Midland Bank and Royal Academy of Music.

Sir, Because Laker took 19 wickets for 90 runs in the fourth Test match, there is a tendency among the armchair critics to say that the soil of Old Trafford ('Oh my Hornby and my Barlow long ago') has suddenly become treacherous and malevolent, and that it is all most unfair. I do not recall a similar wail being raised when Victor Trumper, Archie MacLaren, or Don Bradman used to make fabulous quantities of runs on practically every cricket ground under the sun. Might not the simple explanation of these phenomena be that the one is a devilish good bowler as the others were devilish good bats?

After Agincourt, the French military commentators said it just was not fair and their horses could not be expected to gallop through all that mud; but the fact remains that the English bowmen were in capital form that day.

Yours faithfully,
A. LASCELLES

NOT CRICKET?

From Mr Richie Benaud, 25 August 1967

New South Wales and Australia (1948–64), captain of both.

Sir, As a journalist and television commentator, it hurts to ruin a good story. But having for the sixth time read from my good friend Denzil Batchelor that when I came to England as Australia's captain in 1961 I announced that I had given orders to my team to 'walk' when they knew they were out . . . I think the time may well have arrived.

What I said on board ship that day, in answer to a question by *The Times* correspondent, was: 'We have had a team meeting and the general policy of the team is to walk (to fit in with English practice) but the matter is left entirely to the individual. If any player in the side wishes to rely on the umpire's judgment then that is entirely a matter for him and he will take the umpire's decision as it comes.'

In fact, there were a number in that side who believed and still believe that the matter should be left to the umpire who is there to do that specific job. Later on that tour in a county match, I played at a ball that spun out of the rough into the out-stretched left hand of a diving first slip and the roar of the crowd and the shouts of the players had me two steps towards the pavilion before I realized that in fact I hadn't hit it.

It may have been justice for the 1956 incident, but the 'flexibility of cricket's morality' didn't cut a great deal of ice with me that day for it happened to be my first 'pair' in first-class cricket.

Yours faithfully,
RICHIE BENAUD

In the Lord's Test match of 1956 Benaud, by his own admission, had been caught at the wicket when three, but was given not out and went on to score 97 and help Australia to victory.

ASHES TO ASHES

From Mrs Susan MacRae, 17 July 1975

Sir, After today's debacle at Edgbaston are they going to burn the team rather than the stumps?

Yours faithfully,
SUSAN MACRAE

Australia's victory by an innings and 85 runs, completed by early afternoon on the fourth day, was the first by a visiting country in a Test match at Edgbaston. England had put Australia in to bat, a decision which cost Mike Denness the captaincy.

ABANDONMENT OF HEADINGLEY TEST

Campaigners for the release of George Davis (imprisoned for robbery and assault) dug holes and poured oil on the Headingley pitch during the night, causing the abandonment of the fourth Test between England and Australia.

From Dr R. J. Birts, 21 August 1975

Sir, Bring back the willow.

I am, Sir, your obedient servant,
ROBIN BIRTS

From Mr Will W. Inge, 23 August 1975

Sir, Isn't it amazing that with 22 world class players, 2 umpires, balls galore, and one of the best grounds in England all available (and paid for), and millions waiting for a cricket match there to watch, there should be a decision for *no play*.

Some of us think cricket is a game.

Thank God for Village Cricket which many play and few watch.

Before my blood boils,

Yours once and for ever,

WILL W. INGE

From Mr Dennis A. Brunning, 27 August 1975

Sir, I am amazed that apparently there are Englishmen who equate cricket with mere entertainment and can write of it in such terms as – 'The show must go on'. Sir, cricket is not a circus, neither is it a matter of just belting a ball about a field.

The game and its results depends not only on the skill of the batsmen, the art of the bowlers and the sure-handedness of the fieldsmen but also on the nuances of a particular wicket and on the vagaries of a particular day's weather.

It is quite unthinkable that a match so finely poised as was the Headingley Test, should be continued on another wicket, much less another ground.

So far as the vandals are concerned my immediate thought was that they should be boiled in the oil they had so unwisely provided.

Yours, etc,

DENNIS A. BRUNNING

Davis, who was said to be a cricket lover, was released, but two years later was convicted of another armed robbery.

CENTENARY TEST GUESTS

From the Secretary of the South African Cricket Association,
8 February 1977

Sir, The list of those former England and Australian cricketers who will be guests at the Centenary Test to be played in Melbourne from

12 March has come my way. How interesting it is that the eleven England players all now over 70 years in age who figure in the list make an ideal England team. They are, in batting order:

			Age
1	Herbert Sutcliffe	Yorkshire	82
2	Andy Sandham	Surrey	86
3	Bob Wyatt	Warwick	75
4	Frank Woolley	Kent	89
5	Les Ames (WK)	Kent	71
6	Eddie Paynter	Lancs	75
7	P. G. H. Fender	Surrey	84
8	G. O. Allen	Middlesex	74
9	Harold Larwood	Notts	72
10	George Geary	Leicester	83
11	Tommy Mitchell	Derby	74

The average age of this team, which really does fit all needs for every occasion, is 79 years. Australian Test players seem less likely to make old bones. The best side I can draw up from the guests is: Ponsford, Rigg, Chipperfield, Pellew, Ryder, Barnett (WK), O'Reilly, McCormick, Grimmett, Ebeling.

Although of average age some four years less than their opponents (with a wicketkeeper still but 68) and for all the menace of the Grimmett/O'Reilly combination, most of us would fancy the chances of the team that any one of Fender, Allen or Wyatt might skipper.

Yours faithfully,
CHARLES FORTUNE

THE 77 CLUB

From Mr Robert Lord, 13 July 1977
Of Darlinghurst, New South Wales.

Sir, The 7-7-77 index, the subject of the letters of Mr Petgrave-Johnson (7 July) and Mr D. R. Forrester (9 July), extends to international sport.

The cricket Test between England and Australia commenced at Old Trafford on 7-7-77, which was the 77th day of the Australians' tour. In the 77th over, K. D. Walters took his score to 77, his partner at the wicket being R. W. Marsh, batting at No. 7.

Yours truly,

ROBERT LORD

THE MATCH THAT FAILED

The Centenary Test match in England was marred by a long delay on the third day when the umpires, and captains, considered the ground unfit for play. During the afternoon there was a scuffle on the pavilion steps involving the umpires, some MCC members, and the captains.

From Mr R. S. Alexander, QC, 2 September 1980

Sir, Any ugly moments at Lord's on Saturday are to be deplored. But for every individual who regrettably gave vent to his feelings there were many thousands deeply frustrated not only at the lack of play but also at its consequences for the match. The umpires have borne the blame. The authorities are said to have been imaginative in supporting extended playing hours, despite the fact that the idea of playing until 8 pm on Saturday apparently ignored the lack of floodlights. The plain fact is however that, barring a miracle or a contrived finish, the Centenary Test match has fizzed miserably.

Yet Sunday was fine weather; the crowd could have come. Why was there no play? At the beginning of last week we were told that to play on Sunday in the event of a washout on any earlier day would have been unfair to ticket holders for Monday if the match had finished in three days. This is, on its face, just understandable. But how many Test matches finish in three days? And could it not have been discovered that the groundsman was preparing a wicket which could well prove, as it did in the event, plumb and easy paced?

The weather forecast was for bad weather at the end of the week. By Thursday evening it was virtually certain and by Friday lunchtime clear beyond all doubt that the match could not finish in three days. We all know that there is much preparation for an important cricket match, but this was a great occasion which in the end will have been principally rich only in nostalgia.

It is hard to believe that enterprising contingency planning could not have included the possibility of Sunday play, with a final decision to be taken when the very slight risk of injustice to Monday ticket holders was no longer possible. This would have ensured some reward to those many enthusiasts who were denied play on Friday and Saturday and it would have kept the game more alive.

Yours faithfully,
ROBERT ALEXANDER

From Mr H. Seabourn, 6 September 1980

Sir, None of the controversy would have arisen if the match had been played on the proper ground, the Oval, where the first Test was played.

Yours sincerely,
H. SEABOURN

From Dr O. Caiger-Smith, 9 September 1980

Sir, There was no breathless hush at Lord's on the last evening of the Centenary Test with Australia, as the English innings faded into inanition. Cricket is a game and therefore fun, and this particular match was designed to celebrate this fact and 100 years of cricket fellowship.

As it was, England pursued its Test policy of playing not to lose. Circumstances sometimes justify this policy but it was quite out of place on this sunny day. The result was less important than the game itself, which had a glorious chance of an exciting ending offered by the Australian declaration. Greg Chappell's languid applause at the moment of Boycott's century was, I am sure, not due to lack of appreciation of the skill displayed, but to the fact that England was deliberately letting the game die.

England had the blinding light. It might have had ten to make and the last man in – and cricket.

Yours sincerely,
OLIVER CAIGER-SMITH

From Mr Anthony Bradbury, 27 November 1980

Sir, The MCC has just spent over £2,000 in postage by sending to all its members a short letter saying that those who had misbehaved on the Saturday of the Centenary Test had now been disciplined.

Would it not have been more constructive and appropriate to have used that £2,000 towards the provision of more adequate covering for the playing area?

Yours faithfully,
ANTHONY BRADBURY

HEROES IN RETREAT

England beat Australia at Headingly by 18 runs after following on.

From Mr C. A. Philbrick, 25 July 1981

Sir, The sight of Ian Botham and, on the following day, Bob Willis, having to make their undignified headlong dash for the safety of the dressing room was the only sad aspect of the exciting finish to the recent Test.

It is a player's *right* to be allowed to walk back to the pavilion in the traditional manner after producing an exceptional piece of cricket. It is more moving and emotionally satisfying for the player and spectator alike. I should have felt cheated at not being able to stand and clap my hands off for the full minute such an exit usually took years ago.

Yours, etc,
C. A. PHILBRICK

THE GREATEST INNINGS?

The Times correspondent wrote that Botham's 118 v Australia at Old Trafford was, of its kind, perhaps the greatest innings ever played.

From Mr Michael Croft, OBE, 21 August 1981

Director of the National Youth Theatre.

Sir, I would not take away a jot or tittle from the glory of Botham's Test innings last Saturday (report, 17 August), but I cannot accept it as superior to what I regard as the greatest innings played in my lifetime – McCabe's 232 at Trent Bridge in 1938.

When Botham was out, the game could still have gone either way, as Yallop and Border were later to prove. Not so at Nottingham in 1938. England had declared at 658 for eight and, with Bradman and the flower of Australia's batting back in the pavilion, nothing stood between the slaughter of Australia but McCabe and the tail-enders, Barnett, O'Reilly, McCormick and Fleetwood-Smith.

It was then that McCabe (who had saved Australia often before, not least at Sydney in 1932 with an astonishing innings of 187 against the lethal might of Larwood and Voce) took utter command. From 194 for six he took that score to 411. According to Neville Cardus, he scored 232 out of 300 in 230 minutes, the last 78 runs coming in 28 minutes. He did not win, but he made it possible for Australia to save the match.

Bradman not only called his players on to the balcony to watch. Years later the Don (who, to English players, seemed incapable even of shedding a tear at a funeral) admitted: 'Towards the end I could scarcely watch the play. My eyes were filled as I drank in the glory of his shots. It was the greatest innings I ever saw or ever hope to see.'

We all had the chance to watch Botham's innings last week. In 1938, bound to my school desk in Manchester, I was able only to hear reports of McCabe's masterpiece surreptitiously on radio between lessons; but the memory of it has remained with me ever since.

None the less, Botham has helped to restore cricket to its true glory. After the locust years of dreadful caution and dire mediocrity, heroes are now with us again (not only Botham, but Border too); and nobleness walks, if not 'in our ways', at least in our cricket fields again.

Yours faithfully,
MICHAEL CROFT

From Mr Reginald Bosanquet, 21 August 1981
Son of B.J.T., the inventor of the googly. The 1914 letter, of a general nature, derided golf as being a pleasant recreation rather than a manly game like cricket, football or polo.

Sir, Almost seventy years ago my father wrote you a letter, which you kindly published (4 June 1914), saying that no game which did not require pluck and physical courage could be called 'great'.

I wonder how many people, like myself, notice how Ian Botham goes to the wicket wearing nothing more round his head than his beard, whereas other less exciting and magical batsmen appear looking like a motor-scooter windshield with transistor earphones. Perhaps there is a lesson here, somewhere?

Yours faithfully,
REGINALD BOSANQUET

From Mr R. N. G. Stone, 21 August 1981

Sir, England's retention of the 'Ashes' reminds me of a curious but little-known statistic. Since the war the Conservative and Labour parties have held power for roughly equal lengths of time (18 years 11 months and 17 years 4 months respectively). During the same period England has held the 'Ashes' for 13½ years: of these, 10¾ years (with more to come) have been during Conservative governments, but only 2¾ under Labour.

Cricket-loving patriots will know which way to vote next time!

Yours faithfully,
R. N. G. STONE

One year and five months later, still under a Conservative government, England lost the Ashes.

RECOVERING THE ASHES

From Mr Paul Myers, 20 August 1977

Sir, Having recovered the Ashes in this country first in 1926, the year of the Queen's birth; then in 1953, her Coronation year; and now in 1977, Silver Jubilee year, will we have to wait until the next great event in the Queen's life for such an event to take place again? The year 2002, the Golden Jubilee, seems a long way away.

Yours faithfully,
PAUL B. MYERS

3

CRICKET AND
CONSCIENCE

THE SOUTH AFRICAN CRICKETERS

From Mr G. Lacy, 26 March 1901

Sir, I observe that a team of cricketers is about to leave South Africa for this country. At a time like the present, with the call for young men to put an end to the deplorable state of affairs there, and when we ourselves are sending out the best of our manhood for that purpose, it is, to say the least of it, the most wretched of taste for these young men to leave it on a cricket tour. I trust the British public will take this view of the matter. Next year we should be delighted to see them, but today it seems quite monstrous.

G. LACY

They played no Test matches, but the tour was, in a cricket sense, successful. Their presence in England, however, made little impact on the cricketing public.

SOUTH AFRICA'S CRICKET TEAM

From Mr Geoffrey Lowick, 8 April 1960

Sir, I am distressed to read today, as I am sure most other South Africans are, that demonstrations are being organized against the South African cricket team. I deplore the policy and consequences of *apartheid*, and also play cricket. They are not the same thing. The

South African cricket team are representing their country as cricketers, not as politicians, nor even as an electorate. In fact, in view
of their English background, they probably do not support the Government, but this does not affect the principle at stake. Their
association together as a body is due to their ability at cricket, not to
any political affinity. Whatever their political opinions, however, a
protest against a team is not only wrong but probably harmful.

By demonstrating against a sporting body one is contaminating
with ill-will occasions which should foster friendship. In South
Africa the playing fields are among the few places where Afrikaans
and English speaking people, unhampered by politics, can meet and
understand each other better. It is hoped the same may be said of
South African sides on English fields.

The opinions of South Africans visiting England might indeed be
modified. A demonstration against people whose personal views
are unknown is, however, presumptious. An open declaration of
hostility on arrival will, if anything, drive South Africans away from
the cause of the demonstrators rather than aligning them to it. The
result will be the opposite of that intended, which will, it is hoped,
reflect only on the demonstrators' judgment and not on their
sincerity.

Yours, &c.,
GEOFFREY LOWICK

MCC SELECTION

Basil D'Oliveira scored 158 against Australia at the Oval but was omitted
from the touring party for South Africa.

From Mr Jim Powell, 30 August 1968

Sir, How strange is the decision not to send Basil D'Oliveira to
South Africa this winter.

D'Oliveira's inclusion in the side for the last Test came as a surprise to many; he has batted indifferently for Worcestershire this
season, while his bowling (for which, some say, he was played) is
neither penetrating nor, as it turned out, was it in very heavy
demand for his side. In neither capacity did he in any way replace
the injured Prideaux, an opening batsman, for whom Green or

Sharpe would have been a logical substitute, or Barrington, had an experienced middle-order batsman been required.

Hence, D'Oliveira's inclusion seemed to be purely designed as a make or break match for him as far as the tour was concerned. If he failed, no one could say he was a pawn hard done by; if he succeeded no one could say his selection for South Africa was solely a provocation. The fact that his great innings owed a certain amount to dropped catches is neither here nor there – such is cricket, and a similar case could be made for the omission of Edrich, all but bowled at the beginning of his innings! In any case, most of the dropped catches came after he had scored his century.

That there was an excellent case for D'Oliveira's omission from the touring party prior to last Friday is indisputable, and indeed there is still some case for it now. It may also be that the choice was right for the Oval and not for Cape Town. But that is not the whole point. What is difficult to see is how the selectors could regard D'Oliveira (in Mr Insole's own words) as one of the best 11 players for the England team before his innings, and not as one of the best 15 after it. This apparent lack of judgment and logicality must harm not only their own image, but that of cricket as well.

Yours faithfully,

JIM POWELL

From Mr W. Gething, 2 September 1968
Writing from Hepworth, Huddersfield.

Sir, Mr Richard Wainwright – my MP – is concerned about the omission of Mr D'Oliveira from the MCC South African party.

I have asked him to take up with the Race Relations Board about the omission of Messrs Binks, Hutton and Sharpe, which appears to be a clear case of discrimination against the Yorkshire race.

Yours truly,

W. GETHING

THE D'OLIVEIRA AFFAIR

When Tom Cartwright was ruled out on medical grounds and D'Oliveira was chosen to replace him, the South African Prime Minister refused to receive what he called a team forced upon his country by people 'with certain political aims'.

From Mr Robin Marlar, 19 September 1968
Cambridge University and Sussex (1951–62), captaining both. Cricket correspondent of *The Sunday Times*.

Sir, One aspect of the D'Oliveira affair which deserves further attention is the constitutional one. Under MCC's praiseworthy and unselfish lead, the administration of cricket is becoming a much more democratic business.

However, those who have the responsibility of nominating and voting for members and officers of powerful bodies like the selection committee and the Test and County Cricket Board need some indication of the record of candidates for these important positions.

It may be undesirable that the names of those selectors who voted against D'Oliveira, or for that matter against Milburn, be publicly issued, but they should certainly be made available to county cricket committees. Many members of such committees believe, as I do, that the cricketing grounds on which D'Oliveira was excluded were specious, and that the subsequent statements showed a lack of logic and humanity which was bound to lead to a public outcry.

This outcry has led step by step to the grotesque position in which Dr Vorster has been given some excuse, should he decide on what must surely be the total breach in cricketing relations between this country and South Africa. There is still no sign that the names of those of the eight selectors who voted for or against D'Oliveira's selection will ever be known to anyone. How then are those at the grass roots to decide who should or should not be invited to continue in the game's administration at national level?

Yours sincerely,
ROBIN MARLAR

MR BASIL D'OLIVEIRA

From Marshal of the Royal Air Force Sir Dermot A. Boyle,
21 September 1968

Sir, One cheering aspect of the otherwise sordid D'Oliveira controversy is the impeccable behaviour of Mr Basil D'Oliveira himself.

His modest attitude to the whole affair and his refusal to make capital out of the situation provide an outstanding example of good manners, good sense and, incidentally, good politics, because he has inadvertently done more for the cause against racial discrimination than any marching, slogan waving, rioting crowd could ever achieve.

The publicity surrounding this case has given us a brief glimpse of the character of the man at the centre of the storm and we are the richer for that experience.

Yours faithfully,

D. A. BOYLE

MCC cancelled the tour on 24 September.

RACIAL BIAS AND TEST CRICKET

From Mr Mark Bonham Carter, and others, 24 May 1969
Including the future and past England cricketers, Mike Brearley (Cambridge University and Middlesex, 1961–82), and Frank Tyson (Northamptonshire, 1952–60). Mr Bonham Carter, Chairman of the Race Relations Board 1966–70, is son of Sir Maurice Bonham Carter (Oxford University and Kent, 1902).

Sir, We believe that the majority of members of the MCC Council abhor apartheid. Nevertheless, members of the council who have spoken publicly since the special meeting of MCC which discussed future tours with South Africa have dismissed those who query the wisdom of going ahead with the 1970 tour as 'fanatics'.

They have suggested that the issues are not connected with sport and morality, but only with 'politics'. So, they say, it is no concern of English cricketers if African, Indian or Coloured cricketers in South Africa are denied fair recognition *indefinitely*. We note that this view has been repudiated neither by the Club Committee nor by the Council, nor, apparently, by any of their individual members.

Surely, it is no longer necessary to point out that by standing firmly to a policy that all teams should be selected on merit we do not thereby logically commit ourselves to a 'boycott' of all countries of whose 'policies' one may disapprove. If that were so, there would indeed be little international sport. It is when politics get *into* sport, and control and distort its very structure, as they have done in South Africa, that sportsmen are bound to be concerned.

We who are all concerned for the future of cricket and of race relations which are now closely tied up together, believe that it would be a constructive move if the MCC Committee, and through them the MCC Council, and the International Cricket Conference (with appropriate re-wording) would declare themselves in terms such as the following:–

We believe that racial discrimination has no place in cricket and that international teams should always be selected on merit. For this reason, while anxious to continue cricket relations with South Africa, we are unwilling to go on playing indefinitely under current conditions, that is against sides representative of white South Africans only.

Yours faithfully,
MARK BONHAM CARTER, MIKE BREARLEY,
JEREMY HUTCHINSON, J. P. W. MALLALIEU, MARCH,
IVOR MONTAGU, PHILIP NOEL-BAKER, TREVOR
PARK, ALAN ROSS, NICHOLAS SCOTT, DAVID
SHEPPARD, FRANK TYSON

In September 1969 the itinerary for the 1970 tour was announced and the 'Stop the Seventy Tour' committee was formed. Campaigning started in earnest on both sides; the nation was divided. At Lord's barbed wire went up.

A WORLD ELEVEN

From Mr Alan Gibson, 5 February 1970

Author and broadcaster. Writer on cricket and rugby for *The Times* and *The Sunday Times*, his first (unpaid) cricket report for *The Times* recording a victory for his school, Taunton, over RNC Dartmouth in 1942.

Sir, The prospect of the cricket season must strike dismay into everyone who loves cricket.

The situation could still be redeemed if, as has indeed been suggested in the press, the South African tour were to be abandoned, and its place taken by a tour of a World XI, which would naturally include some leading South African cricketers.

This would have the following advantages:

(1) Since the World XI would be chosen on an inter-racial basis, it would hardly be possible to demonstrate against it on anti-racialist grounds.

(2) Those South African cricketers who are willing to play for the World XI would have made the clearest possible demonstration of their own views on race (and such South African cricketers as I know are liberally-minded on this subject). They would not only increase the esteem in which we hold them as individuals, but they would help to create an image of South African sport altogether more in keeping with the nature of its sportsmen.

(3) The counties, and cricket generally, could look forward to a pleasing financial bonus, instead of the possibility of bankruptcy.

(4) The public would be enabled to see most of the best cricketers in the world, at a high, competitive level. (I see no reason why England caps should not be awarded, and the matches treated as Tests for statistical purposes: this assumes a 'World XI' of sufficient strength could be raised, but that is not impracticable.)

(5) We should all enjoy it so much.

This proposal irritates the extreme left-wing demonstrators, because they would have nothing left against which to demonstrate. It also irritates the extreme cricket-establishment people, some of whom seem to relish the thought of the tour, barbed wire and truncheons and all, to show that they are not going to be dictated to by the long-haired permissives. While both these attitudes are understandable, neither has anything to do with cricket.

The Cricket Council could reasonably and graciously withdraw the invitation to South Africa. There is no question of them having to 'climb down'. They could simply say that they regret the tour is not feasible, which is no more than the truth.

The rugby tour has hardened extreme attitudes, often very unpleasantly. Cricket is a silly, precious, vulnerable game. I love it dearly, so do countless others. Let us try to see it does not suffer the same miserable fate.

I think of the Nawab of Pataudi as the kind of man who could make a tremendous success of leading a tour such as this. How good it would be if we could look back on the season of 1970 as the beginning of a new and happy era in international cricket, and not as a stricken battlefield!

Yours sincerely,
ALAN GIBSON

THE JOB OF REPORTING

From Mr John Arlott, 22 April 1970

Author and broadcaster, his voice synonymous with cricket. Cricket correspondent of *The Guardian* 1968–80. Also wrote for *The Times*. He had said that he would not commentate on the South African tour for the BBC.

Sir, Your leader writer (18 April) is entitled, if not generous, to describe me as 'emotional' for wishing to oppose apartheid. Anyone of mildly liberal views, however, must protest when he argues that the difference in the racial situation in South Africa between the pre-Nationalist period of 1947 and the present day is that 'it simply was not the fashion to notice racial discrimination . . . in 1947'.

It is such ignorance of apartheid that causes some British people tacitly to acquiesce in it: in one empowered to comment on these matters in a national newspaper it is gravely disquieting.

Yours faithfully,
JOHN ARLOTT

PRAYERS FOR RAIN

From the Revd S. W. Wilson, 30 April 1970

Sir, The Bishop of Gloucester asks for prayers that the South African Test matches may be rained off. This is a bit unfair, not least on the farmers in his diocese, for, as the bishop will recollect, the rain falls on the just and unjust.

Has the bishop considered the more dramatic and effective calling-down of fire and brimstone? Or he might make little wax images of the touring team and stick pins in them the night before each Test match is due to start.

Yours faithfully,
SPENCER W. WILSON

RISKS OF GOING AHEAD

From the Bishop of Woolwich and others, 6 May 1970

The Rt Revd David Sheppard (Cambridge University, Sussex and England, 1947–63, captaining all three; Bishop of Woolwich 1969–75, subsequently Bishop of Liverpool) and a distinguished cast from the arts, Church and politics, including Lord (Learie) Constantine, a dynamic West Indies cricketer (1922–45) and Trinidad politician and High Commissioner in London.

Sir, We, who are drawn from a wide range of life in Britain, are profoundly disturbed by the implications of going through with the white South African cricket tour this summer.

We do not wish to enter into any detailed arguments about who is to blame for the situation which threatens us all during this summer. That is past history. To go ahead with the tour now can do no good to the cause of cricket or of sport in general. There is a serious danger that it will result in international cricket disintegrating into a black camp and a white camp. Above all the tour would damage the already strained racial situation in this country.

We therefore appeal to the Cricket Council to demonstrate their sense of responsibility as citizens, and at the same time their concern for the future of international cricket by cancelling, even at this late stage, their invitation to the South African team.

Yours faithfully,
DAVID WOOLWICH, RICHARD ATTENBOROUGH, CONSTANTINE, JAMES MITCHELL, L. OLIVIER, SAINSBURY, REG PRENTICE, JEREMY THORPE, EDWARD BOYLE, EDNA O'BRIEN, TREVOR HUDDLESTON, C.R., EDWARD WOODWARD, NEIL E. WATES, HENRY MOORE, KENNETH CLARK, IAN HISLOP (O.P.), MOLLIE BUTLER

On 21 May the Home Secretary asked the Cricket Council to cancel the tour 'on the grounds of broad public policy'. On 22 May the tour was called off.

BREAK WITH FRIENDS

From Mr Russell Endean, 27 May 1970
Transvaal and South Africa (1945–61).

Sir, The actions which have led to the cancellation of the South African cricket tour will have saddened a considerable section of the white population in South Africa particularly those with backgrounds such as my own. Though having lived the last nine years in England I was born in South Africa of English parents. My upbringing was coloured by references to England as home, that British goods were automatically the best, in fact to buy otherwise was regarded as sacrilege.

During the war my parents, along with countless thousands of other South Africans, threw open their home to the British troops in South Africa. Virtually to a man the country's cricketers joined in the fight against Hitler; all were volunteers for there was no conscription in South Africa. Of the players opposed to each other in the Test series immediately before the war four failed to return – Hedley Verity and Ken Farnes of the MCC party and Dooley Briscoe and Chud Langton of South Africa.

I was fortunate enough to tour England with the South African teams in 1951 and 1955. Although the way of life in South Africa was then much the same as it is now, the teams were welcomed here in the most warming way. Particularly in 1951 it was obvious, because of rationing, that the numerous kindnesses bestowed upon us by the people represented real sacrifices, often involving things that money simply could not buy.

Has the whole position now changed? Admittedly a new generation has emerged nurtured, alas, on the South African image presented by television and the press in which the only news of interest is the bad news. Despite the latest image that brands all South Africans as racist, those who know South Africa are aware that it has its full quota of righteous citizens who by their very presence contribute to a better life for all. Ali Bacher, the South African captain, is, in fact, a doctor who has spent some years in a non-European hospital.

The Government now sees fit to break this cricket tie, a tie dating back to 1888. In doing this it has knocked especially at South Africa's English element. It has struck at a friend, indeed a blood-brother, and has discarded a comrade-at-arms. I believe friendships are precious and that this act is neither statesmanlike nor Christian.

Those who have fought for the cancellation of the tour hope they have struck a blow against apartheid. The issues in South Africa are highly complex and the solutions far from obvious. Ironically, I wonder whether the non-whites would want a multi-racial tour; they could well prefer their own tour in the same way that India and Pakistan tour separately.

So it is all over and what has been gained? I feel sure that it will not influence the South African Government's policies – it will only harden the attitude of all shades of opinion against Britain, even my dear Dad will now think twice about buying British. It will be difficult to assess the non-white reaction; my own feeling is that there will be little elation on the part of the large majority.

On the debit side this will have saddened the hearts of millions with mutual ties between the countries. It has deprived cricket lovers in all parts of the world, black and white, of the pleasure to be derived from the wonderful cricket which was anticipated. In addition, I feel that only ill can come of the deliberate attempts to stir up racial feeling which formed part of the campaign to cancel the tour.

Yours faithfully,
RUSSELL ENDEAN

On 17 June England began a series of five unofficial Test matches against the Rest of the World, whose party included five South Africans, five West Indians, two Pakistanis and one Indian. On 18 June, the day the Lord's Test against South Africa would have started, the Labour Government lost the General Election.

CRICKET AND CONSCIENCE

From Mr Manoranjan Biswas, 11 June 1971

Sir, The South African cricket tour was disrupted by demonstrators protesting against the South African Government's racial policy. The Pakistani Government is systematically slaughtering thousands of innocent and unarmed civilians in East Pakistan. Nearly six million terrified East Pakistanis have already fled to India to escape the slaughter and the flight continues at the rate of over fifty thousand a day.

The Pakistan Test team, on the advice of the Pakistani High Commission in London, refused to sign a cricket bat which the Lord Mayor of Birmingham proposes to auction for an appeal fund for the benefit of Pakistani refugees in India.

Why are there no demonstrations against the Pakistan cricket team by those who demonstrated so energetically against the South African team? Is Apartheid more abhorrent than mass murder?

Yours faithfully,
MANORANJAN BISWAS

BAN ON CRICKETERS

Guyana had refused entry to the Barbados batsman, Geoffrey Greenidge, because he had gone to Rhodesia with the International Wanderers.

From the Chairman, Cambridge University Cricket Society,
7 April 1976

Sir, Your article in *The Times* today (2 April) on the situation in cricket in the West Indies demonstrates very clearly the dangers facing the game there and the possibility of serious international repercussions. Sadly we have now reached a juncture where sport is inseparable from politics, but recent developments in the West Indies can only cause considerable alarm amongst all lovers of cricket.

While it may or may not be right to ban Test matches against South African sides so as to indicate disapproval of the policies of the South African Government, it is surely, as Wes Hall has said, carrying matters too far to impose bans on individuals who play in South Africa. Probably none of the well-known cricketers who have done so in recent years is a supporter of apartheid, and I am convinced that many go there with the highest motives of wishing to promote multi-racial sport.

The Derrick Robins team which visited South Africa in 1973–74 comprised two coloured players who were well received. This in itself was an advance. In 1968 the South African Government was not prepared to allow Basil D'Oliveira to tour with the MCC.

Many cricketers from South Africa itself, such as Tony Greig, Barry Richards and Mike Procter, are well known to be in favour of change. Influences such as these within the country can only produce a good effect. A total interdict on South Africa can only lead to a hardening of attitudes there and the people that would suffer most would be the large number of talented coloured cricketers.

I hope that before any other West Indian governments decide to introduce further bans they will consider, not only the friction such a move would cause between them and the other current Test-playing countries, but also the harm that it might produce in South Africa itself, where there are some signs of improvement.

Yours faithfully,
PETER HORROCKS

In 1981 Guyana expelled Robin Jackman because he had played and coached in South Africa. England left without playing the second Test match.

BAN ON RHODESIAN CRICKETERS

Britain's Minister for Sport forbade the tour of a team of Rhodesian cricketers ('Ridgebacks' after a breed of lion-dog indigenous to Central Africa) according to United Nations sanctions, adding that a tour in 1974 had taken place 'by subterfuge and deception'. The 1976 team stayed on to play as individuals.

From Mr Philip Jones, 19 May 1976

Sir, The Minister for Sport was absolutely right to ban the so-called cricketers from Rhodesia. Their fell purpose was only too obvious, to recruit a private army that they would smuggle back with them as team managers, trainers, masseurs, umpires, sight screen adjusters, scorers, stump polishers, bat oilers, pad whiteners, boot repairers, flannel pressers, crease whitewashers, roller operators and so on. Thanks to the minister's vigilance this foul and traitorous plot has been nipped in the bud. Well done, Mr Howell.

Yours faithfully,
PHILIP JONES

THE FREEDOM TO TOUR SOUTH AFRICA

South African Breweries hired 12 English cricketers to tour their country, which had played no Test cricket since 1970.

From Lord Chalfont, 3 March 1982

Alun Arthur Gwynne Jones, Defence Correspondent of *The Times* 1961–64. Minister of State, Foreign and Commonwealth Office 1964–70. Military historian.

Sir, Will you allow a regular reader of your paper, once one of its regular contributors, to express his grave concern at the confusion and hypocrisy which has characterized much of the reaction to the decision of 12 cricket players to play in South Africa? Whether they should call themselves 'an England Eleven' or 'Boycott's Buccaneers' is a matter of legitimate if not world-shaking concern. There is, however, a much more profound issue involved, and it is important that it should not be obscured by some of the highly coloured and emotionally charged language employed by some politicians, sports officials and journalists.

The practice of discrimination on grounds of race or colour is understandably abhorrent to the civilized mind. Furthermore, it is legitimate to argue, even if it is not universally accepted, that the South African Government is not moving far enough or fast enough in dismantling the political apparatus which institutionalizes such practices. It is also reasonable to hold the view that the most effective way of influencing that Government is to isolate it, so far as possible, from the rest of the civilized world. It is also reasonable to hold the opposite view; and it is for the democratically elected Government of this country to make its judgment and to frame its foreign policies accordingly.

It is *not* reasonable, or indeed tolerable, that citizens of this country should be deprived, by harassment, blackmail or threat, of their freedom to pursue their sporting activities, either for pleasure or for gain, wherever they wish to do so. There is no law in this country, as there is in some others, which forbids travel abroad. United Kingdom citizens are therefore free to go to South Africa whenever they wish, on business or for pleasure.

The Government may, in its wisdom, forbid certain categories of commerce or trade for reasons of state; sporting bodies may justifiably decline to allow representative teams to travel under their auspices. *No one* has the right to tell an individual law-abiding British citizen where he may play his games, earn his living, or enjoy his leisure.

This fundamental freedom, cherished and protected by our own political system, is now threatened by meddlesome propagandists compiling offensive and politically inspired 'blacklists' designed to threaten people with the loss of their livelihoods simply because they have chosen to exericse their indisputable rights as British citizens.

It is claimed that the action of these cricket players might endanger England's future in international sport, jeopardize the forthcoming cricket tours by India and Pakistan, put at risk the Commonwealth Games and even disrupt the next Olympic Games. It would be depressing and deplorable if any of these things were to happen (although it should be noted that at least one of these events will include competitors from countries whose record in human rights is no better than that of South Africa). It would, however, be a small price to pay for preserving the freedom of choice of law-abiding citizens of this country.

There is, to me, only one thing of more profound concern than the denial of liberty in other countries; it is a threat to it in our own. What is almost as disturbing is the fact that no political party in this country seems prepared to stand up to this particular manifestation of the threat without equivocation or compromise.

Yours faithfully,

CHALFONT

The players, eventually 15 in number, were banned from Test cricket for three years. In October 1982 15 Sri Lankans toured South Africa and were banned from Sri Lankan cricket for 25 years. In January 1983 18 West Indians toured South Africa and were banned from West Indian cricket for life.

4

CALCUTTA TO MOSCOW VIA HEIDELBERG

CENTENARY CRICKET ABROAD

From Mr Irving Rosenwater, 29 April 1955
Leading cricket researcher; statistician for BBC and Channel Nine, Australia.

Sir, Mr B. D. F. Beith is indeed correct when he claims a lengthy existence for the Calcutta Cricket Club, which was in fact active for many years prior to 1836. Although the date of formation of this club is, to my knowledge, not certain, we do know that it existed as early as 1792, in which year it challenged both Barrackpore and Dum-Dum. In Calcutta cricket seems to have flourished in the early years more than in any other centre in India, due doubtless to its being the seat of the supreme government of British India and to the influence of the English East India Company. As long ago as 1840 it was remarked of the Calcutta Cricket Club:–

'The Club can turn out a very good eleven, and whilst in full operation "the field" exhibits no peculiar feature to the eye of the English freshman, except the universality of very broad-brimmed white hats made of vegetable pith called sola, which is far lighter than cork, and an admirable non-conductor of heat. The natives do not enter at all into the spirit of the manly game; neither do the servants of the players, if desired to stop a stray ball, think it at all meritorious to risk stinging their hands by staying it while in motion; they amble by its side until it has ceased rolling, and then pick it up.'

The cricket was, no doubt, on most occasions pleasantly lighthearted, but those English residents who comprised the club – membership has always been exclusively European – ought well to have been proud to have belonged to and fostered a club that is today not only the oldest cricket club in India, but indeed one of the oldest in the world.

Yours faithfully,
IRVING ROSENWATER

THE ALL-INDIA CRICKET TEAM

From Dr H. D. Kanga and Mr J. M. Divecha, 5 September 1911
Vice-captain and Hon. Secretary.

Sir, Before leaving at the close of the season we wish to express on behalf of the 'All-India Cricket Team' our sincere thanks to the captains, the managing committees, and the members of all the counties we had the privilege of playing with for the warm welcome and cordial treatment they uniformly extended to us.

It was, of course, not in any spirit of rivalry or competition on equal terms that the project of our tour was originally conceived; the main idea was an educational one, and the experience we have gained here has amply justified it, and will serve in future to direct our efforts to attaining a higher standard of proficiency on the cricket field.

For enabling us to achieve this object we owe a debt of gratitude to Lord Harris, Lord Hawke, the Marylebone Cricket Club, and its energetic secretary, Mr Lacey, without whose assistance we should never have been able to carry out the elaborate programme of this tour.

Permit us this opportunity of thanking yourself and the British Press generally for the impartial criticism and generous recognition of our play, and also the public for the encouragement they gave us.

We are, Sir, yours obediently,
H. D. KANGA
J. M. DIVECHA

Ten of the fourteen first-class matches were lost, the team's capabilities having been overestimated when the programme was arranged. India's efforts to achieve international status, which began with this tour, reached fruition in 1932.

AN INDIAN BOY ON CRICKET

From Mr O. H. T. Dudley, 5 July 1932

Sir, Twenty-five years ago I went out to India to teach English. I have come back with a rich reward in the following sentence from an Indian schoolboy's essay on cricket:– 'Cricket is a very comfortable game: in it we disremember all our Condition.' That seems to me a great saying worthy of the tongue that Shakespeare spake.

I am, &c.,

O. H. T. DUDLEY

CRICKET IN PAKISTAN

From Mr A. H. Kardar, 13 February 1952

Northern India, Oxford University, Warwickshire, India and captain of Pakistan in their first 23 Test matches (1943–58). Later President of Pakistan Board of Control and representative at ICC.

Sir, About two years ago an official spokesman of the Imperial Cricket Conference stated that the membership of the ICC had for the time being been restricted to those countries who had exhibited a high standard of cricket, and that membership to other Commonwealth countries will remain open, provided their cricket attained a high standard. It will be recalled that Pakistan put up a very good show against the MCC touring team in all the five matches that the tourists played here in November, 1951. Pakistan held a commanding lead of 174 runs in the first Test at Lahore, and in the second Test at Karachi Pakistan, 'with cool and firm determination', beat the tourists by four wickets. A certain section of the Press reported that the cause of the MCC's failure in the second Test was bad umpiring when 30 or more appeals were disallowed by the umpires. If such reports are allowed to pass unchallenged they are likely to belittle Pakistan's victory and also may reflect unfavourably on her application for membership of the ICC.

It is almost impossible to satisfy every one on leg-before-wicket decisions. Sir, I learnt my cricket in England, where fair play is an essential factor in the make-up of a first-class cricketer. I happened to be batting for almost three hours on the last day of this match when only three lbw appeals were disallowed. I was the first batsman. Roy Tattersall, the bowler, later apologized for appealing because I had played the ball. The other two batsmen were my partners and I had no doubt in my mind about the correctness of the decisions. It is to be noticed that it is very difficult to hit the stumps on a matting wicket. In fact, I was beaten by nearly every bowler without losing my wicket. With these comments on some Press reports I would at once add that Pakistan's right to the membership of the ICC cannot be challenged, for we have here achieved a high standard which has been proven by our showing against the West Indies in 1947 and against the MCC in 1951. Some had birth right to the membership: we have won it.

Yours faithfully,

A. H. KARDAR

Pakistan were elected on 28 July 1952.

MCC IN WEST INDIES

From Mr W. D. Isaac, 1 November 1947
Writing from Barbados.

Sir, The controversy over the selection of a Bevin boy for the coming visit of the MCC to the West Indies involves a factor to which the attention of your readers has not yet been drawn – the importance of the tour for cementing the friendly relations between the Mother Country and her colonies. Since 1935, the last occasion of an English visit, the West Indian islands have passed through a very interesting phase, characterized by the backwash of ideology and propaganda from the European battle-ground, the awakening to political consciousness of the labouring classes, and the clamour for responsible government in each colony as a prelude to feder-ation and Dominion status.

The MCC visit is therefore peculiarly opportune, but the best results, in every sense of the word, can be obtained only if a representative side is sent. To judge from inter-colonial perform-ances during the past four years, in the course of which the fourth-wicket record was twice smashed in stands of over 500, the West Indian batting is exceptionally strong, and few bowling sides can hope today to dismiss Headley, Stollmeyer, Worrell, Walcott, and Goddard for small scores on West Indian wickets. The MCC tour cannot be regarded merely as an escape from the rigours of an

English winter and the austerity of post-war Europe to perpetual sunshine and lavish hospitality; it is a good will mission, and, unless the imperial policy of the Government has undergone a change, Smithson will be serving his country as loyally on the West Indian cricket-field as in an English mine.

Yours, &c.,

W. D. ISAAC

⁎ The Minister of Labour stated on Thursday that the National Coal Board were prepared to give Smithson leave of absence to enable him to go to the West Indies.

G. A. Smithson, of Yorkshire and later Leicestershire, appeared in two Test matches on the tour, but did not play for England again.

TOO FAR AHEAD

The West Indians, a great attraction in England in 1963, were not due to tour again until 1971.

From Mr A. N. Gasson, 4 July 1963

Sir, Sir Christopher Lighton's letter, published by you on Saturday, 29 June, surely voices the thoughts of many cricket lovers throughout the world.

If the Imperial Cricket Conference cannot alter the touring programme by cancelling a visit from another of our opponents, a measure to be frowned upon by all, why not arrange another Triangular Tournament (as held here in 1912)? To assist arrangements perhaps each rubber could consist of three Test matches of four days' duration. O to see Australia v. West Indies at Lord's!

Yours faithfully,

ANTHONY GASSON

The programme was rearranged so that the West Indians came in 1966. They met Australia at Lord's, albeit in the one-day Prudential World Cup final, in 1975.

CRICKET IN CORFU

Played on the town square since it was introduced by the British after the Napoleonic wars.

From Mr K. L. Harkness, 6 July 1950

Sir, As a member of a team visiting Corfu in 1934, I can confirm that there were 'jagged stones beneath the matting at strategic points.' But whether on such occasions the stones or the matting are arranged with sinister purpose will never be known with certainty in this country. Very properly, all preparations for the game are completed before the arrival of visitors. There is another uncertainty about cricket in Corfu. The game is played without 'boundaries' and batsmen are expected to run until the ball is returned. Around the perimeter of the ground are a number of tables at which the local beauties gather to enjoy the game and light refreshment. Should a stroke by a visiting batsman send the ball among them, it is at once kicked back on to the field of play. If, on the other hand, it comes from a home bat, it somehow disappears among the draperies, and the visiting fieldsman is left to work out for himself just how far the limits of courtesy may be stretched. Whether such partisan conduct is prompted by the will to win or a greater interest in fieldsmen of the visiting team, I shall never know. I was the wicket-keeper.

Yours faithfully,
KENNETH L. HARKNESS

AS SHE IS PLAYED

From Professor James Trainer, 20 January 1983
Professor of German, University of Stirling.

Sir, Mr Ignarski's succinct history of international cricket in Germany (January 13) perhaps helps explain the lexicographical mystery of the proliferation of cricketing terms in Collins's excellent new German dictionary.

It must be the Heidelberg press cricket correspondent (Johann Waldschnepfe?) who finds a use for those crisp phrases *ausgeschlagen während der Schlagmann seinen Lauf machte* ('run out') and *wir gewannen und hatten vier Schlagmänner noch nicht in Einsatz gehabt* ('we won by four wickets').

And why is German cricket so dominated by slow bowling? The only bowling styles listed by the dictionary's compilers are the curious *gedrehter Ball* ('googly') and the surely illegal *Werfer, der dem Ball einen Drall gibt* ('spin bowler'). No great imagination would have been needed to add a *Chinese* (presumably a *Gastwer-fer?*) and Federal Railway terminology suggests *D-Werfer* for fast bowlers.

In the field Collins offers only *Torwächter* ('wicketkeeper') and *Eckmann* ('slip fielder'). New light on *Eckmanns Gespräche*? One assumes that the European Institute for Molecular Biology scored most of their runs with the *Treibschlag* ('drive') or even the abortive off-drive, the unlisted *Abtreibschlag*. *In der Klemme sein* ('to be on a sticky wicket') is surely art imitating cricket.

The definition *aus sein, weil seine Beine von einem Wurf getroffen wurden* ('to be out lbw') was obviously supplied by the current Australian umpires.

Yours sincerely,
JAMES TRAINER

From Mr C. A. Lugten, 26 January 1983

Sir, Among fielders Collins, surely, should have included *das viereckiges Bein* (square leg) and *der Dummkopf in der Mitte* (silly mid-on).

Yours sincerely
C. A. LUGTEN

The most scholarly work on the vocabulary of cricket is also in German – a doctoral thesis by Ernst Burgschmidt entitled *Studien zum Verbum in englischen Fachsprachen (Cricket)*.

DUTCH CRICKET

From Mr R. H. Macdonald, 2 January 1946

Sir, I was much interested to read extracts of a letter written by Mr H. Van. Manen, Chairman of the Netherland Cricket Bond.

In connexion with the 'Save Dutch Cricket' fund, there is a point which I think should be made – namely, that the 'appalling shortage of playing gear' in Holland is due to the fact that the Dutch collected all available cricket gear in Holland and dispatched it to British prisoner-of-war camps in Germany. Mr Van Manen is perhaps too modest to mention this point.

I can personally testify to the shortage, as I had the honour to captain the first British eleven to play against a 'Free Dutch' side 10 days after the liberation of The Hague; our opponents were our old friends The Hague Cricket Club. After all our combined attempts to obtain a cricket ball had failed, a highly polished hockey ball was used. The enormous inducement of 1,000 cigarettes and one German lorry failed to bring forth even an old or worn cricket ball. The Hague scored 70, while we were all out for 17. We did not blame the hockey ball, the patchwork matting, or the 3½-hour lunch.

Yours faithfully,
R. H. MACDONALD

The Royal Netherlands Cricket Association celebrated its centenary in 1983, when memories were revived of a famous victory in a one-day match against the Australians at The Hague in 1964.

KRIKET

From Mr Patrick Howarth, 6 September 1975
Author, biographer of Sir John Squire.

Sir, I think I can tell Mr Michael Vyvyan (3 September) when and where the first cricket match took place in Poland. It was early in the summer of 1946 on a football ground in Warsaw, the two teams being composed of members of the British Embassy staff. The air attaché captained one team and I captained the other. In the eighteenth century tradition we had a wager of 5,000 zlotys on the match, the rate of exchange between the pound and the zloty being at that time a matter of opinion.

Unfortunately for me, shortly before the match two clerks in the air attaché's office had to be replaced, and both their replacements were more than competent fast-medium bowlers. The air attaché's team won.

One of the difficulties we encountered was that of persuading small boys in Polish, without the advantage of a public address system, why they were welcome to throw the ball in after it had crossed the boundary line and not before.

The match aroused a certain amount of interest locally, and it is possible that the seed we then sowed has now flowered in Slovakia. I wonder whether the Slovak spectators whom Mr Vyvyan met were better instructed than the Poles.

Yours faithfully,
PATRICK HOWARTH

CRICKET IN SWITZERLAND

From Captain W. E. Mocatta, 3 July 1929

Sir, With reference to the letter from Mr Gordon Spencer, of Zuoz College, on cricket in Switzerland, which appeared in your issue of 26 June, I feel sure that all lovers of our national game will be glad to hear that not only in the east but also in the south of this country the flag of cricket is being kept flying. In your own columns there was a report of the British Legion's match against Chillon College, while at this school we count cricket to be the most popular game. The enthusiasm for it has been so great that this year, for the first time in the history of the game (so far as I am aware), a team of English schoolboys from Switzerland will play matches in England, as fixtures have been arranged between our first XI [English Preparatory School, Glion] and four preparatory schools on the South Coast for the last week of July.

I am, Sir, yours faithfully,

W. E. MOCATTA

RANJITSINHJI'S AMERICAN CRICKET TEAM

From K. S. Ranjitsinhji, 3 November 1899

Cambridge University, Sussex and England (1893–1920). Later Maharajah the Jam Sahib of Nawanagar; served on the Indian Council of Princes and the League of Nations.

Sir, A statement appeared in one of your columns today that the Metropolitan Cricket League of New York met to consider the charge of discourtesy against myself and other members of the visiting team.

From the second paragraph of the statement I gather that the accusations are that myself and other members absented ourselves from the match, and that we played substitutes the next day.

I am naturally much astonished at this most extraordinary statement, and this is the first intimation I receive in any shape or form of this conduct on the part of myself and the other members. After the first day, as is well known, of the first match against Philadelphia I was laid up with bronchitis so that I was not able to take any further part even in that match. But, feeling slightly better, I left for New York and, not a little against my doctor's wishes, to play against 18 of New York, in which match our conduct is impugned as discourteous. As the travelling brought on fever, I was advised to abandon the idea of playing in the match and of putting up in New York, instead of Staten Island with the rest of the team. I was unable to leave the hotel the whole time I was in New York on that occasion.

I entrusted Mr MacLaren with the control of the team as before. The next day the team, as invited by Sir Thomas Lipton, went and saw the yacht race. I trust that my absence did not lead Sir Thomas Lipton to think that I was discourteous to him, as it evidently did the associated clubs of New York.

The next day the match commenced and all our players took part. In the evening Mr MacLaren telephoned to me that he was suffering from rheumatism and would I mind if he had some medical treatment for it in New York, and that both he and Mr Priestley were coming to see how I was getting on. I was naturally alarmed with Mr MacLaren's condition, and replied, 'Come this evening and stop here.' Both of them came and stopped in New York that night. Next day he had some electric treatment. A wire was sent by Mr MacLaren in the morning to Mr Stoddart to take charge of the team in his absence to the hotel at Staten Island, informing him of the cause of his absence and that he required Mr Priestley's assistance; the latter also that afternoon had to arrange for our berths for the passage back, as we were not to return to New York again till just before our departure for home. The wire was not forwarded by the Staten Island hotel authorities on to the ground, and consequently Mr Stoddart was unable to declare innings till lunch time, having waited for Mr MacLaren. The delay in declaring undoubtedly saved the New Yorkers from defeat. Whether Mr Stoddart asked for two substitutes to field or not I am unable to say, as no mention was made to myself by either my own side or by any of the New York authorities. These, then are the facts of the case. How they can be construed as acts of discourtesy by our opponents I fail to see.

I am cabling today to the Metropolitan Cricket League of New York, the existence of which I only knew through your columns today, for explanation of the matter, and asking them to inform me why I was kept ignorant of their complaint against myself and my team during our stay in America.

I request you to put this rather lengthy explanation in your columns in justice and fair play to the men who did me the honour to accompany me out there, to myself, and for the sake of English cricket, which we represented out there. I take this opportunity of acknowledging our indebtedness to the Philadelphian clubs and the Canadian clubs for their lavish hospitality and kind attention during six weeks of our most pleasant stay among them.

Thanking you in anticipation,

Yours faithfully,

RANJITSINHJI

ALL-AMERICAN CRICKET

From Major E. R. T. Holmes, R.A., 22 September 1943

Oxford University, Surrey and England (1924–55). Test selector and MCC committee member.

Sir, It will doubtless be of interest to readers of *The Times* to know that on 18 September a cricket match was played between two all-American teams, consisting of officers of the Eighth Air Force, each representing an American station in this country. Each side had previously had only three or four practice games, but when the great day arrived it was evident that there was plenty of keenness to be victorious in this match – surely the first of its kind ever to be played in this country.

The two captains tossed up for choice of innings, and then they went at it with true American enthusiasm. The fielders indulged in a ceaseless flow of 'chatter', and baiting the batsman provided everybody (except the batsman) with amusement. Cries of 'Here's an easy man!' would greet the new arrival, and woebetide the outgoing batsman who had failed to score. Englishmen on such occasions are apt to become suddenly engrossed in deep conversation with their neighbour, thereby affecting not to notice the early return to the pavilion of one who has covered himself with inglory. Not so with the Americans. The man becomes the verbal butt of everybody, friend and foe alike, but he merely smiles or makes some fitting retort. In any case, be sure that he feels less uncomfortable than the Englishman in similar circumstances.

However, the point of it all is this. One of the greatest compliments that you can pay a man (or a nation) is to take up his sport, and if you can enjoy it into the bargain, as these 22 Americans did on Saturday, then it is surely a triumph, more particularly so in this instance, because the game was played not as a gesture towards the English, but simply because these Americans thoroughly enjoy playing cricket.

I know, because I was one of the umpires.

Yours, &c.,

E. R. T. HOLMES

Station 112 beat Station 103 by 57 runs. *The Times* said, somewhat ambiguously: 'The batting and bowling were much above the standard expected by the English spectators.'

A TEST MATCH LACKING

From Mr J. L. Weinstein, 30 June 1956

Sir, Let us resist at all costs the proposal of Mr James Plowden-Wardlaw in his letter of 26 June that we should combine with the Commonwealth to provide the best team to play Test matches against America. We have for too long been humbled in the world of sport. At cricket we are still the masters outside the Commonwealth, and our national sporting pride in the game is subject only to occasional family setbacks such as occurred at Lord's this week.

On a summer's day six years ago the world stood sickeningly still. In a far-off continent the United States had defeated England at soccer. Sir, there is only one humiliation left to us in the world of sport: to lose a Test match to the Americans. Let us gird up our insular loins and eschew the sporting suicide which the exposure of cricket to transatlantic challenge would ultimately and inevitably bring. Cricket is a frail and delicate child of English and Commonwealth parentage. It must never be allowed to leave home.

I am, Sir, yours respectfully,

JERRY L. WEINSTEIN

The first English touring team overseas, in 1859, went to North America. Around the turn of the century Philadelphia proved a match for the English counties, but the American game declined until, with an influx of immigrants from the Commonwealth, the United States was elected an associate member of the International Cricket Conference in 1965 and received a tour from MCC in 1982.

NOT CRICKET

From Mr Harold Lockley, 13 March 1959

Sir, Cricketing metaphors are without a doubt perfectly intelligible to English readers who play the game, but are they to the Russians, who do not? What, for example, do they make of the following extract from your leading article on 11 March:–

[Mr Khrushchev] 'feels himself free to lob ideas on Berlin and Germany because he has done most of the bowling since his Note of November 27 and the West – apart from Mr Macmillan's appearance in Moscow – has been stonewalling.'

Yours faithfully,
HAROLD LOCKLEY

CRICKET IN MOSCOW

From Mr A. C. Jenkins, 23 July 1962

Sir, Your correspondent Mr Eason (July 20) is mistaken in thinking his bankers' soft ball affair was the first cricket match to be played in Moscow. On various occasions during the war, the Russians put the Stalin Stadium at the disposal of elevens from the British Mission and Embassy and some stirring if rusty matches ensued on matting wickets with genuine gear. I was detailed off to captain the Mission side and though this afforded me some satisfaction in giving orders to more senior officers it was also a heavy responsibility in view of our sparse but attentive audience of Red Army officers. It was clear from their reaction that our allies despaired of these 'flannelled fools at the wicket' ever putting into effect the long-awaited 'droogoy' front.

Yours faithfully,
ALAN C. JENKINS

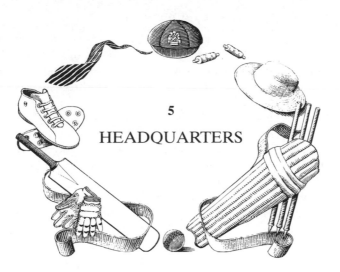

5

HEADQUARTERS

THE DARKS AND LORD'S

From Mr Sidney Dark, 30 June 1937
Editor of the *Church Times*.

Sir, In your interesting MCC Number, and in the subsequent correspondence which you have published, there have been references to my great great uncle, James Henry Dark, who bought Lord's from Lord and afterwards sold it to the MCC.

There may, perhaps, be some small historic interest in the detail of the connexion of my family with Lord's and with cricket. James Henry Dark was one of several brothers who were the sons of a Liskeard sadler. One of his brothers, John Dark, was dust contractor to the old St Marylebone and Paddington vestries. He appears to have known Dickens, and there is a family rumour that he was the original of Boffin, the golden dustman.

Another brother, Ben Dark, founded the cricket bat and ball manufactory which was inherited by my father. The bats were made in a workshop at Lord's and the balls at a factory at Hildenborough in Kent.

James Henry Dark had no children, but his brothers were extremely prolific. When he was a young man, my father had 66 first cousins. The consequence was that though James Henry and his brothers left considerable sums of money, it was divided among so many heirs that the legacies were of small account.

I was born in a house in St John's Wood Road, owned by my

grandfather, which had a private entrance into Lord's. My father had another house next door but one, which also had a private entrance into Lord's; and my grandfather's widowed sister-in-law had a third house, farther east and also looking over the ground. When I was a small child the bat and ball business was known as Matilda Dark and Sons, and I quite remember my great-grandmother, a very old lady, who lived in some rooms over the workshops. St John's Wood Road was, indeed, in those days a veritable colony of my family.

One of my grandfather's sisters married James Bromley, the engraver, who reproduced several of the more famous Landseers. They, too, lived in St John's Wood Road, and the landlord of Lord's Hotel was the husband of one of my grandmother's sisters.

To the west of the hotel there was a building known as the Armory, which belonged to my grandfather and was the head-quarters of the Fifth Middlesex Volunteers, which, when there was no match on that day, always paraded in Lord's before their route march. In those long ago days the 'Licensed Victuallers' Fête and Gala' took place regularly in Lord's in September, and on summer Sunday evenings the hotel did a roaring open-air trade, tables being set out within the grounds.

What is now the practice ground was then a nursery, and I remember the beautiful row of chestnut trees that used to ornament the eastern side of the ground.

The falling in of leases was primarily responsible for the ending of the Dark's connexion with Lord's. Workshops had to be moved elsewhere, and my father, who was a gifted craftsman, had no sort of idea of business, and the once flourishing and almost famous manufactory declined to almost nothingness. Thanks however to the gracious kindness of the MCC, the family connexion with Lord's went on until the death of my father at the age of 85, seven years ago. Darks had been making cricket bats for a hundred years. Since then they have been making them no longer.

Yours very truly,
SIDNEY DARK

Dark in fact bought Lord's from William Ward, who had bought it from Lord.

A MEMORY OF LORD'S

From Senior, 16 August 1919

Sir, I was at Lord's in 1851 and 1852, and saw the following matches – Eton and Harrow; Eton and Winchester; and Harrow and Winchester. In one of these the captain of the Eton eleven was the brother of one of my school-fellows, which gave many of us a desire to see the match. This captain wore a tall black hat, being, I believe, the last non-professional player to do so. The 'professionals' continued to wear the hat much longer. It was in fact a sort of badge of the profession.

In the days referred to the arrangements for refreshment at Lord's old ground were such as would now be considered simple and anything but luxurious. Visitors had luncheon standing up at a long counter in an open shed to the left of the entrance gate. There one could get little, if anything, to eat, except sandwiches and pork pies. Once when I was there a member of the Eton eleven came into the refreshment shed and asked for 'shandy gaff' – the first time that I had ever heard the word.

In the middle of the last century it was a common belief – at any rate in South-Eastern England – that the inhabitants of the 'shires' could not play cricket. The only people credited then with ability to play it were those who belonged to Kent, Sussex, Surrey, Middlesex, Essex, &c.

Your obedient servant,

SENIOR

The catering arrangements are now somewhat improved.

LORD'S

The Times reported on the opening day of the 1900 University match: 'With regard to the cricket, we are able to give only a few general observations. The Marylebone Club executive have recently shown much hostility to the Press at Lord's; and yesterday the cricket reporters were exiled from the grand stand to a position in the north-east corner of the ground, from which it was impossible to secure an accurate idea of the play. Our representative's application to the secretary of the club for a place where the game could be followed was met with a curt refusal.

The Oxford eleven were seen (by the more fortunate) to splendid advantage. . . .'

LORD'S

From Mr Harry Furniss, 7 July 1900

Caricaturist, at this time for *Punch*. Later a lecturer and author of film scripts. Illustrator of 'A Century of Grace' in *How's That?* (1896).

Sir, I am not surprised to read your cricket correspondent's complaint in to-day's issue regarding the unsportsmanlike treatment the Press has received at the hands of the officials at Lord's.

Your readers will recollect how the Empire was nearly shaken to its foundation when the members of Lord's had to decide who was to be the new secretary of the play-ground in St John's Wood! The Queen's-hall was filled with swelled heads, and, judging from your correspondent's note, the swelled heads elected one of their own body. After all, Lord's is to cricket what St Andrews is to golf; but at St Andrews golf is the one thing considered, at Lord's cricket is a mere detail. At St Andrews golfers, lovers of the game, and even mere sightseers, and, may I add, members of the Press, are given every facility to enjoy the game. But, alas! Lord's is fast degenerating from a club of gentlemen cricketers into a show run for the sake of profit.

Under the old management, for many years, Lord's was an ideal retreat for the tired worker and the cricket lover. Then the stranger felt that by paying at the gate he was free to sit in peace, and with the aid of a good cigar it was the ideal place in which to spend a happy day. Not so now, to those seated on the paying stands. Boys, heavily laden with open baskets containing merchandise one sees on Hampstead-heath on Bank holiday or on a third-rate race course, but surely of little attraction to the frequenters of Lord's, trample continually on your toes and screech everlastingly into your ears 'Cigarettes, cigars, chocolates – Cigarettes, cigars, chocolates.' 'Correct card – Correct card.' 'Cigarettes, cigars, chocolates.' 'Correct card.' 'Speshul 'dition – latest cricket scores.' 'Cigarettes, cigars, chocolates.' 'Speshul 'dition – latest cricket scores.' 'Correct card.' 'Cigarettes, cigars, chocolates.' And to offend the ear still further these calls of screeching boys are sandwiched by 'Any seat, Sir, but the first four rows.' 'Any seat, Sir, but the first four rows.'

Why, in the name of reason and peace, cannot the fact that, after paying extra, you can occupy certain seats be written on a placard, or, better still, on the tickets?

In fact, we may soon expect swings erected in the practice-ground, shooting booths under the atrocious erection of the big stand, and knock-me-downs in and out of the many drinking booths now disfiguring the club – a club, once a quiet gentlemanly retreat, now a huge conglomeration of various monstrosities of masonry. In fact, I frankly confess, were I to see the buildings at Lord's, some winter's night, on fire, although I would not be guilty to incendiarism I would certainly not hurry to give the alarm, for, as an artist, I consider even the outside of Lord's Cricket Ground an outrage upon taste and an offence to the eye.

It is not enough that the committee of Lord's should offend the eye by having turned the pretty pitch of old into an ugly mass of sheds and patches of erratic architecture, but they must also offend the ear by turning it into a pandemonium as well.

Many use Lord's Club as a fashionable picnic ground for five days in the year – genuine cricket lovers are absent then and look to the Press to read in detail the doings of the colts – but now it appears that, during the paying-picnic days, the Press is turned out of the stand and relegated to the tool shed, or, perhaps, to the roller horse's stable.

Nearly every sport in this country is being ruined by 'the gate' question – can we not save cricket, and particularly Lord's, before it is too late?

I am, Sir, yours obediently,

HARRY FURNISS

From Mr George Rose Norton, 9 July 1900

Sir, As an old member of Lord's I am rejoiced to see the letter of Mr Harry Furniss in *The Times* of to-day. I have long been looking out for some expression of the kind, and I am thankful that it has at last come. You must not think that the members of the MCC approve of the treatment awarded to the members of the Press. The fact is there is much dissatisfaction amongst the members of the MCC at the manner in which matters have been conducted for the last few years, and the waste of money that has been prodigious. Two hundred new members at £200 each have partly paid for this waste, but otherwise the money might as well been thrown into the sea. Hideous buildings have been erected all over the place, and, as Mr Harry Furniss says, the place which was once 'a quiet gentlemanly retreat is now a huge conglomeration of various monstrosities of masonry'. In fact, I can excuse his not giving the alarm of fire before all the hideous buildings were burnt down, should such a fortunate accident occur. It must not be supposed that the members of the MCC had anything to do with the erection of these monstrosities. We went away in August and when we returned in May the hideous building called the Mound stand stood before us. No one who is not obliged will sit in it, scorched in the sun or drenched in the rain according to our variable climate. The members were never consulted about all this deformation of the ground. No plans were placed before them. The clock was placed where no one in the pavilion could see it. Since then another clock has been placed on one of the hideous buildings, luckily far off, so that it is not constantly shadowing the game; and now the members of the Press have been placed on the top of that building, so that if they cannot see the game they will be enabled, by looking round the corner, to time it. I do not wish to say these things anonymously, so, at the risk of some censure,

I am, Sir, yours obediently,

GEORGE ROSE NORTON

From An Old Cricketer, 12 July 1900

Sir, Mr Harry Furniss in his diatribe against the management of the MCC charges the committee with running the club for profit. Supposing it were run at a loss, would he consider that as a mark of superior management? Mr Furniss also complains that Lord's is no longer 'a retreat for the tired worker'. But it would hardly satisfy the members or the public to turn the place into a sanatorium. Mr Furniss forgets, as do many others, that in the place of the few hundreds who used to attend the matches there are now as many or more thousands, for whom it is the duty of the committee, as far as possible, to provide sitting and seeing accommodation, besides giving them facilities for obtaining refreshments. That the new Mound seats when empty are a thing of beauty no one will contend. Neither will any one, I venture to say, be able to suggest how a fine architectural effect could have been combined with the utilitarian necessities of the case. With regard to the letter of 'B.S.', I would point out that he is entirely in error in thinking that the chances of candidates put down for election were prejudiced by the recent introduction of 200 life members. As a matter of fact, no one's election was put back by a single day, whilst some had their prospect of election actually accelerated by that proceeding.

This was fully explained by Mr Alfred Lyttelton when he presided at the general meeting, at which the resolution was passed by a very large majority.

AN OLD CRICKETER

P.S. Since writing the above I have seen the letter signed 'Sigma' in your impression of to-day, and as regards 'the waste of club funds' in buildings to which he refers, I would observe that, seeing that the Mound stand, which seats many thousands for whom there was no accommodation before, also pays a fair interest on its cost, I fail to see where the wastefulness comes in.

MCC did not reply; but for the Gentlemen v Players match on 16–18 July the Press returned to the Grand stand. Next season a new Press box was opened opposite the pavilion; in January 1906 it was demolished by a severe storm. Thenceforth the Press were accommodated in an extension to the pavilion until 1958, when they were moved to the top of the new Warner Stand – a comfortable but poorly sited location overlooking mid-off or long leg.

LORD'S CRICKET GROUND

From Mr W. H. Fowler, 8 July 1910
Essex and Somerset (1877–84). Amateur golf international and designer of Walton Heath and other courses in England and the United States.

Sir, This ancient home of the game of cricket has of late earned an unenviable notoriety by reason of the long time the surface takes to dry after heavy rain. It will be remembered by many thousands how the Eton and Harrow match of last year had to be left as a draw, although half an hour's play on Saturday would probably have sufficed to give a definite result. Cricket was played on the Oval on that day, and there was no special circumstance why it should not have been possible at Lord's also. Then on Monday last, on a fine day, we saw the start of the Oxford and Cambridge match delayed until 4 p.m. The ground even then was in a shocking state and not really fit for such an important contest. There have been many other cases during the past few years, which go to prove that the wicket and ground hold the water on the surface far too long. The question is, Can anything be done to prevent these tedious delays without tampering with the wicket?

I venture to suggest that a course of treatment similar to that which has been successfully carried out on many golf courses, where heavy clay soils have had to be dealt with, would transform Lord's from a slow to a quick drying ground. The pitch and the outfielding require different treatment. For the former the turf should be removed and the soil taken up to a depth of at least a foot. Then put in a layer of rough clinker at the bottom, and finer above, to a depth of 6in., then fill in with the soil taken out and relay the old turf. This plan would have two advantages from a turf-growing point of view: first, the harm done by worm-casts in the spring would be largely reduced, if not absolutely stopped; and, secondly, the grass roots would become healthier and the turf would stand wet and drought far better.

For the fielding part of the ground, the plan of heavy dressings of 'coke breeze' every autumn would be found to work wonders in the way of helping the ground to absorb heavy rains. The 'breeze' should be spread on thickly at the end of September and rolled in with a light roller. The grass will soon come up through it, and it will remain just under the surface, and by the next cricket season no one would know it was there. The result to the turf, however, would be easily seen, as it would be far healthier, and in a few years it would cure the cracking which is now so often in evidence during hot weather. This treatment would not do for the pitch, as the 'breeze' would be too near the surface.

In making these suggestions, which are based on practical experience, I desire to say most emphatically that I would do nothing to 'doctor' or alter the wicket from what it has been in the past. I would use the same soil, and the only difference my suggested treatment would make would be to produce a healthier turf and ensure the quick drying of the wicket and outfield.

Yours truly,
W. HERBERT FOWLER

The following winter the drainage was overhauled.

DRAINAGE AT LORD'S

From Mr Keith Falkner, 23 June 1964

Sir, Your Cricket Correspondent today laments the present drainage problem at Lord's.

It was ludicrous to all of us watching despondently yesterday to see the falling rain run off the playing area, by hosepipe, to the very parts of the ground which need redraining. It is an elementary thought that the water could have been drained into mobile tanks or containers.

In future may this be considered for the benefit of thousands of cricketers for whom the Lord's Test is the one event each year which takes precedence over all else?

Yours faithfully,
KEITH FALKNER

In autumn 1964 a new drainage system was installed.

INVALID CHAIRS REFUSED ENTRY TO LORD'S

From Mr Arthur Howard, 11 June 1921

Sir, I should be glad if you would make it known through the columns of your powerful paper that the committee of the MCC are refusing to allow wounded officers or men, who cannot walk, into Lord's in their chairs, to see the Test match. I approached a member of the committee, and asked him if a friend of mine could sit in his chair against the Mound stand outside the ropes beside the bowling screen. He seemed to view the matter favourably, and he asked my friend to write to the committee and put the matter before them.

No answer has ever been received to his letter, and I only discovered by inquiring at the gate that no chairs of any description were to be admitted to Lord's for the Test match.

The result is that my friend has travelled 200 miles on a fruitless errand – a journey not lightly undertaken by hopeless cripples like ourselves.

The only reason given for this almost inhuman decree is that a chair takes up as much room as two or three people. Let it! But for the sacrifices similar to that made by my friend, Lord's might now be a fashionable German beer garden!

I may mention that I am a member of the MCC, and am also a hopeless and helpless cripple through wounds. Last year my chair was forbidden to enter the Pavilion to see the University match – in fact, I was debarred from entering my own club to see my own University play!

I am, Sir, yours faithfully,
ARTHUR HOWARD

ACCOMMODATION AT LORD'S

From Mr J. R. Remer, MP, 28 June 1926
Conservative Member for Macclesfield 1918–39. One of the best golfers in the House.

Sir, May I trespass on your columns to enter a protest against the Lord's cricket ground arrangements on Saturday? I was one of the many thousands in a queue which were refused admittance. Eventually, through a friend, I got on to the ground. What did I find when I got there? That there was room for people standing for fully a further 5,000. I know that many cricketing enthusiasts were bitterly disappointed, and there should be, in my opinion, some very straight talk upon the subject.

JOHN R. REMER

From Mr J. A. Haywood, 29 June 1926

Sir, I think the ground on Saturday was full enough. It must not be forgotten that if every available foot of standing room is taken up, it means a number of people sitting in the free seats are without a view of the game. If I may say so, I think the authorities at Lord's are to be congratulated on the greatly improved arrangements made since the last Australian match in 1921.

J. A. HAYWOOD

Wisden agreed with Mr Remer.

SCORE CARDS AT LORD'S

From Mr J. C. R. Johnston, 24 May 1928

Sir, May I call attention to the great delay that always occurs at Lord's (and sometimes at the Oval) in the issue of the cards giving the names of the players on the first day of a match. On Saturday (MCC v. West Indies), although play did not begin until 12 o'clock, the cards were not obtainable at the south side of the ground until 40 minutes after play had begun. During that period there had been two changes of bowling. At other sports (football, &c.) cards can always be obtained before play begins, and they are offered for sale at the entrances: but at Lord's, even on Middlesex match days, cards are never obtainable until long after play has begun on the opening day. I know of a county cricket ground where cards are always available before play begins on the first day, so why cannot Lord's do the same?

J. C. R. JOHNSTON

From the Secretary of MCC, 26 May 1928

William Findlay (Lancashire and captain of Oxford University, 1901–06). Secretary of Surrey CCC 1907–19, MCC 1926–36. Chairman of Findlay Commission into county cricket 1937. President of Lancashire CCC, 1947–48 and of MCC 1951.

Sir, I should like to point out that before setting up the type on the first day of a match the printers must be notified as to (1) the names of the members of the two teams; and (2) the side which will bat first and the order of going in. On occasions this information is not forthcoming until a few minutes before the first ball is bowled, hence the delay. Every effort is made to set up the type at the earliest possible moment.

Yours faithfully,
W. FINDLAY

OVER THE PAVILION AT LORD'S

From Mr P. F. Warner, 25 May 1935

Oxford University and captain of Middlesex and England (1894–1920). One of the game's greatest servants. Chairman of Test selectors. Manager of touring teams. President (1950), Secretary, Trustee and first Life Vice-

President of MCC, serving on the committee almost continuously from 1903. Founder of *The Cricketer*, author and editor of many books on cricket, and writer on the game for several newspapers including *The Times*. Knighted for services to cricket in 1937. He recovered the Ashes in Australia in 1904 and his own ashes were scattered at Lord's.

Sir, It was in the MCC v. Australia match at Lord's at the end of July, 1899, that Trott drove Mr M. A. Noble, the Australian, clean over the pavilion. I was playing in the match and was sitting in the second row of the pavilion seats just behind Mr C. I. Thornton, a giant hitter himself, and I remember it as if it were but yesterday. Just to find the range, as it were, Trott had previously driven the ball twice into the pavilion, and then came this mighty blow – a straight drive – the ball landing in the garden of Philip Need, the dressing-room attendant, and one of the nicest, best, and most faithful servants MCC ever had. I can see 'Alberto', as Trott was called, leaning on his bat as he gazed upward as this sixer climbed the sky.

Earlier in the same year Trott had only just failed to clear the pavilion, an on-drive off F. W. Tate, the father of the present Sussex bowler, hitting the iron scroll work with 'MCC' engraved on it on the top of the South Tower, the ball bouncing back into the pavilion seats below the Committee Room.

Without wishing in any way to lay down the law, I am ready to lay long odds that the only occasion on which a ball has been hit over the pavilion at Lord's was by Trott on the occasion named. Mr F. T. Mann nearly succeeded in so doing, driving Rhodes three times in the course of one over on to the top of the pavilion. That was, I fancy, in the year 1928, and the match Middlesex v. Yorkshire.

Trott's historic hit ruined his batting, for ever afterwards he went about armed with a 3lb 'club' trying to 'carry' pavilions. He was a great all-round cricketer, but, as Mr G. J. V. Weigall would put it, he had 'sawdust in his brain!'

I am, &c.,

P. F. WARNER

In recent times Mike Llewellyn, of Glamorgan, and Kim Hughes, of Australia, have reached the top deck of the pavilion.

From Mr W. H. Fowler, 30 May 1935

Sir, Several of my friends have asked me to write to you on the subject of 'Over the Pavilion at Lord's'. There seems to be consider-able difference of opinion as to what has happened in the past. It is strange that I have never heard of W. G. Grace having done it. I was playing regularly from 1879 till 1890, and all that time I lived under the impression that C. I. Thornton [Eton v. Harrow 1868] and myself were the only two who had carried the Pavilion and also the wall behind. My hit was in 1882, and was off the Derbyshire fast bowler George Hay. The ball went over the top of the flagstaff on the northern end of the Pavilion. Bill Ford told my brother Howard that the ball was travelling faster than any he had ever seen; he was sitting in front of the Pavilion. After the day's play was over, Hearne, the groundsman, and I chained the distance from the Nursery wicket to the base of the wall, and we made it 134 yards [recorded 157 yards elsewhere]. This may be of interest now in reference to where the wickets are now placed. The ball before the one I hit off George Hay for six was bowled by T. Mycroft, and I hit it past mid-off and ran five for it. The match was MCC v. Somerset.

I am, &c.,
W. HERBERT FOWLER

Mr Fowler could have added that he performed the hat-trick in MCC's first innings. The old pavilion, to which he refers, was a good deal lower than its successor, which was opened in 1900 and stands today.

PLOVER AND LEATHER-JACKETS

From Mr Clarence Elliott, 12 October 1935

Sir, I believe that the best and simplest way of getting rid of the plague of leather-jackets which are destroying the turf at Lord's Cricket Ground would be to turn down a dozen or two green plover – pinioned of course – and give them free run of the turf.

The natural food of plover consists of worms, insects, and grubs of various kinds, and leather-jackets. I think it probable that they would eat both the leather-jackets and their parent craneflies [better known as daddy-longlegs]. The plover could be driven, or enticed, into a suitable enclosure at such times as they might be likely to distract public attention from the cricket, and it would probably be a wise precaution to keep them in a cat-proof enclosure at night.

It is a common thing to see pinioned plover – the beautiful Cayenne plover – running about as free pets in gardens in Chile, where they are believed to do much good by destroying insect and crawling pests; and they apparently do no harm to either lawns or flowers.

Yours, &c.,

CLARENCE ELLIOTT

A photograph in *The Times*'s MCC Number shows ground staff working on the ravaged turf but, alas, no plover.

LIGHT BLUE AT LORD'S

From H. H., 11 July 1936

Sir, Various explanations have been put forward to account for the lack of success which has attended Oxford (and Harrow) at Lord's in recent years. Some observers have attributed this to luck, of the toss or otherwise. There is, however, an explanation which I have not yet seen advanced. I refer to the sinister fact that the inside of the scorer's box at Lord's is painted light blue. This is obviously an insuperable obstacle to the success of any dark blue side, but whether it is due to caprice or prejudice on the part of the scorers, or the MCC authorities, has not been revealed to me.

I remain yours faithfully,

H. H.

Light blue has since given way to cream and magnolia.

MCC TOURING SIDES

The MCC Selection and Planning Sub-Committee reported that, because post-war, socio-economic factors prevented selection of the best available sides, future tours should be curtailed and priority given to Australia and South Africa.

From Mr Aidan Crawley, MP, 22 July 1948

Oxford University and Kent (1927–47). Labour Member for Buckingham 1945–51. Parliamentary Under-Secretary of State for Air 1950–51. Conservative Member for West Derbyshire 1962–68. President of MCC 1972. First Chairman of the National Cricket Association 1968–75.

Sir, The report of the sub-committee of the MCC raises two important questions. Is the MCC entitled to say that the best touring side which it can muster in the next few years is unrepresentative just because our standard of cricket is low? Is it certain that every effort has been made to draw upon the best cricketers in this country?

In answer to the first question, the MCC can undoubtedly claim that, since touring sides are club sides, the club has the right to say what they should represent. But that is a legalistic point of view. It was the MCC which gave countries like New Zealand and India 'test-match status', and the tourists from those countries have striven manfully to maintain their standards even when talent has been lacking. It will surely seem most unfair to them that, when England strikes a bad patch and gives them a chance to take their revenge, the MCC should withdraw from the contest.

In answer to the second question, surely the contrast between English and Australian cricket is significant. In Australia the number of three-day matches is so limited that any club player who turns out regularly on Saturdays has a chance of being selected and of arranging to take time off for big matches. In England club players never come within the preview of the selectors at all. Yet every cricketer knows that there are first-class players turning out every Saturday who, if representative cricket was differently organized, would jump at the chances of playing a few three-day matches a year.

Such a reorganization would involve changes in the county championship and in the financial basis of cricket; but unless it is tackled, for all the reasons given in the sub-committee's report, English cricket is unlikely to regain a satisfactory standard. An alternative would be for the Club Cricket Conference to select a representative side, find backers and challenge the world in the spirit of the first Australian team that came to these shores. Their side would certainly be 'representative' of more strata of English cricket than present MCC touring sides, and who will say that it would be less successful?

Of course, such a challenge would bring into question the position of the MCC as the arbiter of cricket, but so, surely, will the policy suggested by the sub-committee. What oversea cricketing community will continue to accept the authority of a club which, so far as they are concerned, admits that it is only second rate? It is to be hoped that the MCC will think again.

Yours, &c.,
AIDAN CRAWLEY

WHITE ENSIGN AT LORD'S

From Mr M. N. Kearney, 10 August 1950

Sir, The guardsman who dropped his musket on parade is forgotten – outclassed. To-day at Lord's, during the Royal Navy v. Royal Air Force match, the White Ensign flew above the pavilion upside down! From before the match until the luncheon interval 'Older Glory' hung on her mast, immediately above the Navy's dressing-room, limp and listless in the still breeze, shy or sad because of the indignity imposed upon her; but occasional puffs of wind displayed her sorry state – while two commanders and one lieutenant, R.N., smote the ball with vigour and squadron leaders and flight lieutenants scurried to and fro, oblivious of the heinous crime perpetrated before their eyes at the headquarters of cricket's majesty.

It was not until a mere civilian pointed out the error that it was rectified. Thereafter the Ensign was lowered, and re-hoisted, the right way up, at 13.38 hours, amid the faint cheers of the few spectators viewing the spectacle. In case this memorable occurrence has skipped your notice I venture to record it. No doubt Wisden will mark it with reverence in due course.

Your obedient servant,
M. NEVILLE KEARNEY

Wisden remained silent.

SCORING AT LORD'S

From the Revd W. H. Murray Walton, 26 May 1953

Sir, May I suggest to the powers that be in the MCC that they celebrate the year of the Coronation by erecting a new score-board on the south side of what I presume is the premier cricket ground in the world? The present board is a confused jumble of figures, a jumble now made the worse by the addition of the numbers 1–11 and S, squeezed in at the top to denote the fielders. The spacing and arrangement of words and figures would bring a blush to the cheeks of even a third-rate printer.

Yours faithfully,
W. H. MURRAY WALTON

The scoreboard was replaced in 1969, nearly 80 years old. The MCC annual report opined that it 'had reached the end of a most useful life'.

INFLATION AT LORD'S

From Mr L. H. Razzall, 22 July 1961

Sir, This afternoon, on the last day of the Varsity match, I arrived at Lord's at 4.20 and on tendering the prescribed entrance fee of 3*s*. was informed that if I waited until 4.30 I should save 1*s*. 6*d*. Remembering Mr Getty's prudent philosophy I decided to wait. On peering through the gate I saw that the playing area was deserted, as the tea interval was in progress.

Surely, Sir, the MCC does not include the tea interval in the hours of play, and, if it does, is it not adding to the inflationary spiral?

Yours, &c.,
LEONARD HUMPHREY RAZZALL

MUST RAIN STOP PLAY?

Seventeen hours and twenty minutes of playing time in the England v. Pakistan Test match were lost to the weather.

From Mrs John Tayler, 26 June 1971

Sir, There is a recurring mystery which I am confronted with every year around this time. And I wish to goodness someone would solve it.

I have the misfortune to have unwittingly tied myself for life to a cricket fanatic; I have just been dragged back from our annual holiday in time for the first Test match at Lord's only to have the master of the house turn, as he always does on these occasions, into a neurotic mass, pacing Hamlet-like from room to room, chasing to the window to check cloud formations and to the telephone for the latest dismal recorded announcement. Eventually, of course, comes the inevitable realization that rain, as usual, has stopped play.

I understand that there has been cricket at Lord's for the past one hundred years, and so, incredible as it seems, the wives of W. G. Grace fans must have suffered the same traumatic conditions. And this is the mystery: why, in the name of reason, in that complete century while Edison, Marconi, Fleming and countless other great men were making contributions to the benefit of mankind, has no one asked an inventor to invent something to keep the grass dry at Lord's when it rains? It cannot be anything as simple as lack of money, for I am sure every member of the MCC, for a start, would happily subscribe £5 towards the enterprise – (my husband has already lost more than this in unused tickets this week alone, and I hear today that the MCC are £16,000 down on lost takings).

Please could *someone* do something before 22 July – even if it is only organizing the requisite number of enthusiasts to stand cheek by jowl over the whole area with their umbrellas up.

Yours faithfully,
ANNE TAYLER

22 July was the first day of the England v. India match. Rain again intervened, preventing play after tea on the final day with India needing 38 runs, and England two wickets, to win.

A GOOD DELIVERY

From the Curator of Lord's Cricket Ground, 27 March 1980

Sir, I realize that Britain's role in the world has changed somewhat since the days of, say, Dr W. G. Grace, but it was still a shock to receive a letter addressed to 'Lord's Cricket Ground, London, Ontario'.

I must, however, congratulate the Canadian and British Post Offices on delivering it safely.

Yours faithfully,
STEPHEN GREEN

6
MONEY IS THE ROOT OF ALL EVIL

CANTERBURY CRICKET WEEK

From A Man of Kent, 12 August 1892

Sir, I have been a regular attendant at the Cricket Week for 44 years. Till recently lookers-on could see all they wished of the game, and, moreover, if they regarded the great annual county meeting in merely a social point of view, had every opportunity of meeting their friends, as, with the exception of the necessary markers' tent, the whole circuit of the ground was open to the public.

A great change, I regret to say, has taken place for the worse in consequence of the proprietors allowing private tents to be erected, which now, being about a score, and increasing in number annually, monopolize a good third of the ground, and thus deprive the public of both seeing the cricket and, at the same time, enjoying the society of their friends.

Many tents with a capacity for 30 or 40 occupants may be seen with less than a dozen. True, there are a limited number of covered seats for subscribers and their friends, but the great mass of visitors who pay their shilling (and these were said to be yesterday upwards of 8,000) are deprived of half their pleasure by this dog-in-the-manger love of exclusiveness. I venture to make known through your columns this public grievance in hope of some remedy being adopted.

> I am, Sir, your obedient servant,
> A MAN OF KENT

A PROTEST

From Mr George Brann, 5 April 1926
Sussex (1883–1905). England football international.

Sir, Will you spare a small amount of space for the lament of an ancient cricketer with reference to the appalling amount of 'pen-swishing' from an advance guard of Australian writers as published by a section of the English Press?

What it all means one fails to understand, and one feels that the majority of the English cricket-loving public cares less. The Australians, hitherto, have come over without all this boosting and self-advertisement and have beaten us – so to speak – off their own bat. The actual players themselves surely cannot like it. Cricket to a cricketer is a game – not a spectacle. If it is to be turned into a species of circus show, why not adopt prize-ring methods, and as each player steps on the field at Lord's appoint a master of ceremonies, armed with a megaphone, to announce his name, his family history, and the deeds of daring he has performed on the cricket field?

We have six weeks to go before the Test matches are begun, and if this ink-slinging is to continue until that time all good cricketers will be nauseated with the clap-trap, and heartily wish that the word test – as applied to cricket – had never been coined.

I am, Sir, yours truly,
GEORGE BRANN

'BRITAIN'S FIRST CRICKET POOL'

From Mr John Murphy, 28 May 1934

Sir, On the occasion of the match between Lancashire and Somerset at Old Trafford last week, there was distributed to spectators leaving the field an envelope containing a description of 'Britain's First Cricket Pool'. The claim was made that this 'Cricket Totalisator Pool' 'presents the follower of cricket with an opportunity to make money in summer to the same extent as the football follower made in the winter'! The scheme is twofold, giving people the chance of gambling either on the counties' matches or on the Lancashire League Saturday contests. Further, the counties pool has two competitions involving forecasts, in the one case, of the number of runs to be scored by leading batsmen, and, in the other, of the more successful bowler of a pair who are set against each other. The promoters of the pool take 10 per cent in addition to 'working expenses'. The betting must all be done by post; so that those who take part need never see a game.

I am conscious that some will regard me as a sentimental fool when I say that my heart sank as I saw these people lay their hands at last upon our great game; but there are multitudes in England, of many shades of opinion on the abstract question, who will view this encroachment upon it with profound disquiet and disgust. Greyhounds and a mechanical hare, the football teams, and now our great cricketers. These men, who have been to us personalities, regarded with a kindly interest and affection, without anger or spite in their 'successes' or 'failures', lifting us above our partisanships in our admiration or sympathy, are to be mere instruments in a gambling system, and to be the subjects of the mean passions which are stirred by the winning and losing of money in this way. It is a degradation of personality from which we should protect the men, and protect our honour as a sport-loving people.

There is the more obvious and far-reaching evil that we have here a profit-making company whose single commercial aim is to induce more and more persons to gamble; and the profits are so good, the organization so simple, and the risk to the promoters so trifling, that these concerns will spring up – and are indeed springing up – like mushrooms; and there is no legal limit to them at present. The class which is appealed to, as is shown by the small stakes asked, is mainly the poorest of our people; and once more their desperate anxiety to make a few shillings is exploited. The inevitable result, which is so often forgotten, is that, since the losers must always be in the majority, vastly more distress is caused than pleasure given. The demoralizing influence which so impressed the Royal Commission, and also the Government, as to produce the clause in the Lotteries Bill designed to abolish football pools, is to be extended into the field of the national summer game. One is moved, therefore, to appeal to Lord Londonderry and the National Government either not to withdraw this portion of the Bill or to introduce some safeguards which will deliver our people from this gratuitous temptation and our finest sport from degradation. One respects every man's liberty; but this would be an act of moral sanitation.

Yours, &c.,

JOHN MURPHY

TIMELESS TESTS

From Mr W. B. Franklin, 8 February 1937

Cambridge University and Buckinghamshire (1911–46). President of the Minor Counties Cricket Association 1954–68, Chairman 1945–57.

Sir, Will you allow me to voice the opinion of many cricketers who like myself view with increasing concern the continuance of what have become known as 'timeless Tests'? The only advantage, if indeed it can be called an advantage, is that they attract large attendances, at least in Australia, though it is extremely doubtful whether in this country the result would be the same, and consequently large sums are acquired for the respective promoters.

In other words, the great game of cricket is being hopelessly and deliberately commercialized.

There are two other great disadvantages:–

(1) Time is of no consequence and the whole essence of the game as played since its inception is lacking; that is, to make more runs than the other side in a given time. Gone is the art of making a subtle and successful declaration; gone is the attraction and excitement of making runs 'against the clock' and then finding that it is not possible even to effect a meritorious draw. Anyone who has played cricket in the great spirit and tradition of Francis Ford, Jessop, or Woolley will realize at once what a pitiful loss is being sustained in international cricket to-day. And for what? Merely that more and more money should be made. What a mockery of the game of cricket!

(2) Far too great an importance devolves upon the result of the toss. One distinguished cricketer has recently put it at not less than 100 runs. The side that bats first on a good dry wicket has apparently only one object under the prevailing conditions, and that is to stay at the crease as long as possible, wear down the bowlers, and, by no means least, wear away the wicket, in order that in the fourth innings not great bowling shall prevail but the vagaries of an uncertain pitch.

That, Sir, is not a real test of the game, quite apart from its obvious reduction of enjoyment for the players and spectators alike. Surely those who control the game in this country can take a stand against turning cricket into a business proposition?

The last Test Match at Adelaide was played for six days without any interruption from the weather! It is not difficult to imagine a match lasting even 10 days with bad weather. It is enough merely to state these facts in order to show up the absurdity of not fixing some reasonable time limit before it is too late to rescue future matches from a creeping paralysis of inactivity.

It took years of argument and talk to change the size of the stumps and the leg-before-wicket rule, but the 'timeless' Test has done more to change the whole game of cricket than these two rules put together.

The answer no doubt from those in authority – I almost wrote from the 'big bosses' – will be: We cannot afford to return to three or four days, and there, Sir, you have the true answer naked and unashamed.

Yours faithfully.

W. B. FRANKLIN

Until 1927–28 all Australian domestic first-class cricket was 'timeless' i.e. played to a finish.

From Mr A. H. J. Cochrane, 13 February 1937
Oxford University and Derbyshire (1884–88). Writer of verse and books on cricket

Sir, Mr Franklin, writing about modern cricket in a strain of fashionable melancholy, deplores the commercialization of the game as if it were something new. The association of cricket with finance is of considerable antiquity, and in its present form dates from the middle of the eighteenth century when the public first thought it worth while to pay money to watch first-class matches. The same spirit under other aspects may be traced through those heroic days when Lord Frederick Beauclerk made £600 a year by his skilful play, and Lord's Pavilion was the centre of a betting ring. In our degenerate age we can console ourselves by reflecting that the profits of cricket, if there are any, go to the treasurers of impoverished county clubs, instead of to bookmakers, and that professionals are now paid to win, instead of being paid to lose. There are silver linings to most clouds.

As regards the Test matches against Australia, the real problem is that of getting more definite results when these contests take place in England. The conditions which prevail when our representatives uphold our standard in Australia differ so much from those which prevail when the Australians visit this country that it is hardly necessary to suspect that pecuniary motives must underlie any efforts to bring them into harmony.

Three-day matches suit our crowded domestic programme, and when teams are constantly meeting each other, as the counties are, the fact that half of their engagements are left unfinished, as was the case in 1936, does not matter much. But, when the chosen champions of Australia cross the world to demonstrate that they play cricket in their own land better than we do in ours, there is something to be said for settling the issue of that challenge as fairly and as conclusively as it is possible to settle it. The decision is designed to depend upon the issue of five separate matches. In 1926 it depended upon a single finished match, and in 1930 and 1934 it depended upon the best of three finished games. This is to say that of the last 15 Test matches in this country against Australia no fewer than eight have been drawn, and the question is whether these statistics form a reliable criterion of success or failure.

Our cricket authorities have already recognized those international encounters as being in a class by themselves. Four days have been allotted, in place of three, to Australian Test matches, and the final match, if the rival teams enter upon it with an equal number of wins, is now played to a finish. This arrangement has hitherto worked out quite well, and has provided a settlement of the rubber which, though it may not be thorough, is better than no settlement at all. But it has certain disadvantages which may at any time become obvious. A side robbed by weather of victory in the first four games may, when it comes to the fifth, find itself beaten after a protracted struggle. In this untoward event some sense of grievance would be felt that the rain, which had prevented earlier triumphs, was now powerless to avert defeat. Again there is no particular reason why the loser of two matches to one should not, now that Test matches last four days, win the fifth within the prescribed time, and so, by making the result two all, render the campaign inconclusive.

It might be a more satisfactory plan to extend each of these matches in England to six days, and to play them all under the same conditions. No more interference, if a Saturday start were made, would be caused to county cricket than is caused at present, and the extra time would allow of some margin against interruption by the weather.

Your obedient servant,
ALFRED COCHRANE

CRICKET AND ADVERTISING

From Sir Brian Batsford, 14 June 1974
Chairman of Council, The Royal Society of Arts

Sir, Much of the enjoyment of watching cricket, especially on television, is now marred by advertising.

The batsman's stroke, the bowler's run up or the catch in the slips is no longer seen against the traditional green of the cricket field or the white rails of the pavilion, but instead against the incongruous and garish board of an advertisement.

Is there no authority in the world of cricket, of advertising or of government which can halt this steady deterioration in our standards?

Yours faithfully,
BRIAN BATSFORD

TEST MATCH OVER RATES

From Mr Kenneth Gregory, 15 June 1976
Compiler of *The First Cuckoo* (a general anthology of letters to *The Times*) and author of books on cricket and other subjects.

Sir, Whenever a member of the opposing side is dismissed nowadays, our Test cricketers oblige with a creditable rendition of the Polovtsian dances, which may explain why – physically and emotionally exhausted – they are incapable of bowling only 85 overs in a day. With the Lord's match soon to take place, it is worth recalling that on this ground in 1926 England (three-quarters of whose bowling was done at fast or brisk medium pace by Larwood, Root and Tate) managed on the first, six-hour, day to get through 140 overs.

Perhaps gamesmanship accounts for the modern over rate. At long last, and forty years too late, it seems that we have discovered how to prevent a Bradman from scoring 300 in a day: when heavily punished for a single alter the field placings, re-tie one's boot laces, polish the ball, remove one's sweater, rough up the bowler's foot holds, appear aggrieved that the sun has gone in or come out – in short, *Don't bowl at him.*

Yours faithfully,
KENNETH GREGORY

In December 1981 India bowled only 67 overs in a full day at Delhi. For the 1982 and 1983 Tests in England a daily minimum of 96 overs was stipulated.

123

THE PACKER EPISODE

In May 1977 it was announced that Kerry Packer, an Australian business-man who had been refused exclusive rights to televise cricket in Australia, had signed up 35 of the world's leading cricketers to play in a series of matches in Australia in conflict with established Test cricket. The enter-prise, called World Series Cricket (WSC) but soon dubbed the 'Packer Circus', put the world of cricket in turmoil. An 'agent' for Kerry Packer had been the England captain.

TONY GREIG'S DISMISSAL

From Mr Stephen Hodges, 17 May 1977

Sir, In his article on the decision to dismiss Tony Greig as England Test Captain (May 14), John Woodcock writes, 'no one is likely to be convinced that he has acted less than miserably as the reigning captain'. Mr Woodcock is wrong in his assumption that his views are shared by the world, if such an attitude is rather pompous, it is, nevertheless, relatively harmless. What is inexcusable, in my opinion, is the way in which Mr Woodcock explains Greig's 'mis-erable' conduct.

'What has to be remembered, of course, is that he is an English-man not by birth or upbringing, but only by adoption. It is not the same thing as being English through and through.' At best this might be a misguided attempt to rationalize what Mr Woodcock sees as a lack of patriotism on Greig's part. At worst this is shabby and objectionable chauvinism, which ill becomes *The Times* front page.

Yours faithfully,
STEPHEN HODGES

The intervention of World Series Cricket brought in new sponsors to support the traditional Test matches in England and ultimately raised the level of earnings for players and umpires. Meanwhile WSC players were faced with a ban from Test and county cricket.

MR PACKER'S CRICKETERS

From the Editor of Time Out, *18 July 1977*

Sir, Will you please refrain from dignifying Mr Kerry Packer's commercial adventure through your continued description of his proposed artificial cricket matches as a 'Test series'?

Yours faithfully,
RICHARD WILLIAMS

From Mr George Speaight, 20 July 1977

Sir, Will you please refrain from dignifying Mr Kerry Packer's commercial adventure with the title of such a traditional and honourable form of entertainment as the Circus.

Yours faithfully,
GEORGE SPEAIGHT

From Dr E. H. Kronheimer, 22 July 1977

Sir, Will you please refrain from dignifying Mr Kerry Packer's commercial adventure through your continued description of his proposed activity as 'cricket'?

Yours faithfully,
ERWIN KRONHEIMER

CRICKETERS' RIGHT TO EARN

From Mr P. T. Logan, 30 July 1977

Sir, A (professional) cricketer has no continuous contract with any authority that governs the selection of national teams. No retainers are paid. A cricketer does not know whether he will ever be selected again. It depends on absence of injury, his form, the form of rival candidates, the balance needed in a touring team between players with different skills, and so on. *If* the MCC are about to go on tour abroad in the following winter, an aspiring player will not know in July whether he will have employment with them.

In these circumstances the International Cricket Conference has acted in a high-handed and spiteful manner towards those players who have signed contracts with Mr Kerry Packer. In effect they have said, 'We do not guarantee employment, but, by God, if you work for anyone else you shall suffer'.

I trust that the counties will ignore the suggestion that they should act in the same way. If they do not ignore it some of the county teams will indeed not look 'first-class'. Perhaps the fact that their support and income depend largely on their successes will have a salutary effect. Who, for example, will be prepared to risk missing the final at Lord's of a one day competition with all its financial advantages and the fun and excitement for the supporters?

If Mr Packer's venture fails the authorities will have nothing further to worry about. If it succeeds they will have to compete with him in a way that will benefit the players. They have set about it in the wrong way.

I am, Sir, Your obedient servant,

P. T. LOGAN

The bans were contested in the High Court and the verdict in favour of the players on the grounds of 'restraint of trade' left the cricket authorities to pay costs of £20,000. The WSC matches attracted little support and the authorities, having decided not to appeal, expressed hope of eventual compromise with Mr Packer.

FUTURE OF ENGLISH CRICKET

From Mr Oliver Popplewell, QC, 11 February 1978
Cambridge University (1949–51). Member of MCC committee. Knighted 1983.

Sir, Mr Subba Row's judgment (February 9) on cricketing matters always commands respect (even if he did run me out once in the University Match!) – but while negotiations and compromise are normally much to be commended, it is impossible to see how much further the authorities can go, even though they can now speak from a position of strength.

For English cricket there are two immediate problems – the county matches this summer and the Australian tour in the winter. The counties have been allowed to make their own decision in the attitude they adopt to the Packer players but it would be quite unreal not to recognize that the strength of feeling among the majority of county players and cricket lovers is likely to manifest itself even more forcibly before the season is over, whatever discussion there may be.

Next winter England visit Australia. The arrangements for this have been known for a long time. At the same time Mr Packer will be operating in direct and deliberate competition. Both cannot contain the same players.

The only practical area of compromise is for those English and Australian players good enough for the Test series to be released by Mr Packer, but they would have to be available for the whole tour. No doubt if Mr Packer is willing he will notify the authorities. Until then I believe they should stand firm and beware the siren song of compromise.

Yours faithfully.
OLIVER POPPLEWELL

After much international upheaval of players, administrators and sponsors while both varieties of cricket contended for spectators' attentions, Kerry Packer achieved in April 1979 his original aim of exclusive television rights. Next month one of his companies was awarded the contract to promote Australian cricket for ten years. World Series Cricket was disbanded.

THE REAL TEST

In Test matches between New Zealand and West Indies Michael Holding kicked down the stumps, Colin Croft barged an umpire, and the West Indians threatened to go home before the tour was completed.

From Mr Raman Subba Row, 29 February 1980
Cambridge University, Surrey, Northamptonshire and England (1951–61), captaining Northamptonshire. Chairman of Surrey. Member of MCC committee. Manager of England touring team to India and Sri Lanka 1981–82.

Sir, I expect that many cricket lovers will deplore the declining standards of behaviour in international competition. Although not the only sport to suffer from this decline, cricket has so long been synonymous with sportsmanship that there are real dangers of the game losing its hard core of support if the present state of affairs is allowed to continue.

Pressures on international cricketers today are greater than ever before, and so are their rewards from playing and commercial sources. That is one of the reasons why the game needs a strong international management structure which, had it existed three years ago, would not have enabled a rival cricket system to emerge.

Other reasons such as the increasing complexity of international tours programming, financial arrangements between countries and, not least, the marketing of the game throughout the world, highlight the importance of a modern management approach.

If cricket is well run internationally, it will inevitably bring respect from those who work in it. The stark truth of the converse is plain to see.

Yours faithfully,
RAMAN SUBBA ROW

UMPIRES' DECISION ON TEST PITCH

From Mr John Carlisle, 3 September 1980

Conservative MP for Luton West, subsequently Luton North. Ardent campaigner for renewal of official cricketing links with South Africa.

Sir, While deploring the unruly behaviour of MCC members at the Centenary Test, as an interested spectator I must express some sympathy with their frustrations and that of the large crowd.

There might indeed be some parallel, as indicated by Ian Botham, with the game of soccer. Cricketers are now highly paid, sponsorship is an essential part of the game's finance and even the officials, including umpires, have taken a public image similar to those of team managers and referees. This indicates that their actions will attract publicity and it has not gone unnoticed that umpires now assume a stance more akin to showmen than silent adjudicators of old.

That this new attitude extended to the decision by two men to deny entertainment to 22,000 people is nevertheless regrettable. They must have expected an antagonistic response and in the circumstances it is not undeserved.

Yours faithfully,
JOHN CARLISLE

KNOCK-OUT CRICKET

MCC put up a County Champion Cup in 1873 to increase interest in the game. However, only Kent and Sussex entered and the competition was discontinued. In 1945 a competition of three-day knock-out matches, with a four-day final at Lord's, for 'The Cricket Cup' was proposed.

From the Archdeacon of Ipswich, 4 April 1945

Sir, Many lovers of cricket must view with regret and dismay the proposal to start a knock-out competition on the lines of the FA Cup. They feel that, far from increasing a healthy and intelligent interest in the game for its own sake, it will only tend to encourage systematic betting and such things as cricket pools.

No doubt it might increase the gate money and draw larger crowds to the matches, but this would be due to interest in the betting rather than in the cricket. True lovers of the game will surely hope that the proposed scheme may be found unworkable and so be abandoned.

I am, Sir, yours, &c.,
ERIC REDE BUCKLEY

From Canon J. M. Swift, 6 April 1945
Cheshire and Lancashire second XI.

Sir, I hope, and believe, that Archdeacon Buckley's fears about knock-out cricket are unfounded. As one who has played competitive cricket, and seen much league cricket, my experience is that the game gains more than it loses by keen competition. Those who wish to bet can always find an opportunity, and it is very doubtful if knock-out cricket will encourage systematic betting. The uncertainty of the game does not encourage the average backer.

Those who know the facts about county cricket finance are naturally anxious about the future; they realize that something must be done to attract larger crowds. True lovers of the game wish to see cricket played and enjoyed by the greatest number of people, and some of us are prepared to run many risks in catering for the masses rather than allow our great national game to become a 'class' pursuit.

Yours faithfully,
J. M. SWIFT

This plan was shelved, but the Knock-Out competition (later Gillette Cup) began on 1 May 1963.

From Mr J. R. Reid, 16 July 1963

Sir, The county cricket knock-out competition has so far proved to be a success. Perhaps therefore MCC might consider extending its scope next season. In the FA Cup a good deal of interest comes from the fact that the small clubs get a chance to try their luck against the larger and more famous ones. It might be that a comparable system in the knockout competition would increase its popularity still further. Perhaps the Minor Counties, who have at present no opportunity of playing against first-class counties, would welcome the chance of entering, especially as there is always a sneaking suspicion that luck may have some part in the results.

Yours faithfully.

J. R. REID

Five minor counties were admitted in 1964 and by the end of 1982 Durham, Lincolnshire and Hertfordshire had beaten first-class opponents.

SUNDAY CRICKET – COUNTIES

From Mr Neville Cardus, CBE, 12 October 1965

Music critic and the outstanding writer on cricket, mainly for *The Guardian* (formerly *The Manchester Guardian*). Special correspondent for *The Times* in Australia 1946–47. Knighted 1967.

Sir, Might I suggest to county committees who are in favour of Sunday cricket that, first of all, they should see to it that their teams play cricket on Mondays, Tuesdays, Wednesdays, Thursdays, Fridays, and Saturdays.

Yours sincerely,

NEVILLE CARDUS

The first Sunday of county play took place on 15 May 1966 at Ilford where 6000 spectators watched Essex play Somerset.

From the Revd David Sheppard, 29 June 1966

Sir, Your reports on the experiment of some counties' playing first-class cricket matches on Sunday have spoken without qualification of their 'success'. There are factors on the other side which should be mentioned unless the case is to go by default.

Both in conversation and in correspondence a number of cricket followers have told me how upset they have been by the introduction of first-class cricket on Sunday. The journal *The Cricketer* conducted a poll of its readers this summer; asked whether they approved of Sunday cricket the majority said 'Yes'. Thirty per cent said 'No'. A minority, but a significant minority, who care very much that the character of Sunday is not altogether changed.

The Crathorne Committee was concerned too: 'A substantial relaxation of the restrictions on spectators' sports would do more to alter the character of Sunday than a relaxation in relation to entertainments. . . . We should like to limit Sunday sports to those in which the particpants receive no payment and which are likely to attract only a comparatively small number of spectators.' There is no entirely logical line to draw here, but the Wolfenden Committee's distinction in its report on 'Sport and the Community' was followed, the line 'between private or semi-private enjoyment and organized commercial sport'.

The Crathorne Committee said that the Wolfenden Report on Sunday sports was quoted by several organizations that submitted evidence, including the Central Council of Physical Recreation, the British Council of Churches and the National Association of Youth Clubs, 'and it appeared to set out a general approach that received widespread support'.

Because first-class cricket has some great financial problems, cricketers should not ignore their responsibility to the community as a whole. I love cricket very greatly, but the need of the community to have a 'different day' is more important to me than any possible advantage to the game; to keep a day when men are free to do what they choose argues, in my judgment, against counties requiring their players to play for their living on Sundays.

What an unfair position it puts an aspiring young cricketer in, who wants his Sunday to be a different day, and who must play on Sunday if he is to play in a three-day match for his team.

Yours faithfully,
DAVID SHEPPARD

In 1969 the John Player Sunday League was instituted.

SUNDAY CRICKET – TEST MATCHES

From Mr C. F. Corbould-Ellis, JP, 20 July 1926
Clerk of the Worshipful Company of Founders.

Sir, Is there any really cogent reason why four days cannot be set apart for the remaining Test matches by the inclusion in each of a Sunday? The doing so would give numbers of people the opportunity, otherwise lacking, of seeing one or both of the matches and might lead to a match being ended. We all play tennis, golf, croquet, bowls on Sundays and go on the river or fish or motor. If it is a matter of ecclesiastical sin to play a cricket match on Sundays, why so is receiving a cup of tea from an overfed and underworked butler in a deanery garden. Why should we be balked of enjoyment on the best and most care-free day in the week?

Yours faithfully,
C. F. CORBOULD-ELLIS

From the Bishop of Norwich and Lord Robertson of Oakridge,
14 November 1980

Sir, On 12 November your columns reported the proposal that there should be Sunday play in some of next year's Test matches. Recently there have also been suggestions that some Football League matches should be played on Sunday.

Whilst recognizing that there are factors, mainly financial (as you rightly say, 'Money is clearly at the basis of the plan') in favour of Sunday sport, we believe there are other points which should be considered by the sports authorities before final decisions are taken.

In the first place, to hold Sunday sporting events on the scale proposed would affect the quality of life not only of participants, spectators and those others, such as transport workers and police, who would have to work extra time on the Sundays concerned, but also people living near by who would have to put up with the invasion of sporting crowds in their neighbourhood, with all that this entails.

Secondly, from a specifically Christian point of view, no avoidable hindrance should be placed in the way of the growing number of people who wish to set apart Sunday as a day when the main priority is the worship of their God, both corporately and individually. Furthermore, it would be sad if cricket and football were to lose the wholehearted support of those among the millions of churchgoers, who are enthusiastic supporters, as indeed we are, of our two great national sports.

Lastly, and more generally, let us try to keep Sunday, as far as possible, a day when we can have a respite from the weekday pressures of life and a day when families can relax together and enjoy each other's company in peace.

Yours faithfully,
MAURICE NORVIC, ROBERTSON OF OAKRIDGE

The first Sunday of Test cricket in England was 21 June 1981 against Australia at Trent Bridge.

FLOODLIT CRICKET

An England XI met the Rest of the World at Bristol City football ground.

From Mr Derek Batten, 26 September 1980

Sir, Alan Gibson's scathing report on floodlit cricket (18 September) omits to mention its two main advantages.

First, the ball can be seen very clearly by the spectators throughout the whole of the match no matter how fast the bowling or how high the hit. A colleague of mine with failing eyesight who still watches cricket, although hardly seeing anything of the ball, was amazed at the difference. I am sure he is not alone.

Second, Mr Gibson should not forget that he is one of the very privileged few who is actually paid to watch cricket. The vast majority of cricket lovers have to work during most of the hours when the game is being played. Evening floodlit games enable us to see first-class players at an obviously convenient time.

Of course, the football ground scenario makes the game a travesty at the present time. The floodlighting of county grounds will remove most anomalies and I welcome the news that the Test and County Cricket Board is looking at the whole matter.

Yours faithfully,
DEREK BATTEN

From Mr Jeremy Sanders, 29 November 1980

Sir, It seems, then, that the Test and County Cricket Board have finally sold their collective soul to the world of advertising and television. Whilst 'traditional' one-day cricket was still very much the same game as first-class cricket, quite what this new [floodlit] competition planned by the TCCB (report, 21 November) will be is rather a matter for speculation.

The combination of matches being played on a basis of ten overs per side, and their being played on football grounds, which will effectively limit boundaries to about 25 yards, will mean that virtually the entire match will consist of batsmen swinging wildly at every ball, in an attempt to hit a four or a six to either square-leg or cover point. With such short boundaries, even mis-hits would often go for six. This is the sort of mutilation of cricket which even Kerry Packer would not have dared introduce.

There is nothing wrong with altering the conditions under which cricket is played. Such innovations as floodlit cricket, white balls and even coloured clothing will, no doubt, be taken for granted within a few years, but this is a very different matter from completely altering the game itself. The new competition planned by the TCCB may be many things, but it won't be cricket.

Yours faithfully,
JEREMY SANDERS

The competition was abandoned after one season.

7
DESCENDANTS OF KING SOLOMON OR REINCARNATIONS OF JUDGE JEFFREYS

WHITE COATS

From Mr F. C. Robertson, 11 July 1919

Sir, Mr R. H. Lyttelton is quite right in stating that Mr W N Powys delivered the ball with the left hand, over the wicket, just clearing the bails, and that he was a very fast bowler.

In a match in 1878 on Chislehurst Common between the West Kent and Assyrians Clubs Powys bowled for the latter, and I found it difficult to see the ball, owing to his peculiar delivery. This difficulty was increased by the black garments of our West Kent umpire, whose figure considerably interfered with one's view of the ball. On being requested by me to stand clear, he replied, 'Can't stand back no farther, Sir,' so I had to make the best of matters. This led to my suggesting in *Bell's Life* or the *Field* – I forget which – that umpires should be clad in white; and shortly afterwards, to the general amusement of the spectators, the umpires at the Eton and Harrow match appeared in the white robe which adds so much to the dignity of those functionaries and enables the batsmen to get a better sight of the ball.

Yours faithfully,
F. C. ROBERTSON

THE DUTIES OF UMPIRES

From Mr P. F. Warner, 29 June 1909
Captain of Middlesex.

Sir, *The Times* of to-day, referring to the leg-before-wicket incident at Lord's in the Middlesex v. Notts match, says:– 'Mr Jones protested, and there was a discussion between Mr Warner, Mr Jones, and the umpire, when Mr Jones took exception to the proceedings altogether. If the facts were as we have stated, we think Mr Warner ought not to have permitted Tarrant to continue his innings. . . . It is setting up a very bad precedent to permit a batsman to take any part in a discussion at all. . . . The umpire only reversed the decision because the batsman made a protest.'

May I be allowed to state that Tarrant made no protest, and took no part whatsoever in the discussion between Mr Jones, Roberts, the umpire, and myself?

On being given 'out' in the first instance by Roberts, Tarrant walked promptly away from the wicket; but when he had got about four or five yards from his crease in the direction of mid-off he said, quite quietly, 'I hit it.' The remark was addressed to no one in particular – if to any one person more than another, to mid-off – and certainly not to Roberts, and I am convinced that Tarrant had no intention of influencing him. In the discussion which followed – in which, I repeat, Tarrant said not one word – I told Roberts that if he was in any way influenced, however slightly, by Tarrant's remark, he was bound to give Tarrant 'out'.

Roberts declared emphatically that he was not so influenced, and repeated his declaration more than once, and that, on considera-tion, he gave Tarrant not out because, in his opinion, he had played the ball.

This is the correct version of what took place. I happened to be in batting with Tarrant at the moment, and I do not see how in the circumstances I could have insisted on Roberts adhering to his original decision of 'out'. That would have been an extraordinary assumption of the umpire's duty on the part of a captain.

I am yours truly,
P. F. WARNER

From Mr A. O. Jones, 2 July 1909

Cambridge University and captain of Nottinghamshire and England (1892–1914).

Sir, I should have been well content to let the Tarrant incident drop until the powers at Lord's had given their decision, but as Mr Warner has thought fit to give his version of the affair, I think, on behalf of the Notts County Cricket Club, that I ought to give mine, which differs considerably from Mr Warner's.

I was fielding at 'silly' third man, and perhaps had a better view of the incident than any one else on the field. Iremonger, the bowler, and Oates, the wicketkeeper, both appealed for leg-before-wicket; Roberts put up his hand giving the batsman out; Tarrant immediately (not, as Mr Warner says, after walking five yards towards mid-off) said in an undertone, 'I hit it,' and walked towards the pavilion. On passing the other wicket he again said, 'I hit it,' and Roberts then altered his decision.

Mr Warner makes a strong point of the fact that Roberts states that he was not influenced in any way by Tarrant's remark. Does Mr Warner infer that the decision would have been reversed had Tarrant walked to the pavilion without saying anything? My objection is to the principle of the decision. The object of the rule allowing umpires to alter a decision is only to enable them to correct a slip; but a slip, if made, should be corrected instantly, and not after a batsman has left the wicket and has given his version of the incident to the umpire.

I am, Sir, yours truly,

A. O. JONES

A PLEA FOR BETTER PAY

From Mr Frank Mitchell, 2 July 1930

Cambridge University, Yorkshire, Transvaal, England and South Africa (1894–1914), captain of Cambridge and South Africa. England rugby international. A journalist who wrote on cricket, rugby and war.

Sir, May I be allowed in *The Times* to call attention to the position of umpires in first-class cricket? The nature of their duties must be well understood. Physical fitness and complete concentration are necessary for men who have to stand in the open from 11.30 a.m. until 6.30 p.m. with but an hour's break. On them more than on anyone else depends the well-being of the game, and it says much for their capability that things run so smoothly; but it may be pointed out – and with truth, for I speak and write as one having experience – that their position is a precarious one. A faulty decision may bring down on their head a bad mark in the report made by the captains or one of them after a game. Against this there is no appeal.

It is, however, the financial side of their position that I have in mind. Their pay is £9 10s for a match beginning on a Wednesday and £10 10s for a week-end match which covers four days. They, unlike the players, are never at home because they do not umpire in games where their own county is concerned. They are unable to obtain cheap fares, as do the others who have their third-class fares paid for them. I gather that during the summer, on an average, each man has 22 matches, £220 in all, out of which all his expenses have to be paid. We can take it that they are away from home for 154 days. Including railway fares their expenses must come to about 15s a day, so that the margin is small. They receive no winter pay, as do the players, so that they are the worse off all round. Again, in the Test matches the fee of £25 [players £40] is paid; as standing in these games means missing two county matches, the umpires, who presumably are absolutely at the head of their profession, are only a mere fiver to the good. Is this fair?

I strongly advocate that their remuneration during the summer should be the same as that of the players themselves. Such a body of men are well worth better pay. I am glad to say that I played with most of the present list, and am only too glad to endeavour to assist them, for I count many genuine friends among them.

I am, Sir, yours truly,

FRANK MITCHELL

A scheme for umpires' cheap fares, promoted by MCC and 'a famous firm of ticket agents' in 1931, was rejected by the Railway Clearing Office. By 1980 an umpire's pay for a season's county cricket was equivalent to that of a capped county player. Fees for Test matches, with players' equivalents in brackets, have been: 1950: £50 (£75); 1976: £165 (£200); 1978: £750 (£1000); 1983: £1125 (£1500).

VILLAGE UMPIRES

From Mr Charles Ponsonby, 12 August 1935

Sir, I am glad that Mr Aidan Crawley has called attention to the horrible suggestion made by Mr F. G. J. Ford that alterations in the leg-before-wicket rule should apply to village cricket.

Umpires in village cricket are all honourable men and try to temper their judgments with discretion, but they often suffer from defects both in training and physique. The majority of them have no training in the art of umpiring; some have never played cricket themselves, and many would frankly admit that they are unfit for cricket, too old, too fat, or too slow. Some even have defective dental arrangements which interfere with a quick decision.

I was playing in a match last year and as the bowler delivered the ball the umpire ejaculated 'brrr', and after a pause, 'I beg your pardon, I meant to say no-ball, but I dropped my teeth.'

Of course not every village umpire suffers from defects. Some are very good and all do their best in this very difficult position.

Yours faithfully,
CHARLES PONSONBY

A PROBLEM OF CRICKET

From A Puzzled Foreign Sportsman, 14 July 1932

Sir, On a recent visit to your beautiful England I went to see your national game of cricket. Kind friends told me how the game was played, but I could not find out why the umpire could not give a decision without being appealed to. In other games one considers it unfair to ask the umpire for a decision. Will you kindly explain to me why it is so in cricket.

A PUZZLED FOREIGN SPORTSMAN

From A Student of Cricket History, 18 July 1932

Sir, I can answer 'A Puzzled Foreigner' as to the reason why an umpire in present-day cricket cannot give a decision unless he is appealed to. It is a matter of history and tradition.

Years and years ago an umpire merely counted the balls and signalled the byes, &c. It was always understood that should a batsman think he was out he immediately went back to the pavilion, or in those days the tent. It was the only gentlemanly thing to do. Hence the expression 'not cricket' being synonymous with anything ungentlemanly from the Englishman's point of view. However, this chivalrous conduct spoilt so many games that it was mutually agreed that if a doubt arose the burden of asking for a decision from the umpire should lie with the bowler, thus relieving the batsman from the embarrassing situation of being called unsporting. It was found to be so satisfactory that eventually it was embodied in the rules. Incidentally an umpire does make decisions without being appealed to – namely, no balls, byes, &c.

I am, Sir, yours faithfully,
A STUDENT OF CRICKET HISTORY

'HOW'S THAT?' PENALTY

From Mr Ben Travers, CBE, AFC, 6 January 1973

Novelist and farceur. *A Bit of a Test* (1933) concerned an English cricket tour of Australia. Spectator at Test matches from 1896 to 1980.

Sir, I, like many other cricket lovers in this country, have always firmly believed that whereas English umpires are the direct descendants of King Solomon and Solon, those in all other cricket-playing countries are reincarnations of Pontius Pilate and Judge Jeffreys. And while your Cricket Correspondent shows his customary reliability and moderation in paying tribute to the impartiality of the Indian umpires, it is obvious from his reports that they have been guilty of some curious aberrations. But it looks as if they have had a good deal to put up with.

If and when the legislators of the cricket world take steps to reorganize the system of appointing umpires for Test matches wherever they are played, they might also consider some project of assuaging the umpire's burden by clamping down on the ever-increasing number of vociferous and often wildly optimistic appeals.

What about this? In the event of any unsuccessful appeal against a batsman by any member of the fielding side (except in the case of an appeal for run out), the umpire shall, on stating his verdict of 'not out', signal to the scoreboard and one run shall be added to the extras in the total of the batting side. This extra shall be in addition to any runs scored from the delivery in question. The run will be entered in the score-sheet under the heading AD (appeals disallowed) in the list of extras.

Would such a scheme, I wonder, tend to modify an umpire's tribulations? I also wonder whether a captain ever tells his side 'Don't accompany your appeals by war-dances and gesticulations calculated either to intimidate or to bamboozle the umpire'. If so, I wonder whether that captain ever wins any matches.

I am, Sir, etc.,

BEN TRAVERS

'NO-BALL' ORDER IN TEST

From Mr Fred Trueman, 28 June 1976

Yorkshire and England (1949–68). First bowler to take 300 wickets in Test matches. Broadcaster.

Sir, I write with reference to the article by Marcel Berlins in *The Times* of June 24. In this he reports Mr E. C. Phillipson's denial of the revelation in my book *Ball of Fire* about instructions apparently given in 1963 not to 'no-ball' Charlie Griffith for suspect action, because of concern over racial tension.

I can only repeat what I said in my book, that I heard this conversation going on and that when Mr Robins realized that I had done so he asked me to promise not to disclose what I had heard. I am surprised that Mr Phillipson denies that Mr Robins gave these instructions because Mr Robins told me that he had been talking to the umpires. It could have been that he said 'umpire' and not 'umpires' and in that case he would have been talking just to Sid Buller who was the senior of the two. At no point do I say that an *official* instruction was given by MCC or any other official body.

Yours faithfully,

F. S. TRUEMAN

A PRETTY PASS

From Mr Stephen Corrin, 23 July 1976

Sir, In the course of his report on the Gloucestershire v. Hampshire match (July 20), Alan Gibson writes: '. . . I confess I passed the time of day with a pretty umpire's wife, severely knitting.' Since when has it been the custom to comment on the umpire's looks? And what business has a cricket correspondent knitting, grimly or otherwise?

Yours sincerely,
STEPHEN CORRIN

OVERDRESSED

From Mr J. W. E. Blanch, 13 July 1978

Sir, In a recent Test match one of the umpires was required to carry a fielder's protective helmet in addition to various sweaters and caps, etc.

What would happen if the umpire declined to be a clothes horse and refused?

Is there any other sport in which the officials are asked to act as cloakroom attendants in addition to their proper duties?

Yours,
J. W. E. BLANCH

Umpires soon refused to carry helmets, which players now place behind the wicketkeeper or boundary.

APPEALING PROSPECT IN THE CRICKET FIELD

From Mr Gavin Drewry, 4 September 1982

Sir, Understandable professional diffidence has inhibited Louis Blom-Cooper (2 September) from carrying through his proposal for appeals against umpires' decisions to its logical conclusion.

With so much at stake it would surely be necessary to set up, not just a first instance 'panel of cricketing experts' but also a second-tier tribunal to unravel particularly tricky points of law. Natural justice demands, of course, that all interested parties be legally represented before these bodies.

The scope for jurisprudential argument will be endless. To take just one example, the level of compensation 'in the award of additional runs' would have to be higher for a wrongfully-dismissed Botham than for a similarly aggrieved Willis. But *how much* higher?

Only the gradual accumulation of relevant precedents can provide satisfactory answers, unless of course Parliament takes the bull by the horns and supplies legislative guidelines.

Think of the added suspense as the outcome of a Test series hangs upon an appeal to the House of Lords three years hence. Think what the European Court of Justice might make of the violation of leg spinners' human rights by unjust lbw laws. Think what Lord Denning might have achieved in this area of jurisprudence had he not retired so prematurely. Think, above all, of all those legal fees.

Yours faithfully,
GAVIN DREWRY

UMPIRES' BURDEN

From Mr A. F. Harlow, 8 September 1982
Member of the Association of Cricket Umpires.

Sir, Having read John Woodcock's report (30 August) I do wonder if Imran Khan [captain of the Pakistan touring team who, with the manager, complained about the umpiring in the Test series] realizes the intense mental and psychological pressure under which Test match umpires operate? It requires concentration of the highest degree to umpire throughout a six-hour day, in the knowledge that every decision will be subject to protracted analysis through television replay. No wonder mistakes are made: it is only remarkable that the errors are so few.

Writing as an occasional club umpire, I believe the Test and County Cricket Board should consider seriously appointing two pairs of umpires for each Test match, to officiate alternately for 50 overs or a similar convenient period. Such an arrangement would lighten the load of individual responsibility and enable umpires to remain mentally fresh; if the experiment was a success it should not be difficult to persuade other countries to follow suit.

I do not believe that an international panel of neutral umpires is a practicable proposition. Such a concept is grandiose, expensive to operate, and based on a false premise: the vast majority of umpiring errors are not due to bias on the part of the umpire, but to a momentary lapse of concentration.

Yours faithfully,
A. F. HARLOW

KEEPING AN EYE ON THE UMPIRES

The scoreboard at the Melbourne Cricket Ground had been replaced by a giant television screen, on which could be shown controversial incidents of play.

From Commander C. M. J. Carson, RN, 6 January 1983

Sir, The presence of a video recording for all to see has put the Test match umpire in an invidious position. Seconds after he has made a split-second decision with his mark one eye ball, the monitor either confirms it or broadcasts his error to the millions watching – or listening via critical, in hindsight, commentators.

As these large screens are obviously going to be an essential feature of the future Test match, may I suggest that cricket looks to horse racing for the answer to the umpires' dilemma. As well as the umpires on the field of play there could be two others off the field, equipped with a monitor with views from both ends of the wicket. All four could be in communication by simple radio.

Whilst the umpires on the field would retain overall charge and make all straightforward decisions, they could, as in horse racing, have recourse to the camera when there is sufficient doubt in their minds for them to want a second opinion.

This simple expedient would, I hope, stop the histrionics of the aggrieved gladiators, eliminate automatic appealing and revert Messrs Lewis and Trueman back to being sensible commentators from their present role as whingeing Poms.

Yours sincerely,

C. M. J. CARSON

8
ENTERTAINMENT
FOR LAYABOUTS

The county championship, which is dated by most authorities from 1864, is a well-gnawed bone of contention. It was put on an official footing by the leading counties at the end of 1890, although the Press was awarding the accolade of champion county as early as 1827. By 1983 some 20 methods had been used to decide the order of precedence.

CRICKET REPORTING

From F. G., 23 August 1887

Frederick Gale, a prolific writer on cricket; known as 'The Old Buffer'.

Sir, I will preface this letter by saying that I have nothing to do with the management now of any club in England and am a unit in the army of Englishmen who take a delight in cricket as a grand English game. I use the word 'game' advisedly, for cricket is a game and not a business. The cricket reporters who provide us every morning with the result and account of matches all over England are worthy of our respect and thanks, but many of them are making a great mistake in using the titles of 'first-class' and 'second-class' counties, 'according to the taste and fancy of the writer', as Sam Weller remarked when asked whether his name was spelt with a 'V' or a 'W'. In the first place, as the Marylebone Club have refused to define any order of precedence and declare that a county is a county and nothing more, we may be sure that all real heart and soul English cricketers accept the verdict of the MCC, the managers of which for a century past have been and are noblemen and gentlemen who have won their spurs from the days of their school matches, until the time when they lay aside their bats after many years of hard fighting on the bloodless battle-field against the best gentlemen and professionals in England.

The objection to the words 'first' and 'second' class as they appear in print is twofold. First, unless there is a recognized authority who has power to classify counties, they are as valueless, in the eyes of real cricketers as the title of 'captain' conferred by the ring on a betting man who for a short time held a subaltern's commission in the Army is in the eyes of real sportsmen. Secondly, in the eyes of the οἱ πολλοί, whose money is as valuable as that of real cricketers who follow the game, the printed title of 'second-class' cheapens a match and keeps very many from attending matches in which there is much first-rate cricket; and now it is an admitted fact that the expenses of county cricket are so great that it could not go on but for gate money. Rising counties have a hard struggle for funds, and the expenses are often a heavy tax on the private purses of liberal patrons, and empty titles and idle words constantly repeated in print are like arrows shot over a house, and we do not know whom they may kill on the other side. Just so 'second-class' as a title hurts a rising county.

The remarks which I have made in respect of first and second class equally apply to a new 'fad' about 'champion counties' used by the same self-constituted authorities, who take on themselves against the *dictum* of the MCC to classify counties. Their theory is that any one of their own 'ear-marked' first-class counties – provided they play not less than eight matches among each other without defeat, shall take precedence and be champion over any other which suffers a defeat – *ex. grat.,* this award last year was the championship to county A [Nottinghamshire], which played 14 matches and two extra matches against Australia. County A's record being as follows:– Seven wins and nine matches drawn, more than one of such draws being admitted much against county A. County B [Surrey] played 16 matches and two against Australia, and their record was 12 county matches won, three lost and one drawn, and a double victory over Australia.

The moral of this is that provided a competitor never loses he may spin out matches for a draw as much as he pleases instead of taking an honest licking like a good cricketer and sportsman.

If the MCC should ever unfortunately consent to classify counties and award championships, it will possibly be a case of exit old English cricket, enter the betting ring.

Quis custodiet ipsos custodes?

Yours truly,

F. G.

From A Cricket Reporter, 24 August 1887

Sir, In his letter on the subject of Cricket Reporting, published in your issue of to-day, 'F. G.' objects to the division of counties into first and second class, but he does not suggest any alternative. When county clubs and county matches were few there was no occasion to make any distinction; but to-day there are quite 20 such clubs, and I am unable to say how many such matches. To say that all counties are now equal is to make a statement entirely at variance with the facts. With the exception of three games that were drawn in consequence of rain, all the matches this year between 'second-class' and 'first-class' counties have, I believe, resulted in favour of the latter. The classification is made with the concurrence of cricket players and writers generally, and it, or something like it, is inevitable, unless county cricket is to be thrown into a state of chaos. The emulative spirit would disappear if there were no competition among counties, and few batsmen or bowlers would care to persevere if averages and records were swept away, or if we were to pretend that a performance accomplished against, say, Cumberland were ranked as highly as one against Surrey or Lancashire. 'F. G.' need not fear the influence of betting. Cricket is played for honour, and will so continue; but honour implies renown, and how is renown to be gained except in a defined and eager competition among rivals of approximately equal skill and ability?

The cricket public recognize the differences between great counties and small ones, and the immensely increased interest in Surrey cricket is due to the fact that the powerful northern elevens can now be met with a good chance of success. There is no desire among cricket reporters to injure the prospects of the younger and less important county clubs. We wish to do justice not only to them, but to the great counties that have for many years fostered and encouraged the game, and we are only doing – in default of any authoritative classification by the Marylebone Club or the new County Cricket Council – what, after careful consideration, we think is fair to all concerned and in the best interests of the game. We have not, nor can we have, any other desire.

Yours truly,
A CRICKET REPORTER

THE COUNTY CRICKET CHAMPIONSHIP

From A. C. W., 16 July 1896

'A Cambridge Wrangler'? Or perhaps 'A Cricket Wag'?

Sir, Your Cricket Correspondent, after explaining the method adopted by the MCC for placing the counties, suggests that a more equitable plan would be to take the proportion of games won to games finished.

Undoubtedly this would be the fairest, as well as the simplest, plan. But your Correspondent overlooks the fact that the counties are placed in exactly the same order by the complicated arithmetic of the MCC as by the simple proportion of wins to games finished. If a be the games won, b the games lost, $a+b$ are the games finished, $a-b$ the 'points', and $\frac{a-b}{a+b}$ the fraction fixing the position of the county in the competition.

Now $\frac{a-b}{a+b} = \frac{2a-a-b}{a+b} = \frac{2a}{a+b}-1$. But $\frac{a}{a+b}$ is the proportion of games won to games finished. Hence a simple rule: – Work out the proportions of games won to games finished $\left(\frac{a}{a+b}\right)$ for the several counties; double these proportions $\left(\frac{2a}{a+b}\right)$ – the order will not be changed; next subtract unity from each of the results – clearly the order will be still unchanged. But now we have arrived at the MCC proportions $\left(\frac{2a}{a+b}-1, \text{ or } \frac{a-b}{a+b}\right)$.

The MCC method then is only a clumsy way of arriving at the fairest and simplest result.

Your obedient servant,
A. C. W.

From the Secretary, Lancashire CCC, 10 April 1912

Sir, Many Lancashire cricketers will highly appreciate the conclusion at which your Correspondent in his article on the prospects of the coming season has arrived, when he declares that 'first-class cricket now is a very different game from first-class cricket of even 20 years ago, and one cannot but think that the suggestions for discussing the whole scheme of the championship with a view to drastic alteration should be welcomed.' After the recent rebuff from the Advisory County Cricket Committee, such weighty words printed so prominently in *The Times* come as 'rare and refreshing fruit' to those who are candid enough to admit, and base their opinion on their experience, that if the cricketing counties of the country are to steer clear of the Bankruptcy Court there must be some effort to keep pace with the times.

It is now common knowledge that Yorkshire has induced a majority of the counties to express the view that 'it is inadvisable to consider any proposal for altering the present system of arriving at the county championship until the end of the cricket season of 1913'; and a Yorkshire contemporary goes into ecstasies over the 'defeat', as it styles it, of 'the fresh attempt to disturb the basis of the championship'. Yet three years ago Yorkshiremen felt so strongly on this subject that they canvassed all the counties in support of an elaborate scheme of classification, as unworkable as it was unsatisfactory, because it divided the counties into two divisions of equal merit. From Warwickshire, with its new halo of glory, we also hear expressions of contentment, as though Mr Foster was going to live for ever and Warwickshire had taken a lien on the championship in perpetuity. It should not be overlooked that Warwickshire in arriving at their present distinction did not meet Kent, the champions of the previous year, or even Middlesex, who were third on the table in 1911. These very facts alone are sufficient to condemn the Yorkshire amendment. To wait until the end of 1913 before even an attempt is made to consider the reform of a palpable anomaly is itself absurd, especially when it is remembered that such delay means that the season of 1915 (not 1914) must be upon us before any such 'drastic alterations' as that commended by *The Times* can possibly come into force. Well may a prominent cricketer of an older time, who has played for Yorkshire and Lancashire, exclaim when he heard of the defeat of Lancashire's resolution, 'Why, cricket will be dead by then.' Drastic reforms take time. In negotiating with county committees months slip by and fixtures meanwhile have to be arranged.

Lancashire's plea for the appointment of a committee to consider the general question of the championship and to devise an alternative scheme is not based on such misleading grounds as those advanced by your Yorkshire contemporary. For all that Lancashire care the method of reckoning by points and percentages, as now, may be incorporated in any new idea. It may be that my signature may be recognized, and therefore I hasten to say I write quite unofficially; but, as one knowing the views, the unanimous views, of the Lancashire authorities, I may be permitted to say that their sole aim before 1915 is to provide a real championship which shall infuse life and vigour and enthusiasm into the game. By a coincidence I received during the holidays from my friend Mr Borrodaile a copy of the annual report of the Essex County Club. It tells the old, old story of troublesome finance and wracking anxiety; in the same Yorkshire paper to which I have referred I read that Worcestershire, Somerset, Leicestershire, and other counties are unable to make ends meet, that they must inevitably drop out from the fighting line, and it is common knowledge that two or more counties would not have dared to enter into engagements for 1912, to say nothing of 1913 or 1914, if there had not been great financial expectations from the Triangular Tournament.

We in Lancashire know only too well that our membership has declined by 800 during the course of nine years, that in spite of the dry weather of 1911 our 'gates' fell away tremendously, and that motoring, golf, tennis, and other pastimes are levying toll on cricket enthusiasts. We know also that taxation is increasing and that deficits on the year are recurring with an unpleasant frequency. We see also that other sports, where the real, live competitive spirit is introduced, do something more than pay their way and we marvel at the supineness of cricketers who see the danger signal but will not heed it. Lacrosse, which is quite a foreign game to English sportsmen, is making rapid strides in this country. It is essentially an amateur sport, yet its devotees recognize the divisional system with its flags and its cup competitions.

This is an age of competition. The old easy-going days have gone, and, if the inspiring words of your cricket contributor, which I quote above, should help cricketers all over the country, to rise to their responsibilities, they will not have been published in vain. To wait till the end of 1913 before reconsidering the position, with the

months of discussion which must follow, is to many of us trifling with
the subject.

'If it were done, when 't is done, then 't were well
It were done quickly.'

Yours, &c.,
T. J. MATTHEWS

CRICKET OF THE FUTURE

From Mr George Drummond, 21 December 1921

Sir, Surely the counties have made a great mistake in again turning
down Lord Harris's registration scheme? One did really hope that
the tragedies of last summer [3–0 beating by Australia] would have
done something to have weaned them from their parochial out-
look. If we are going to find future MacLarens, Jacksons, Fosters,
Richardsons, and Braunds, we cannot start about it too soon.

Take our Chapmans coming down from the University or Public
School with no qualifications for a first-class county. Such men have
now got to miss the best two cricketing years of their lives, and ones
which can never be replaced for moulding them into Test match
players. In these days the leisurely cricketing life of an amateur
finishes at the very latest when he is 25, and it must be in the best
interests of the game that he should not miss a single first-class
match if it can be avoided. If he has played first-class cricket for two
or three years the Selectors will know his form, and he and they will,
I take it, endeavour to make arrangements so that he can play a bit
of first-class cricket when next we welcome the Australians or South
Africans. I am sure, moreover, that if you choke him off for two
years you will in most cases choke him off altogether.

Take our Braunds. Will they prefer to play League cricket, or to
qualify for another county? If they adopt the latter course, how
many counties could afford it? If another county had qualified
Morfee we might not have lost the Test matches. Take Mr Mc-
Donald [the Australian fast bowler who played for Lancashire from
1924 to 1931, having completed the two-year residential qualifica-
tion]. Are the other counties going to be debarred playing against
him for two years? Do not McDonalds help to increase attendances,
and to produce other McDonalds, and also to teach our star
batsmen to play forward? Take the case of Mr Jupp [who had

moved from Sussex to Northamptonshire]. He is now lost to first-class cricket for two years, which incidentally adds 100 per cent. to the burden of the county struggling to keep in the line. If one county goes, others go too.

Yours faithfully,
GEORGE DRUMMOND

SCORING IN COUNTY CRICKET

From Sir John Murray, 9 August 1927

Senior Director of John Murray (Publishers) Ltd. and for many years editor of the *Quarterly Review*. High Sheriff of London 1914. KCVO 1932.

Sir, With much diffidence I venture to make a suggestion. The present system of scoring gives no credit for a plucky attempt to retrieve an initial disaster, which is sometimes due to accident. I suggest that in drawn matches the average of runs scored from the bat per wicket taken, and of runs made per balls bowled, should be drawn, and for each of these averages, say, two points should be given for the best. For a full win, say, eight or ten points should be given. This would afford some incentive to both sides to 'play the game' to the end.

Your obedient servant,
JOHN MURRAY

THE RULES OF CRICKET

From Sir Harold Bowden, 19 June 1928

Chairman of Raleigh Industries. High Sheriff of Nottingham 1933. Chairman of British Olympic Association 1931–35.

Sir, For many years now the bat has been beating the ball, and, not in first-class cricket alone, an excessive number of matches have been drawn for lack of time in which to play them out. Will you allow me to suggest, for the consideration of cricketers and cricket lovers, a very simple modification of the existing laws which should go some distance towards reducing the number of games drawn on account of slow scoring or inflated scoring?

The recent Lancashire v. Surrey match, in which 1,155 runs were scored for the loss of 14 wickets, has been generally regarded as a *reductio ad absurdum* of county cricket. In this game Surrey scored 567 in 161 overs and Lancashire 588 in 221 overs, the average rate of scoring being thus approximately 3.15 runs an over by Surrey and 2.67 by Lancashire. A week earlier Lancashire scored 385 runs in 173 overs (average, 2.22 runs an over) against Yorkshire's 473 runs in 187 overs (average 2.52). During the same three days Oxford University, with an over-rate of 4.4 runs, comfortably beat Glamorgan, having scored 494 runs in 112 overs in their first innings. A survey of your cricket reports suggests that it is not unreasonable to ask for a scoring rate of 2¾–3 runs an over in the opening stages of the game.

My suggestion is this: that the length of the first innings of each side should be limited to a definite number of overs, which in the case of a three days' match might be 100. Roughly speaking, a match which lasts the whole three days comprises 400 overs. With a first-innings limit for each side of 100 overs, the third innings of the match would start not later than the middle of the second afternoon, and thus leave a pretty good chance of finishing the game on the third day. For the third and fourth innings there would be no over-limit. The law as to 'declaration' would remain as at present.

The suggestion of a time-limit for batsmen has frequently been made in various forms, but I believe that the 'over-limit', which is similar in principle, has the advantage of being much easier to work, and its application to the first innings only puts a premium on fast scoring in the first half of the match, but leaves the Shrewsburys of our day to play their due parts on and after the second afternoon.

I should add that I attach no special virtue to the figure of 100 overs, which I have put forward merely in order to make my suggestion definite, but it should enable even a Lancashire to knock up a total of 250 and not rule out a score of 400.

Finally, the principle might well be applied to one-day and especially to half-day cricket, and I should like to see it recognized as a regular practice for the captains to agree before the spin of the coin that the first innings for each side was to be limited to X overs, the value of X being dependent upon the number of hours likely to be available.

I am, Sir, yours, &c.,
HAROLD BOWDEN

In 1974 the first innings of county championship matches was restricted to 100 overs. The rule was in force until 1980.

ACCOMMODATION AT THE OVAL

From the Revd A. J. Hutton, 17 July 1929

Sir, A visit to the Oval last week shortly after one to Lord's gave one occasion to wonder how it is that, while at Lord's we are all so well provided with seats out of the sun or the damp of a shower, at the Oval there is no cover at all for the ordinary spectator, who cannot afford 2*s* 6*d* or 5*s* in addition to his gate money. To sit on a stone wall with no rest for his back in a blazing sun for six hours on end is hardly the height of bliss. There is a clientele of working men at the Oval that is surely worthy of some more consideration than is yet being given. If the authorities at the Oval have not the means to put up a cover over some of the seats, surely they might manage to free that large 2*s* 6*d* pavilion at the far end of the ground, which was almost entirely empty last Wednesday afternoon. If nothing can be done by the authorities to improve the seating accommodation, there is surely a real opportunity for one of our wealthy Londoners to become a real benefactor by giving a few hundreds towards covering in a stand for all lovers of cricket and of Surrey.

ALFRED J. HUTTON

THE COUNTY CHAMPIONSHIP

From Mr W. F. Esse, 4 September 1929

Sir, The fight for the championship among the first-class counties has been followed by all lovers of our national game with intense interest. There is one fact, however, which does not emerge – namely, how is a second-class or minor county to attain first-class status?

Originally the first class consisted of ten members only. This was gradually increased to 17. Of the additional seven, only Leicestershire has succeeded in getting into the first 10 this year.

Has not the time arrived when, say, the last five counties should be relegated to a second class, and the first seven counties among the minors added to these five to form a second class? Each class would then only be called upon to play 22 matches, which would probably admit of those amateurs who are obliged to give up the game now, finding time to play in most, if not all, of the county fixtures. There are obvious reasons why each of our 40 counties should be encouraged to form a county team.

Your obedient servant,

W. F. ESSE

The total has remained at 17; Devon applied unsuccessfully for first-class status in 1949.

DECLARATIONS AT CRICKET

By declaring their first innings at equal scores – or no scores at all – in rain-affected matches several counties contrived to contest 15 points for an outright win rather than five for first-innings lead in a drawn match.

From Mr R. C. Robertson-Glasgow, 13 August 1931

Oxford University and Somerset (1920–37). Celebrated cricket writer and special correspondent for *The Times* in Australia and New Zealand 1950–51 when 'Beau' Vincent was taken ill.

Sir, The 'freak' declarations, which began with the Pact of Sheffield, continued with the Diet of Cowbridge, and culminated in the Concordat of Cardiff, raise a most interesting ethical problem – interesting, but simple. Have they been in accordance with the true spirit of the game? That they are, at present, legal is indisputable, but irrelevant.

Matches of cricket are intended to be brought to a finish, win or lose, at a price, not of money, or gainful rivalry – there is no English equivalent to πλεονεξια – but of physical and mental skill and effort, at a cost, so often, of self-effacement, but never of self-respect. Examine the motives of the captains in these matches. They have, we are told, been 'out to have a finish somehow'. Why? It may be (1) for the joy of the game as a game; (2) for the good of the game as a financial concern; (3) for the acquisition of 15 points, somehow; and (4) to please the crowd. If the motives have been (1) only, or (1) and (4), well and good. If (2) or (3), or both, the game has suffered harm. The low state of most county exchequers may account for such a motive, but does not, therefore, excuse it. A true craftsman, be he statesman or carpenter, physician or cricketer, practises his art best when he is independent of gain or money. As to (3) there is little, or nothing, to be said. These 15 points bid fair to prove a greater nuisance than the 14 of the late President Wilson. Is it fair to rise in the championship on such wings as these? Most county

155

captains, I fancy, think otherwise. Such a scheme would have delighted Uriah Heep without appealing to Betsy Trotwood.

Yours, &c.,
R. C. ROBERTSON-GLASGOW

GOOD CRICKET

From Mr H. K. Foster and brothers, 16 May 1946
The survivors of the seven brothers who all played for Worcestershire ('Fostershire') before the First World War.

Sir, May we, through your columns, be permitted to express our intense pleasure, and our congratulations to the county captains concerned, at the sporting results of the early county matches of the present season?

We have always felt that the success, or otherwise, of county cricket, and the support of the public for it, lies in the hands of the county captains. 'The game' is far more important than the relative position of the counties in the championship table, and so long as the captains are determined to make the games, win or lose, sporting contests and not long-drawn-out agonies with no chance of a close finish, so long will the game flourish throughout the country and public support be assured.

Yours, &c.,
H. K. FOSTER, W. L. FOSTER, B. S. FOSTER,
G. N. FOSTER, N. J. A. FOSTER

From Lieutenant-Colonel D. C. Robinson, 22 May 1946
Essex and captain of Gloucestershire (1905–26).

Sir, The Robinson family of cricketers of Gloucestershire, who have played since 1878 yearly, with war breaks, salute the Foster family of Worcestershire and only regret they could not produce a family XI to play us as the Graces did in 1891. The glorious game of cricket will be kept alive if all captains of counties will go out for a win. First-class cricket will be killed if 'pot hunters' – a county percentage – and personal batting or bowling averages enter into the picture. Cricket is too good a game to allow this.

Yours, &c.,
D. C. ROBINSON

COUNTY CRICKET

From Mr A. A. Milne, 19 August 1947

Sir, Under the present scoring system when a match begins nobody knows whether it is for the division of 16, 12, four, or no points – which seems a little odd. If a county at the bottom of the table is playing one at the top and has had to follow on, it does not matter to it whether it saves the match or loses it, and yet the result of the championship may depend on which it does; which also seems a little odd. Finally, if a match is rained out after the first over both sides are regarded as having lost it – and that is the oddest feature of the whole fantastic system.

To suggest a less fantastic one is easy. Here it is. Probably it has already been used and was discarded because some lacrosse or water-polo player complained that cricket wanted brightening. Every championship match once on the fixture list to be worth eight points: to be divided 8–0 if played to a finish; 5–3 if there is a first innings result only; and 4–4 in any other event.

The fairness of this method of scoring should be obvious. Any last lingering doubt will be removed when I add that on their present record Kent and Sussex, the love of my youth and of my old age, would actually suffer by it.

Yours, &c.,

A. A. MILNE

From the Provost of Worcester College, Oxford, 9 September 1954

John Masterman. Athletics Blue; England hockey and lawn tennis international; toured Canada with MCC. Leading figure in wartime intelligence for which he was made OBE. Vice-Chancellor of Oxford University 1957–58. Knighted 1957.

Sir, In a leading article in your issue of 4 September you tell us that the system of scoring points in the county cricket championship has been 'altered some 17 times since the championship proper began'. On page 4 of the same issue appears the final championship table, with the counties placed in order of merit according to the points which they have amassed. Is it not worth noting that the 17 counties would finish the season in precisely the same order if the number of matches won was the only figure which was taken into account? Is it just possible that a simple tally of wins is as good a criterion as any one of some 17 more elaborate systems of scoring points, and that the county which has won the most matches outright is the most worthy holder of the championship?

I am, Sir, your obedient servant,

J. C. MASTERMAN

DROPPED BOWLERS

From Mr Roy MacNab, 7 June 1955
Author and poet.

Sir, Several of my fellow-countrymen from South Africa who have come over here to follow the fortunes of the Springbok cricketers are surprised and dismayed at a curious new turn in English gamesmanship. I refer to the practice among county team selectors of dropping their international bowlers for matches against the South Africans. The aim of this presumably is to allow the English bowlers to preserve their tricks as a surprise for the South Africans when they meet in the Tests.

The MCC omitted every bowler of note, except Bailey, from its side in the recent match at Lord's and now Lancashire, the latest team to meet the visitors, has left out both Statham and Tattersall. Much of the interest in these county matches is thus lost, and one begins to wonder if there is any point in staging these cricket tours, when all that seems to matter is the Test series. Can we not, Sir, have an end to these selectors' antics and a return to the days when cricket was still regarded as a game and the spectator counted for something?

I am, Sir, yours truly,

ROY MACNAB

The practice of 'resting' leading players against touring sides had reached such a pass by 1982 that offending counties were threatened with the loss of their fixture.

FREAK DECLARATIONS

From Mr Dudley Carew, 26 August 1958
Distinguished member of the editorial staff of *The Times* as writer on cricket, football, drama; book reviewer; fourth leader writer; and film critic. Wrote novels and books on cricket.

Sir, In commenting on the Essex v. Hampshire match, *The Times* writes of 'declarations referred to as freak, sporting or challenging according to the point of view', and goes on 'if there are those who say that the tactics adopted on this occasion contrived a false finish. . . .' This is altogether too tolerant and broadminded. The declarations were freak (as in other matches played that day), the finish was false – there is not, and cannot be, any two opinions about it.

It is surprising, and salutary, to reflect that when such batsmen as Trumper, Ranji, Hutchings, MacLaren, Jessop, and J. T. Tyldesley were revelling in their genius and when Fry was propounding the theory that the best way of coping with Barnes was 'to drive him hard for four over his own head' declarations were few and far between. And the weather was then as it is now. The challenge was then a positive one conceived in the terms of cricket between ball and bat, the ball bowled not to keep runs down but to get the batsmen out (and what Warwick Armstrong did at Trent Bridge in 1905 does not affect the general picture), the bat determined to play the appropriate stroke, not a mathematical calculation concerned with, and concocted for, the gaining of points.

The irony is that the points so gained are counterfeit, debasing such value as the legitimate currency can claim, and that the artificial contortions so ingeniously gone through after luncheon on the third day could be avoided if, from the first ball of the first, bowlers and batsmen concentrated on the essentials of their tasks. England, under a superb cricketer, is as strong as she has ever been, and the way for the counties is, or should be, clear.

I am, Sir, your obedient servant,

DUDLEY CAREW

COUNTY CRICKET

The Clark committee recommended a county championship of 16 three day matches and a separate one of 16 one-day matches. The counties rejected them.

From Mr Richard Gordon, 28 January 1967

Sir, Such layabouts as authors, strikers, clerics, fugitive prisoners, out-of-work actors, and out-of-office politicians are terribly spoiled by the present county system. Any summer weekday there's a game handy somewhere. In Australia it can be quite difficult to see a cricket match. There is grade cricket, played as a serial on successive Saturdays, but the Sheffield Shield clashes are comparatively infrequent and long-heralded affairs.

If our counties combined into five groups like the Australian states they would certainly lower costs and possibly heighten standards. Hampshire could bundle up with Sussex and Somerset, Lancashire and Yorkshire entwine their roses, and Middlesex (which doesn't exist) join Surrey (partly London postal area) with Kent (which has no county ground anyway) to play at Lord's. Then they could build flats on the rest of the Oval.

I am, &c.,

RICHARD GORDON

A redevelopment plan for the Oval had been announced on 9 January 1967 and now awaited approval by the Greater London Council.

FUTURE OF THE OVAL

From Mr Christopher Booker, 30 July 1973

Award-winning journalist; essayist and author. First editor of *Private Eye*.

Sir, I am surprised that more public concern has not been expressed over the future of the Oval. Many cricket lovers will have heard the broadcast interview on the first day of the present Test match, in which Mr Geoffrey Howard, Secretary to Surrey Cricket Club, expressed the hope that the redevelopment plan for the Oval, despite its recent rejection by Lambeth borough council, will still be pushed ahead as fast as possible. This scheme involves the complete reconstruction of the ground, to include two blocks of flats and an office block larger than Centre Point.

The crux of the Oval scheme, however, is the fate of the ground itself. The playing area is to be reduced by almost half. The 75 yard boundary of this new circular ground will be the bare Test match minimum (making the Oval the smallest Test ground in the world). Even Mr Howard has admitted that to provide an adequate ground for the rest of the year's programme, when the pitch has to be moved anything up to 30 yards nearer to the boundary, will present his successors with 'considerable difficulties'.

If Surrey were to obtain any direct financial benefit from this scheme, it might have some more obvious justification. As it is, they are to receive little more than a new set of seating and a new pavilion (which Mr Howard admits will 'not be ideal'), in return for which they are to lose almost half their ground, and all the Oval's traditional atmosphere.

The only real beneficiaries from the scheme would appear to be the freeholders, the Duchy of Cornwall, and the builders of the huge office block. Why have Surrey, whose lease does not expire for some years, allowed this to happen? There are surely some questions here which require a public answer.

Yours faithfully,
CHRISTOPHER BOOKER

The Greater London Council rejected the plan in September 1973.

NOT CRICKET?

Apparent time-wasting by the Yorkshire captain, Brian Close, ensured that Warwickshire failed by 9 runs to score 142 in 100 minutes for victory.

From Mr A. W. B. Taylor, 23 August 1967

Sir, Yorkshire want to win the county cricket championship.

If they can gain points by playing bright cricket, they will play brightly; if they can gain them by delaying tactics, they will be obstructive. What county, given the circumstances of last Friday afternoon, would have done otherwise?

The blame for any distasteful manoeuvres of the Yorkshire fielding side lies with those who framed the regulations, making it more profitable to draw than lose.

Yours, &c.,
A. W. B. TAYLOR

GRACE'S WAY

From Mr N. J. Hodgkinson, 29 August 1967

Sir, In July 1911, when playing in a charity match I sat next to W. G. Grace at lunch and he told me the story of how he got out a batsman, who looked set for a century, by saying to him 'Look at yon bird' pointing up at the sun. The batsman looked for the non-existent bird, was temporarily blinded and was bowled by W.G. next ball! I do not recollect that W.G. was dropped from Gloucestershire in consequence!

Yours faithfully,

N. J. HODGKINSON

Yorkshire won the championship – and an official censure; Close, the reigning England captain, was passed over for the winter tour of West Indies.

YORKSHIRE CRICKET TROUBLES

From Mr Geoffrey Boycott, 18 October 1978

Yorkshire and England (1962–   ). Outstanding opening batsman and highest runmaker in Test cricket. Captained England in four of his 108 Tests and Yorkshire 1971–78. After years of strife within the club he was dismissed from the captaincy on 29 September 1978 but was asked to stay on as a player.

Sir, In June my letter to you publicly declared my intention to play for Yorkshire and England as long as I could maintain my ability. This is still my wish.

Trueman's leak about the invitation by a member or members of the committee to Hutton to captain Yorkshire made on 28 July 1972, in my second season as captain, is informative.

Even after Hutton's departure at the end of 1974 my captaincy continued to be seriously disrupted. I formally discussed this situation with two high officials of the club in February, 1975; I was assured that action would be taken and this assurance was confirmed in writing. Some action must have been taken because, in relative calm, my young team and I were able to have a splendid season.

However, the disruptive elements reappeared and continued unabated from then on until the culmination at Northampton and my subsequent dismissal from the captaincy. I believe it was only my century of centuries that saved me from dismissal last year.

My team has never had a chance (and they are beginning to be a real force in county cricket), for no team can serve two masters and gain success; disruption and success are poor bedfellows.

I sincerely hope, for the sake of Yorkshire County Cricket Club, that its all powerful general committee will see fit to resolve

matters this week [they met on the following Monday] so that I can
fly to Australia knowing that my efforts to eradicate disloyalty have
achieved success.

Yours faithfully,
GEOFF BOYCOTT

From Mr Fred Trueman, 21 October 1978
Who was elected to the Yorkshire committee in January 1979.

Sir, Geoffrey Boycott's letter in yesterday's *The Times* (18 October)
is manifest rubbish. If, as he claims, he intends to play for Yorkshire
'as long as he can maintain his ability' all he has to do is to accept
the Yorkshire committee's offer of a contract and make his batting
talent available to the team. One hopes he will, but fears he won't. If
he doesn't perhaps he will tell us why.

He has no divine right to the captaincy of Yorkshire. He has held
the appointment for eight seasons during which time Yorkshire's
results have been the worst for one hundred years. Since 1878
Yorkshire's position in the championship table has been in double
figures only eight times and five of those have been during Boycott's
captaincy. My only quarrel with the Yorkshire committee is that
they have put up with Boycott as captain for too long.

Yours truly,
F. S. TRUEMAN

The general committee reaffirmed their decision and, despite subsequent
strong lobbying by the pro-Boycott Reform Group, the captaincy changed
hands. Boycott, however, remained as a player.

From Mr C. F. A. T. Halliday, 25 October 1978

Sir, Mr F. S. Trueman (21 October) declares that under Geoff
Boycott's captaincy, Yorkshire's playing results have been the
worst for a hundred years.

Surely he must realize the main reason for this apparent failure?
For years the other sixteen first-class counties have been relying on
the services of players imported from overseas, whereas Yorkshire
have continued to make birth in the county the first qualification.

Yours faithfully,
CHARLES HALLIDAY

COLONIAL PLAYERS AND COUNTY CRICKET

From Mr C. E. Green, 24 August 1909

Cambridge University, Middlesex, Sussex and Essex (1865–79). President of MCC 1905.

Sir, I have seen it reported in several of the newspapers that inducements have been offered by one or more of our first-class counties to Mr W. Bardsley, the brilliant batsman and cricketer now with the Australian team, to qualify to play in English county cricket.

In face of the very widely expressed condemnation some two years ago of this system of qualifying colonial players for our county cricket, I can hardly credit the rumour as being correct. But in case there is any foundation for the report, I would venture, as an old cricketer and one who has taken a very active interest in the welfare and maintenance of English cricket, and especially county cricket, to make a very strong protest against this action, which, in my opinion, and that of many other cricketers and supporters of our great English game, does so much to prejudice and do away with the real character and best traditions of county cricket and the *esprit de corps* which should exist in this class of cricket, for not only is it unfair to the Colonies that inducements should be made to deprive them of any of their players, but it is also most unfair and discouraging to our home-bred players that their places should be taken in county teams by those who have not learnt their cricket in England.

Real county cricket is the backbone of our English cricket, and every possible endeavour should be made to keep this as genuine and real as it is possible and to prevent it ever becoming merely a gate money business affair, which the engaging of outside 'star' players to strengthen a county side must ultimately cause it to be.

Should there be any truth in the report, I would venture to suggest that all the other counties should abstain from making fixtures with that county which induces a colonial player to qualify.

I would like to say that I have written this in no unfriendly spirit towards our colonial cousins, who have shown us splendid cricket during their tour in this country, and have played the game in the most thorough and sportsmanlike manner at all times. I have merely been prompted to write as I have done in the best interests of real and *bona fide* county cricket, and in the hopes of seeing its very best traditions maintained.

It is with hesitation that I have written this letter, but I feel very strongly upon this subject, and I know that my opinions and sentiments are shared by a very large number of influential supporters of the game.

I remain yours truly,

C. E. GREEN

Warren Bardsley never played county cricket but other Australians – notably W. L. Murdoch, S. M. J. Woods, A. E. Trott and F. A. Tarrant up to 1914 – did after serving the two-year qualifying period. Murdoch, Woods and Trott all went with English teams to South Africa and played in matches which were retrospectively awarded Test status; Tarrant was selected for a Test trial.

TARRANT AND INTERNATIONAL CRICKET

From Mr C. E. Green, 28 June 1911

Sir, Together with a great many others who are interested in cricket, I have been much surprised at the inclusion of Tarrant's name in the list of players to represent 'England against the Rest', which match has been arranged to assist the selectors in choosing an English team to visit Australia in the autumn, and also to represent England in the triangular contests arranged for next year. I should at once like to say that I am writing this letter in no unfriendly spirit towards Tarrant, for whom as a cricketer I entertain the highest admiration. It is well known, however, that Tarrant was born and bred in Australia, where he learnt his cricket, and it will be remembered that after he had qualified for Middlesex he went back to Australia, where he played for Victoria and in other matches against the last English team visiting that country, and I have reason to believe he was willing, if selected, to play for Australia in the Test matches. This position was, however, so anomalous that it was decided at headquarters that a telegram should be sent to Tarrant informing him that if he continued to play for an Australian State he would forfeit his county qualification for Middlesex. Even if by any recently amended rules Tarrant might now technically be qualified to play for England, surely it is against the spirit of international cricket that England should be represented by a player born and bred in Australia. That England as the home of cricket and with all her wealth of cricketers should go outside her own players to represent the Mother Country seems to me to be wrong in every way, and makes international cricket absolutely farcical. Personally I would even prefer to see England defeated with a team composed entirely of home-bred players than successful with an eleven assisted by a Colonial player.

C. E. GREEN

Tarrant never played for England – or Australia – but overseas players continued to qualify for counties. The decision in 1968 to allow their immediate registration opened the floodgates. Immediately the best of them dominated the county scene.

UNSPORTING?

From Mr G. H. G. Doggart, 20 September 1980

Cambridge University, Sussex and England (1948–61), captaining first two. Won Blues for five sports. President of MCC 1982 and President of English Schools Cricket Association. Headmaster of King's School, Bruton.

Sir, Am I alone in being a trifle saddened by the final word of the cricketing headline on your sporting page this morning (September 9), which reads: 'Averages point to dominance of foreigners'? It was cricket, surely, as much as anything that once made those 'at home' think of those in Commonwealth countries, South Africa included, not as foreigners but as friends. Is the use of the word 'foreigners', I wonder, a reflection of a new ecumenical feeling, a rare fall from grace on the part of *The Times*, or, even, in the light of current Anglo-French friction, a Freudian slip occasioned by the name of the leader in those averages – Lamb?

Yours faithfully,
G. H. G. DOGGART

THE CAPTAINS' TABLE

From the Hon. T. C. F. Prittie, 24 February 1982

On the staff of *The (Manchester) Guardian* 1945–70; Cricket Correspondent 1946. Author of books on cricket and politics.

Sir, I learn from your columns today (17 February) that Norman Featherstone (Zimbabwe/Rhodesia) will not be captaining the

Glamorgan cricket team this season and his place may be taken by Javed Miandad (Pakistan).

Worcestershire are being captained by Turner (New Zealand), Nottinghamshire by Rice (South Africa), Gloucestershire (up to last season) by Procter (Zimbabwe/Rhodesia), Kent by Asif (Pakistan), Leicestershire by Davison (Zimbabwe/Rhodesia), Lancashire by Lloyd (West Indies). I suggest that this is a ludicrous situation, with nearly half the English first-class counties captained by men who are not qualified to play for England.

Cricketers from overseas add lustre to the first-class cricket field in this country, but it should be axiomatic that only cricketers qualified to play for England should captain county sides and be given the experience needed to make them candidates to captain England. This is neither racism nor chauvinism, but strict common sense.

Yours faithfully,
TERENCE PRITTIE

By the 1982 season controls had been tightened with the aim of restricting counties to one player not qualified for England.

GOOD FOR A LAUGH

From Mr Ned Sherrin, 10 July 1976
Producer, director and writer.

Sir, I was interested in your diarist's suggestion that to mention the name of a newspaper from the stage is the easiest way to make an audience break spontaneously into laughter. Over the past ten weeks I have been researching this point conscientiously at the Mermaid Theatre. I find at least three far more certain laughter provokers. The phrases are 'The Liberal Party in the House of Commons'; 'Sir Harold Wilson's Honours List'; and 'Angela Rippon'. A bonus is that these combinations of words have only to be spoken to produce the desired effect. It is not necessary to add a funny or an exact comment in the manner of Sir Noël Coward when writing about *The Times*. (A close runner-up is 'Ladies mentioned in Paul Getty's will'.)

May I make double use of my 8½p stamp? Is there no way in which Richards of Hampshire could be coopted into the English

Test side? Can no patriotic English girl be persuaded to marry him? He is quite personable and surely such a sacrifice would qualify him for selection. Failing that could not some elderly gentleman adopt him?

Yours faithfully,
NED SHERRIN

Barry Richards, who had played for South Africa before their ban from Test cricket, did not play for England; but, sustained by rulings on parentage or residential qualifications, the South-African-born Tony and Ian Greig and Allan Lamb and the West-Indian-born Roland Butcher and Norman Cowans had been selected by the start of the 1983 season.

9
GENTLEMEN AND PLAYERS

HIGH SCORES AND DRAWN MATCHES

From A Bowler in the Fifties, 29 August 1899

Sir, I believe the great majority of old players will concur in the views you express in your leading article of the 25th. The fact that the record of county cricket for the present year is now: finished matches, 80; drawn, 106; shows that the situation should be at least considered. I sincerely hope the proposed committee will be appointed, and write to call attention to an aspect of the question which has not been touched upon by 'An Old Blue'.

I refer to the extent to which professional is superseding amateur cricket in the county matches.

The following statement gives the numbers of the two classes playing in the games to be decided to-day.

	Amateurs	Profes-sionals		Amateurs	Profes-sionals
Kent	8	3	Essex	5	6
Gloucester	7	4	Lancashire	4	7
Middlesex	7	4	Yorkshire	4	7
Hants	7	4	Notts	4	7
Somerset	7	4	Surrey	3	8
Worcester	6	5	Warwick	1	10
Sussex	5	6			

I fully admit that professional bowling is a necessity. Without it amateurs could not have brought batting into its present state of perfection, and if the county matches were played by amateurs only the number of finished matches would be much smaller than it is at present; but some limit should be placed on professional batting, which is too often of the 'stonewall' order. An amateur can play what game he likes, even when a draw is the only chance for his side. Thus you record today, 'Ranjitsinhji made 57 out of 69 in 75 minutes', under such conditions. A professional cannot do this, he is paid to keep up his end and has his average, his captain, and his committee to consider, and hence the Fabian tactics he adopts.

But apart from this a preponderance of professionals means that county cricket has become a question not of which county produces the best cricketers, but of which county can pay best and so attract the best available talent from elsewhere. In short the counties receiving the largest amount of gate money will always lead in the competition, as a glance at the present statement of wins and losses will show.

The present system also works badly in another way, as the following incident will show. The committee of my own county had to dismiss a young professional for insubordination. He took the matter lightly and said he could do better for himself elsewhere. This he promptly did and after a brief qualification has continued to play for another county. It was more than suspected that he had his offer in his pocket and that his offence was committed for the purpose of obtaining an excuse for his departure.

I hope the committee if it meets will consider this question, and I venture to make two proposals. First, that at least six, or still better seven, players in each county team should be amateurs; and, secondly, that the residential qualification of a professional player changing his county should be not less than two years.

My excuse for writing is that I have first played and then watched cricket for half a century, and I sign myself

Yours faithfully,
A BOWLER IN THE FIFTIES

PRESENT-DAY CRICKET

From Mr A. G. Steel, KC, 25 June 1909

Lancashire and captain of Cambridge University and England (1877–93). At his peak second as an all-rounder only to W. G. Grace. President of MCC 1902.

Sir, I know something of captaincy of a cricket team, as I have been captain of my school (Marlborough), captain of my University team (Cambridge), captain of Gentlemen v. Players, and captain of England v. Australia. These are my credentials. Well, I cannot understand the present-day captains in this respect – they will not change their bowlers quick enough. Today they often use a bowler for 40 or 50 runs with no wicket without a change, and sometimes two bowlers at the same time with the same result. This is as a rule bad captaincy. Again, when things are in a knot with the bowling side, it seems strange that the captain does not think it advisable to change ends for a bowler who has not been successful at the end he began at. The last Test match at Lord's was an instance of this. Again, when the best bowlers have been unsuccessful, why not try the worst for a couple of overs – as I often used to do – *sometimes* with success? It is always worth a trial.

As for batting, I am convinced that a straight bat is still the best, in spite of the pull stroke. Jumping in front before the ball reaches the bat is and must be radically wrong. The once best bat on the present Australian side has spoilt his play by continually playing with a cross bat to a straight ball. Grace never did this, and though I was never in the same class with him, I think I never did it.

Schoolboys, *verb. sap.*

I am yours truly,
ALLAN G. STEEL

PROFESSIONALS IN CRICKET

From Sir Home Gordon, Bt, 24 January 1925

Cricket journalist virtually from leaving Eton in 1887 until shortly before his death in 1956; publisher and industrialist. Said to have been influential with England selectors. For services to Sussex, of which he was President in 1948, he was awarded an honorary county cap. Contributor to *Encyclopaedia Britannica*.

Sir, As perhaps the most intimate of all Lord Hawke's friends, may I be permitted briefly to touch on the cricket controversy at issue about him, while he is on the high seas *en route* for Ceylon. No other lover of cricket has ever done so much for the professional as Lord Hawke. It has always been admitted that to him more than to all others is due the modern high status of cricket professionals, and among them I have many valued friends. That he should have intended to have cast a slur on them is unthinkable. What is clear is that in making an impromptu reply to a vote of thanks, he phrased clumsily what I know is his view – namely, that if first-class cricket has not the leaven of amateurs with professionals it would lose its truly national character. A careless sentence from an admittedly diffident speaker ought not to be allowed to outweigh a lifework of devotion to the best interests of professionals in cricket.

I am, &c.,

HOME GORDON

Lord Hawke was reported to have said: 'Pray heaven no professional may ever captain England.' What he meant, it was said, was: 'It will be a bad day for England when no amateur is fit to lead the side.'

THE WINE OF VICTORY

Jack Hobbs was brought a celebratory drink by his captain, P. G. H. Fender, when he equalled W. G. Grace's record of 126 centuries at Taunton on 17 August 1925. He broke the record the next day.

From Mr R. T. Knight, 19 August 1925

Sir, Hobbs richly deserved, and I hope enjoyed, his goblet of champagne at the wicket. When in Birmingham the other day I saw him announced as a total abstainer, but he evidently was not in his moment of victory. In this he was on another par with the great W. G. Grace. Whoever saw him walking in his prime down the steps at Lord's or the Oval can ever forget the physical splendour of the man, the tireless energy, the world of concentration he threw into his batting, or the boyish gaiety with which he shuffled to the crease? And what individual ever deserved or enjoyed his glass of wine more at lunch and dinner than did 'W.G.'? He not only enjoyed it, but throve marvellously well on it!

R. T. KNIGHT

From Mr M. C. Salaman, 21 August 1925

Sir, Mr R. J. Knight's letter calls to my memory W. G. Grace's splendid figure at the wicket on that day of May 30 years ago when he made his 100th century. Happening to be in Bristol, which was all agog for the event, I hurried up to the cricket ground in time to witness the consummation; but the champion proceeded to make a second century. Then, from the pavilion came his famous brother, Dr E. M. Grace, all smiles, carrying a magnum of champagne, a gratulatory gesture which happily created the precedent followed the other day by the Surrey captain when Hobbs achieved his triumph. But Hobbs, after quaffing his goblet of champagne, added only one run to his century; Grace drank his bumper with a difference, adding 88 runs to the 200 he had just celebrated.

MALCOLM C. SALAMAN

From Mr W. Drewett, 22 August 1925

Sir, One whose recollections of the Oval go back to the '50's of last century may be permitted to recall the custom prevailing there on the occasions of big matches when Mr Burrup was hon. secretary of the Surrey CCC. If the batsmen had collared the bowling and were giving the fieldsmen a warm time on a hot day, Mr Burrup would be seen to leave the pavilion carrying aloft a huge two-handled cup, with a waiter following him similarly loaded. Suspension of play followed and the cups were circulated among a thirsty group, giving complete satisfaction to those who drank therefrom. There was no tea interval in those days.

W. DREWETT

From Lieutenant-Colonel H. J. Stone, 25 August 1925

Sir, Champagne, apparently in large quantities, seems to have been most efficacious in assisting 'W.G.'s' run-getting propensities according to Mr Salaman's account. In the 80's he came up to Oxford to play for MCC against the University. At the end of the first day's play he had made 64, not out. It looked as if things were going badly for Oxford. Some of us put our heads together and decided it was necessary to try to put the Doctor's 'eye out', so we invited him to dine with us and plied him with, among other things, brands of Oxford champagne – some ill-natured people said it was manufactured locally. However, he took everything very kindly and kept us all amused. The next day he continued his innings and carried his score to 104 before losing his wicket. Later he said to me, 'That champagne we had last night did me a lot of good.'

HY. J. STONE

From Lieutenant-Colonel C. H. Jones, 28 August 1925

Colonel Stone might have gone on to say that 'W.G.' that same day, June, 1886, took all ten wickets also – and for 49 runs.

C. H. JONES

From Canon A. H. Sewell, 2 September 1925

Your readers may be interested to learn that the correspondence on this subject started on an entirely false assumption. In response to an inquiry from the secretary of the Western Temperance League, of which I have the honour to be president, Hobbs has written to say that on the memorable occasion when he equalled W. G. Grace's record at Taunton, his captain did not bring him out champagne to drink. As a fact, the glass contained nothing more intoxicating than ginger-ale. Hobbs has been an abstainer for some years, and remains so.

A. H. SEWELL

BALL AND BEARD

From Mr Arthur Porritt, 10 August 1944
For many years editor of the *Christian Herald*.

The evidence concerning the time-honoured story of Ernest Jones sending a ball through 'W.G.'s' beard is curiously conflicting. I collaborated with W. G. Grace in writing his *Cricketing Reminiscences and Personal Recollections*, and in 1899 spent hundreds of hours with him as he revived his memories. He never mentioned the 'ball and beard' incident, and no specific reference to Ernest Jones appears in the book. 'W.G.' had an ingrained objection to fast bowlers who, bowling short, bumped the ball high and dangerously (Ernest Jones and Arthur Mold were notoriously addicted to that practice), and my own theory, for what it is worth, is that when Jones bowled the ball that flashed past 'W.G.' face-high 'the long-whiskered Doctor' (as Francis Thompson called him) expostulated testily and drew from Jones the apologetic 'Sorry, Doctor, she slipped.' This may indeed have happened more than once.

ARTHUR PORRITT

From Sir Pelham Warner, 15 August 1944

Sir, In his letter which was published in *The Times* of 10 August Mr Arthur Porritt wrote 'W.G. had an ingrained objection to fast bowlers who, bowling short, bumped the ball high and dangerously (Ernest Jones and Arthur Mold were notoriously addicted to that practice).' This would seem to imply that W G disliked fast bowling. May I say, with respect to Mr Porritt, that no one ever played fast bowling better than W.G., and it would be a slur on the champion's memory if the idea were to prevail that he disliked it. He simply revelled in it, and in the seventies and early eighties of the last century, when the wickets were often none too perfect, he simply 'murdered' it, and to the end of his days he continued to do so.

It was the slower bowlers who caused him most trouble at the end of his career, when increasing weight made him less quick on his feet. I remember once asking him which type of bowling, if any, he liked least, and I recall the exact words of his reply. 'I didn't mind what they bowled if I was in form, but the faster they bowled the better I liked 'em.' Ernest Jones every now and again bowled what may be called 'a quick riser', but Mold, with his easy action, perfect body swing, and smooth approach to the crease, concentrated on length. Even as late in his career as 1898 and 1899 I saw W.G. play the bowling of Jones, Richardson, and Lockwood with a mastery and ease which his far younger contemporaries may perhaps have equalled but certainly did not surpass. To support my contention I would call as a witness Sir Stanley Jackson, who has got himself involved in this interesting Ball and Beard controversy. The only thing W.G. had an ingrained objection to was the Zeppelins, and when Mr H. D. G. Leveson Gower said to him 'But, W.G., you didn't mind the fastest of bowlers,' his reply was 'Ah! but I could see 'em.'

If ever there was a champion, it was the Bearded Doctor.

Yours, &c.,

P. F. WARNER

From Mr Peter Johnson, 16 August 1944

If the ball from Jones had literally gone through W.G.'s beard it would have touched it and therefore been recorded as a leg-bye. I understand this was not the case and suggest that the umpire's decision should, as always, be final.

PETER JOHNSON

LORD HARRIS'S BIRTHDAY MESSAGE

From Lord Harris, 3 February 1931

Sir, I appreciate, I assure you, the suggestion that I might like to send a message of good will to all my cricketing friends on my eightieth birthday and I gladly, in the words of Rip Van Winkle, greet them and 'their wives and families, and may they live long and prosper'.

Only there is something a bit ominous about the suggestion. Does it convey a hint that it is time I said farewell to cricket? If so, I have no intention of complying with it. Cricket has been too good a friend to me for nearly 70 years for me to part with it one moment before I have to. I cannot remember a time when it did not convey its friendly welcome. In school at Eton the tapping of the bats in Sixpenny assured me of happy hours to come, and reminded me of happy hours in the past. I have been fairly busy for most of my life, but never so busy that the thoughts of cricket and my companions were not an inspiration to get on with the work that I might the sooner enjoy the invigorating capacity.

And my message includes youth, and I advise them to get all the cricket they can. They will never regret it: I might apply to it Mr

Jorrocks's commendation of hunting: 'It's the image of war without its guilt, and 25 per cent of its danger.' And in my message to youth I will repeat what I said to the half-holiday cricketer, 'You do well to love it, for it is more free from anything sordid, anything dishonourable, than any game in the world. To play it keenly, honourably, generously, self-sacrificingly is a moral lesson in itself, and the class-room is God's air and sunshine. Foster it, my brothers, so that it may attract all who can find the time to play it; protect it from anything that would sully it, so that it may grow in favour with all men.'

Thus, Mr Editor, thanks to your kindness I have the opportunity of sending my greetings to all my friends round the world, both those I do not know as well as those I do, for we are all comrades in the world of cricket.

Yours faithfully,

HARRIS

'LE ROI EST MORT . . .'

From the Revd Hugh Hunter, 26 August 1938
Vicar of Riddlesden, Yorkshire.

I called out to a very small boy in the village here this evening (24 August) as he was slogging a ball up the street, 'Hello, Bradman!' He replied, 'I'm not Bradman, I'm 'Utton!' I apologized instantly.

HUGH HUNTER

On 23 August Hutton's 364 against Australia at the Oval had broken the previous Test match record of 334 by Bradman.

PERFECT PITCHES

From Mr Pascoe Thornton, 6 September 1938
An announcer at the BBC.

Dr Lyttelton's letter published in your columns on 2 September reminds me of a remark made to me a year or two ago by a well-known cricketing journalist – a first-class bowler himself. He had recently had the misfortune to bowl to Bradman at the Oval. 'It was like bowling to God on a concrete pitch,' he said.

PASCOE C. THORNTON

A GREAT DAY AT THE OVAL

To celebrate the centenaries of Surrey CCC and the Oval, Surrey played a one-day match against a side comprising ten former England players and Brooks, the old Surrey wicketkeeper. The historic ten were: Sutcliffe, Sandham, Woolley, Hendren, Jardine, Fender (captain), Knight, Tate, Holmes and Allom; the umpires were Hobbs and Strudwick. The King and 15 000 others revelled in the post-war festivities.

From Mr P. G. H. Fender, 25 May 1946
Sussex, Surrey and England (1910–35), outstanding captain of Surrey. Scored the fastest first-class hundred, in 35 minutes, and wrote several books on cricket.

Sir, May I claim the hospitality of your columns to express to the thousands of enthusiasts who gave 'Old England' such a wonderful reception at the Oval yesterday the sincere and heartfelt thanks of all those who were privileged to play in that side? There are many others who should have played and we realize that we were the lucky ones, and that the tribute was to the game rather than to a few individuals.

May I, at the same time, record a thought which, more than once while we were fielding came to my mind, and which, I am sure, in one form or another, was in the mind of each of the other players in the 'Old England' side? The warmth of the welcome, the size and the enthusiasm of the great crowd, and, above all, the presence of His Majesty, seemed to me to convey a message to all the younger generation of cricketers, not only in this country, but all over the world. A message telling them that, in spite of the old adage, and where cricket is concerned, public memory is not short. A message to inspire all young cricketers, and to urge them to achievements in the game greater even than their wildest dreams had yet conjured up.

Such a welcome as was given to 'Old England', collectively and individually, must surely be a public assurance that those who can carve for themselves a little niche in the greatest of games can always be sure of a warm place in the hearts of all lovers of cricket.

Yours faithfully,

PERCY G. H. FENDER

SOME THOUGHTS ON THE GAME

From Mr Ken Barrington, 17 August 1968

Surrey and England (1953–68). Test selector and manager of England touring teams. Died of a heart attack in 1981 during the tour of West Indies.

Sir, I wonder if I might be allowed the courtesy of your column to express a cricketer's observations on the first-class game today.

I think most cricket lovers will agree that there is as much interest in cricket as a game – and even in the first-class county championship – as ever, but there is little doubt that the value of the first-class game as a spectacle has declined and that all too often the spectator finds himself looking at a game he can no longer understand. I am all too aware that I myself played many innings which to the average onlooker must have been baffling and have provided little enjoyment. It is the batsman who is subjected to the greatest criticisms, although I suggest that it is often the restrictions that are placed upon him by the bowlers and the tactics of the fielding team which perhaps contribute more than is apparent on the surface.

The game has become very professional, not only in the sense of the absence of the amateur but of the study by professionals of the techniques of the game which has resulted in a development of the defensive skills, out of which has emerged the dominance of the medium paced bowler. His skills, which are considerable, have been assisted by the present surfeit of grassy pitches and grassy outfields, and I am afraid his licence to polish the ball to his heart's content; and, alas in some cases, to interfere with the seam of the ball, for which he has no licence.

Whilst I know that there are valid arguments in support of the present lbw law, I am quite certain that it has encouraged medium paced bowlers to shift the direction of their attack from the off stump to the leg. There are a lot of batsmen today who would quickly demonstrate that they could play the game attractively if the direction of attack was the off stump.

There is obviously little, beyond comment, that a player can do to influence the preparation of wickets and the control of outfields, both of which need a change of method, but I feel that most players who think about the game and its future would like to see the present defensive trends discouraged by a complete removal of the right of the bowler – or anyone else – to interfere with the ball in any way, and a limitation of the onside field. I would argue for a limitation to five, with not more than two behind the wicket as this would force the bowlers to direct their attack more on the off stump, and would rid the game of many of its present frustrations.

I am convinced of the need for fast, true wickets which to be both must be dry, and therefore would support far more covering by all the county clubs. I would also suggest that there be one rule which all counties should adhere to, as at the present time clubs seem to suit themselves. But I would go further, and suggest an exploration of the possibility of developing artificial wickets. I would make a start by insisting that there should be one such wicket available on every ground where county cricket is played as an experiment. So much research has been made into the use of artificial substances for all sorts of playing surfaces that I am sure some expenditure in this direction would yield dividends for the benefit of the game.

I firmly believe that three-day cricketers must be brought to a realization that it is the cricket on the first day of a three-day match that matters, for it is on this day that most people contemplate their watching. I would unhesitatingly restrict the number of overs in the first innings of a three-day match in such a way as to assure that in good weather each side would have completed its first innings on the first day. I would go further and limit the number of overs any one bowler could bowl. I realize only too well that these or other limitations would lessen the opportunities of middle order and, indeed, all batsmen to play a long innings but I regard this as of secondary importance to the recapture of the interest of spectators.

So far as the structure of the county championship is concerned, I firmly believe that there is a place for the three-day championship and am content with the proposed 1969 reduction to 24 matches. I am anxious, however, because I feel that Saturday attendances may be affected by the introduction of what will, I am sure, be exciting time-limited league championship matches on Sundays. I am sure that a better approach to the problem might be to play not 16 but 32 one-day league matches and to play them on Saturdays and Sundays, leaving three-day cricket to mid-week.

I have no knowledge or experience of fixture making, but believe that if this structure is possible it would do a great deal for the game so far as the spectator is concerned, and provide sufficient three-day cricket to assure that players of international standing have sufficient two-innings match practice to match the skills of other Test match countries. Obviously room has to be found for the Gillette Cup, matches against the tourists, and this might involve some lengthening of the season into September; a prospect which I think most cricket lovers would welcome. We must challenge soccer, not keep out of the way.

> Yours faithfully,
> KEN BARRINGTON

MIGHTY HITTERS

From Mr Laurence Meynell, 9 May 1953
Author of books on many subjects, including cricket.

Sir, Surely Mr Adlard achieves a masterpiece of meiosis in saying that Gilbert Jessop 'should be included among the mighty hitters'? It is like saying that St Peter's must find a place among the big churches of the world.

> Yours, &c.,
> LAURENCE MEYNELL

THE CROUCHER AND HEIR

From the Principal, Bishop Otter College, Chichester, 23 May 1974

Sir, Alan Gibson's tribute to a Gloucestershire father and son (Sportsview, 18 May) recalled a hot west-country morning in the early fifties. Opening the attack for the University of Bristol against a touring Cambridge college, I was deluded, by a few quick successes, toward a vision of early lunch and an afternoon swim. A slight delay, a buzz from the pavilion, and a portly figure emerged with a look of mild surprise, fostering our hunch that we might be 'through' the real batting.

What followed was a sharp lesson in line and length, as the best we could offer was peremptorily dismissed to all parts of the ground. Withdrawn, chastened, from the rout, to ruminate at third-man, near the score box, I enquired after my mysterious assailant. 'Reverend G. L. Jessop', came the grinning reply. 'We were a bit short, so we picked him up on the way over.'

Self esteem repaired, I felt – like Mr Gibson at his Cornish revelation – briefly in touch with the Immortal.

Yours faithfully,
GORDON McGREGOR

Alan Gibson had seen the Revd Jessop score, in the manner of his father, a vigorous 80 for Dorset against Cornwall.

COACHING OF TEST CRICKETERS

From Mr E. R. Dexter, 8 April 1978
Cambridge University, Sussex and England (1956–68), captain of each. All-round sportsman. Writer and broadcaster on cricket.

Sir, I was naturally flattered to read John Woodcock, your Cricket Correspondent (13 March), when he proposed that I should be considered for inclusion in the England Test team for the tour to Australia later this year. However, whilst the idea of returning to the front line to help retain the Ashes has emotional attractions, it is contrary to my conviction that top class cricket is increasingly a young man's game; and that we have much young talent from which to choose.

Your correspondent's diagnosis is that, whilst our bowling and fielding are first rate, our batting is not. His solution is to encourage a more buccaneering approach. But the 'buccaneering touch' is only the outward sign of the confidence and positive thinking which arise from genuine skill. To bat effectively in Test cricket a variety of attributes are needed including talent, courage, technique and know-how and it was these latter elements of higher education which used to be handed down man to man – that is until Kerry Packer so dramatically removed almost an entire generation of senior England Test batsmen.

I have just completed and costed a detailed plan of action to bridge this sudden gap in the normal process of education and communication. Roughly, it would consist of a short end-of-season course at which the cream of the country's young cricketing talent would be subjected to instruction and counsel by the best cricketing brains; coupled with an award scheme for the season's best performances, based on technique, skill, etc, rather than sudden flashes in the pan.

I have discussed the proposal with leading members of cricket's governing bodies who have given their approval in principle.

I now need an astute businessman who can see the advantage to his company and its products of sponsoring England's reply to Mr Packer – but at a cost which works out at no more than one of Messrs Rolls-Royce's more exotic motor cars. And if we are going to improve England's Test chances, I must meet my astute (and patriotic) businessman soon.

I am, Sir, Yours sincerely,

TED DEXTER

A year later Commercial Union Assurance put up £40,000 for four youth cricket projects with Ted Dexter as entrepreneur.

SIR T. INSKIP AT THE WICKET

From Mr P. F. Warner, 17 March 1936

Sir, In these rather grim days it may be some slight alleviation to recall a game of cricket in which Sir Thomas Inskip, the recently appointed Minister for the Coordination of Defence, took part. The match was Lords and Commons v. the *Morning Post*, and the Solicitor-General, as Sir Thomas was then, was batting for Lords and Commons. Mr H. A. Gwynne, the captain of the *Morning Post* team, had more faith in my bowling than any other captain under whom I have ever played, and Sir Thomas remarked to me, 'I had no idea you were such a good bowler, Warner.' Having said this he promptly on-drove me for six, but as I am, or strive to be, an accurate chronicler of matters appertaining to cricket the truth forces me to add that in the next over I 'had' him with a slow one.

That match is full of memories. I remember Major Lloyd George telling me that though Lord Howe's driving had been likened unto that of Jehu, the son of Nimshi, he was, none the less, the safest driver of a motor-car he knew. Major Lloyd George himself played a very good innings of some 30 odd, and Mr Hogben sent my middle stump flying with a ball that came back some three or four inches and in so doing clung to the turf. Then there were the late Mr Tom

Griffiths, the Labour Whip, who averred that he had 'worn out the seat of his pants watching cricket at Lord's'; and the MP who, in the tense silence of the tense moments of a keen match, appealed for lbw *from short-leg* and simultaneously apologized for such un-parliamentary conduct!

Finally Mr Gwynne's drive over the bowler's head which caused me to say – I was in with him at the time – 'That one reminds me of A. C. MacLaren' – a compliment which he assured me he would never forget.

I have ventured to recall a match which, if its venue was neither Lord's nor the Oval, remains with me as something of a landmark in a long and happy experience of the incomparable game.

I am, &c.,

P. F. WARNER

From Major Gwilym Lloyd George, MP, 19 March 1936
Liberal-Conservative Member for Pembroke 1929–50; later Member for Newcastle-upon-Tyne; Minister of Fuel 1942–45; Minister of Food 1951–54; Home Secretary and Minister for Welsh Affairs 1954–57. Created Viscount Tenby 1957. Lloyd George *was* his father.

Sir, I feel sure that all who took part in the match between the Lords and Commons and the *Morning Post* will be grateful to Mr Warner for reminding them of a singularly pleasant day's cricket.

There was one incident, however, which Mr Warner did not mention. It is true that he referred to Mr Gwynne's drive over the bowler's head. Surely he cannot have forgotten an even greater drive of Sir T. Inskip's over mid-on's head, the only difference being that in Sir Thomas Inskip's case it was the bat, and not the ball, that sailed through the air.

I am, &c.,

G. LLOYD GEORGE

NOT CRICKET

From Mr Ayton Whitaker, 26 September 1977
Umpire with Lords and Commons CC.

Sir, Mr Nicholas Scott is one of the leading batsmen for Lords and

Commons cricket. It is therefore unthinkable that he should be dislodged by his constituency.

Yours faithfully,

A. R. WHITAKER

Ayton Whitaker, quoted elsewhere, added: 'Cricket is more important than the niceties of Tory politics'. Mr Scott, Member for Kensington and Chelsea, kept his wicket intact.

10
CHANGE

CRICKET

From F.G. [Frederick Gale], 12 September 1884

Sir, I fear that cricket is so conservative – that is, the MCC, the trustees or conservators of the game, are so sensitive about any change – that things will go on as they are.

There are one or two remedies in cricketers' own hands: 1. Amateurs, if they have the will and capability, can by hard work and practice acquire the art of true, quick, and good bowling quite as well as the players, and provide more changes of bowling, which would shorten matches. 2. The captains may always agree to play five-ball overs instead of four, and many of the first bowlers in England have repeatedly told me there is no reason to prevent it except loss of gate-money by shortening matches. 3. They can, if they please, agree to have two wickets prepared and toss for choice, and each eleven would bat on its own wickets and this would avoid the everlasting excuse about the eleven who goes in second playing on a broken wicket. 4. They can, if they please, commence at 11 o'clock on the second and third days, and this, added to the five-ball over system, would much tend to decrease 'draws'.

The fact is, and it is high treason to say so, that cricket is now so common that it is a mere trade with very many of the players, and a lounge second to some other amusement with many of the amateurs; so that the heart and will to 'play up' and waste no time are not the mainsprings of some of the modern matches.

In unfinished 'day matches' in Philadelphia, when more than two innings are played, and the match is unfinished, they decide their victory by dividing the aggregate of runs by the number of wickets down, and the best average decides the match.

Yours obediently,

F.G.

CRICKET

From X.Y.Z., 7 May 1892
Of Birmingham.

Sir, May I suggest, in the interest of cricket, that the three days' matches, instead of commencing as they now do on Mondays and Thursdays, should commence on Saturdays and Wednesdays? It is very rarely that a three days' match extends to the afternoon of the third day, and the consequence is that on Wednesday and Saturday afternoons practically no opportunities are afforded for witnessing first-class cricket matches. Saturday afternoon is a general holiday and Wednesday afternoon is a general school holiday. How often in the season can first-class cricket be viewed on Saturday afternoons either at Lord's or the Oval?

I know there are objections to the alteration I propose, but the increase in gate money and in the public interest in cricket would be enormous if, in the leading grounds in the country, county and first-class cricket could be seen on Saturday and Wednesday afternoons.

Your obedient servant,

X.Y.Z.

Saturday and Wednesday starts were instituted in 1920.

COUNTY CRICKET

From Mr J. P. Pringle, 14 September 1885

Sir, Now that the results of the season's cricket are made up, and the present method of awarding county precedence shown up in all its absurdity by some grotesque results, perhaps you will allow me to point out another defect in our mode of procedure which is not likely to receive all the attention that it deserves. I mean the method of comparing the merits of bowlers. The present method is a very rough and inaccurate one, which may be summed up as runs per wicket. Now, every cricketer knows that the system of crediting a bowler with every wicket caught or stumped without discrimination, results in absurdities quite as great as those which exist in our mode of determining county precedence. When will English cricketers condescend to adopt from America the bolometer method, which was started five or six years ago in Boston, and has given great satisfaction wherever it has been adopted?'

This method was devised by Mr Langley, of Boston, and is described in the 'American Cricketer's Annual'. I myself have used it in a club near this [Old Windsor], and can strongly recommend it to the authorities of the MCC.

I am, Sir, your obedient servant,

J. P. PRINGLE

Both the MCC and C. C. Morris (Philadelphia) Cricket Libraries were stumped by the bolometer.

HIGH SCORES AND DRAWN MATCHES

From The Captain of the Eton Eleven in 1836, 25 August 1899
Robert William Essington, also captain of the school and Eton's first over-the-shoulder (or round-arm) bowler.

Sir, The laws of cricket were framed for batsmen, to whom a blow on unprotected legs was a serious matter, and for underhand bowlers. The use of pads makes it necessary to enact that any ball stopped by anything except the bat, when on its way to the wicket, should be fatal to the batsman, although it was a twister. The permission to bowl, first over shoulder, and then overhead, should have been accompanied with an increased height of the stumps, proportionately to the increased rise of the ball.

But proper as these alterations would be, something more is required, if matches are to end in one day, as they did formerly, and ought to do. The increased science of the batsmen, more marked even than the improvement in the bowling and fielding, makes it necessary to settle all matches in one innings.

THE CAPTAIN OF THE ETON ELEVEN IN 1836

'AUDI ALTERAM PARTEM'

From K. S. Ranjitsinhji, 25 February 1903
At this time captain of Sussex.

Sir, Some years ago, when a controversy on the subject of affording some assistance to the bowlers was in progress, one of the most famous cricketers of our time made a remark which has always remained in my memory. 'Whatever changes are made by the authorities of the game,' wrote the Hon. F. S. Jackson, 'I hope that no interference with the implements of cricket is contemplated.' I cordially agreed with Mr Jackson's view at that time, and I have seen no cause to alter my opinion since.

It is not with any desire either to rush into print or to pose as an authority that I write these lines on the present proposal to widen the wickets. My sole desire is to point out, both to the public and to the cricketing fraternity generally, the advisability of considering this matter on its real merits, instead of jumping at conclusions based on 'the ascendancy of the bat over the ball'. It is perhaps a little unfortunate for the cause that I advocate that I happen to be a fairly successful batsman, whose interests might be supposed to lie in the direction of deprecating, as I do, any change in existing conditions.

As far as I am aware, the dissatisfaction as to drawn games refers principally to first-class cricket. It would be highly injurious, therefore, to alter the existing state of things in order to remedy an evil which exists only in the highest class of cricket, provided we admit that there is an evil due, primarily and absolutely, to the ascendency of the bat. First-class matches form but a small proportion of the world's cricket, however important an item it may be. It would be very injurious to sacrifice the interests of the rest of the community, even for the sake of an important minority, thereby introducing, to use a political phrase, class legislation. The game, whether it is called first-class or otherwise, is cricket, and any measure can only be a half-measure which aims at differentiating between the classes of cricket.

It seems to be taken for granted by those in favour of the change that it is in the best interests of the game that every match should be fought out to a finish. If this were so, I feel sure that the game would be shorn of much of its greatest charm—of that "glorious uncertainty" which is admittedly one of its brightest jewels and best points. For unless the element of luck – *e.g.*, in the way of weather – steps in to the help of the weaker side, the stronger opponents will emerge from the contest with almost a certain win. Some of the best contests which it has been my pleasure and privilege both to play in and to witness have been those wherein the weaker eleven has struggled gamely to avoid defeat and the stronger one has striven its uttermost to bring the game to a definite conclusion within the allotted period.

The majority of drawn games are not nearly as much the result of inferior bowling or superior batting as of downright bad fielding. This is largely due to the prominence given by the Press and the public alike to batting and bowling alone. Often the committees even err in not giving due consideration, in the selection of men, to those who are the better fields, with the result that the cultivation of good fielding, and practising the same, are being left severely alone.

All but one of the drawn first-class games in which I took part last season were unfinished thanks to bad fielding on the part of one and often both sides in most games, and in the remaining one owing to the weather. I may add, by way of parenthesis, that for the last three years the average of easy catches dropped by one county team holding a high position in the championship during Whitsun week alone, at the lowest computation, cannot be less than 13.

In affording legislative aid to the bowlers by making the proposed change you will be, theoretically and practically, lowering the standard of bowling, because, however infinitesimal the increase in the width or height of the stumps, it will be necessarily easier for the bowler.

Of recent years, with the exception of the last, there has been a long succession of dry summers. Consequently we have had more good and hard wickets than formerly; and bowlers in this country – with but few brilliant exceptions – who have gone in for length rather than for head work, have found themselves at sea. But it has had its good effect, inasmuch as it has taught them to realize by degrees – thanks especially to the magnificent example set to them by nearly all the great Australian bowlers (who have visited this country during the last 12 years to my knowledge, and who are accustomed to bowl year after year on true pitches) – that something more than mere length is requisite to obtain wickets on good, dry, hard pitches. In some cases, in this country, I am happy to be able to say that the progress has been even more manifest, inasmuch as the Australian methods of bowling have been copied with success. Bowling on good wickets will train their brains, as it has already done in the case of the Australian bowlers. Batting is, in all conscience, slow enough as things are; but the very fact of increasing the width of the wicket will, I fear, not only render slower those batsmen who are already slow, but may also import the element of tediousness into the comparatively few at present noted for brilliancy, and will certainly not encourage the multiplication of unique hitters of the Gilbert Jessop type. In theory it is safe to assume that the proposed change will put batsmen more on the defensive. Hence batting will be less attractive, and the alleged reform will impose a penalty by putting a premium or handicap on the great players of the day.

Much capital is made out of the fact that at the last meeting of county captains there were only two dissentient voices with regard to the alteration. The Press all over the country, for some reason that I do not understand, seem pledged, as it were, to support this innovation; and their radical proclivities were well illustrated when criticizing the action of some of the county committees in deferring to the opinions of their captains. Now I venture to say, with little fear of contradiction, that not a single captain discussed the matter with his committee, or came with a mandate from them to move in the matter. This proposition was suddenly sprung upon the captains' meeting, and it resulted, as I gather, from a conversation between two of the party present. I am betraying no confidence in stating that one or two captains supported the motion with the sole object of accepting the lesser of two evils, which they evidently feared would again be brought up owing to the increasing craze for changes which are being agitated for from time to time without the necessary excuses to justify their adoption. The other evil to which I refer is the question of the lbw rule, which came up for discussion one or two seasons ago.

In point of fact, the captains are requested by their respective committees to meet at Lord's annually with the sole object of selecting umpires; and it is only since 1899 that on their own initiative they have made suggestions to the MCC regarding alterations in the game. No notice or circular is ever given or sent out by any captain to the rest of any change which he may desire to suggest before the meeting takes place, with the result that the discussion on a suggestion made is more often than not both hasty and scanty, and the judgment often prematurely given.

I have now expressed my views, which are entirely in agreement with the dissentient captains, Messrs. MacLaren and Foster. But if it be decided by that great and august body the premier club of cricket – which rightly holds the destinies of the game in its hands and which, I am happy to say, is conservative, slow, and deliberate in such matters – that in the best interests of cricket this change is required because of the ascendancy of the bat over the ball, then the legislation proposed, in my humble opinion, is wholly inadequate. I have it on the highest authority that the wickets, which according to rule should be 8in. in width, are in reality 8½in., so that the alteration would make an addition of ½in. to the present size. I submit in all earnestness that on good wickets this will be wholly inadequate, while on bad wickets it is generally admitted that no change whatever is required. To cite only one instance to convince anybody of the truth of the latter statement, I would only like to draw attention to the fact of last year's powerful Australian eleven falling victims to the bowlers in successive matches for totals of 36 and 23 on pitches affected by rain. Any change will therefore, I hope, be such as to fulfil the desired object on good wickets. I learn from the Press of the comment of the Australian authorities to the change; but I would like to point out that the Australian summers, in the matter of climate, are reliable, and consequently the change will not affect Antipodean cricketers in the slightest degree. English summers, on the contrary, are notoriously unreliable, and we cannot omit that fact from our consideration.

The present proposal can only be deemed an attempt at tinkering with the laws of the game. The great radical change – for it is reasonable to suppose that when wickets are sufficiently wide all matches will be finished within the prescribed period – will, as I have already pointed out, deprive the game of its greatest charm of uncertainty, a consummation which I feel sure is not desired by true lovers of the game all over the world.

There remains the financial aspect. From this point of view it will be not less unsatisfactory for the majority of county matches to finish either early on the third day or, possibly, on the second. In this connexion I note with pleasure the sensible view taken by the committees of several counties, whose sound businesslike attitude on the subject makes them appreciate the situation and entitles them to view with disfavour the proposed change. County cricket is a costly undertaking; and, with ever-increasing expenses to keep up with the times, anything that tends to decrease the annual income will seriously militate against the clubs' chances of successful competition in the future.

I also note with intense pleasure that one of the most well-reasoned, sensible, and temperate views on this subject comes, fittingly enough, from Dr W. G. Grace. It is peculiarly appropriate that such an opinion should be expressed by the great master of the great game on whose judgment so many of us younger players, but old admirers of his, rely.

May I add, in conclusion, that in writing the foregoing I have had no desire to provoke a controversy? On the other hand, in the interests of the game to which I am devoted, I have endeavoured to present, as briefly as possible, some of the more obvious points of the other side of this question which have not hitherto been placed before the public.

I remain yours faithfully,

RANJITSINHJI

NEAR AND WIDE

From Professor Thomas Case, 29 March 1906

Professor of Moral Philosophy and President of Corpus Christi College, Oxford. Played for Oxford University and Middlesex (1864–68). Treasurer and President, Oxford University CC.

Sir, As an old cricketer before men began to spoil the game both for players and for spectators by leaving the ball alone, I would suggest a simple reform. As the umpire cries 'wide' when the ball is out of the batsman's reach, so, when it is within it but is left alone, let him cry 'near'. While 'wides' are scored by addition to the batsman's side, 'nears' should be subtracted from the batsman's own score, which in some cases might become an actual *minus* to the side. Cricket would then not be so dull, because it would be once more a game.

I am, Sir, yours faithfully,

THOMAS CASE

'THROWN OUT'

From the Revd C. A. F. Campbell, 31 August 1906

Rector of Street, Somerset. Took pride in the village's victory over a Bridgwater XI which contained eight men who had played for the county, including Sammy Woods.

Sir, In your account of the Middlesex batting in today's report you describe how before Mr Warner could get back to his wicket 'Mr Hutchings, going at practically top speed, gathered the ball with his right hand and threw the wicket down.' What you graphically describe in 19 words is unknown to the public, who in so many papers read, or only can read, in the score 'Mr P. F. Warner, run out, 66.' May I ask, are we never to have the name of the man who brilliantly throws down a wicket immortalized in the same way as the name of a man who catches an easy catch? Do the laws of the Medes and Persians forbid it? If there is one respect in which hundreds of wickets are lost every day in county matches it is by a careless throw-in. In spite of the infallible arguments urged to the contrary, I firmly believe that it would encourage smart fielding if the fact that a man has run out a batsman by a smart throw-in were duly recognized in the obvious way. 'Run out' conveys so little. It is only half the truth.

Yours,
COLIN A. F. CAMPBELL

WHERE CREDIT'S DUE

From Mr Mike Faber, 30 April 1983

Sir, A main pleasure of following cricket in the newspapers is the comprehensive picture of play given by the scorecard. But there is one type of event, of increasing influence, in the description of which the scorecard is defective. That is the run out.

No matter how brilliant the feat, no matter how decisive the incident, the perpetrator of it remains anonymous. It is as if the early designer of the scorecard assumed that run outs only happened through the idiocy of the batsmen, and the less said about that the better.

Could you not persuade your Cricket Correspondent to take the lead in remedying this defect?

The convention, 'RO Parker: Gould'', or "RO Parker' if he did it unassisted, would convey over a season lots more information at the cost of little extra space.

And while he is about it, he should right the wrong hitherto inflicted on the substitute fielder. 'Ct sub' is unworthy. Your Football Correspondent does not treat Mr Fairclough, of Liverpool, that way. 'Ct *Smith' would do it.

Yours etc,

MIKE FABER

Many statisticians do record these details but not the agencies responsible for transmitting scores to newspapers.

THE LAW AS TO A 'NO-BALL'

From Mr B. J. T. Bosanquet and others, 29 April 1911

Including one current county captain – Douglas (Essex and England, 1901–28; Olympic middleweight boxing champion); two former county captains – Lucas (Surrey and Essex, also played for Cambridge University and England, 1874–1907), Foster (Worcestershire, also played for Oxford University, 1894–1925); a former MCC President (Green, 1905); and four county players – Mordaunt (Hampshire, Middlesex and Kent, 1886–97), Roller (Surrey, 1881–90), Rutty (Surrey, 1910) and Weigall (Cambridge University and Kent, 1891–1903).

Sir, At the forthcoming general meeting of the MCC it is proposed to alter the law regarding 'no-balls' in such a way that two runs shall be added to the score, and that the 'no-ball' shall be 'dead' on its being called – in other words, that there shall be no more scoring off no-balls. This is the result of the *impasse* created last year by certain umpires' decisions, under which a batsman was given 'run out' when in playing at a 'no-ball' he had gone out of his ground – in other words, he was given 'run out' when, if 'no-ball' had not been called, he would have been given out 'stumped'.

Whatever is to be said in favour or otherwise of such decisions, it is too late to enter upon the discussion now, but the fact remains that under the new proposals a very drastic alteration is to be made in the conduct and playing of the game, and we feel that this old-established and unique feature of cricket should not be abolished.

The cricketers of all grades to whom we have mentioned the matter unanimously condemn this suggested change in the laws of cricket. While a few agree with the aforesaid decisions, a very large majority are equally emphatic that they were wrong and deserving at least of censure. Nearly all, however, confessed that they were unaware of what was proposed, and so we hope to be allowed through your columns to appeal to cricketers who may be similarly ignorant of the change in the spirit of the game that may be imminent to do what they can to retain a popular feature of the game.

Notice of an amendment has been given by Mr A. P. Lucas to the effect that the laws affecting 'no-balls' shall remain as before with the additional words added to Law 16, 'He shall not be given out "run out" under any circumstances under which – had the ball not been a "no-ball" – he would have been given out "stumped" under Law 23,' and, consequently, the necessary alteration in Law 23 (the 'run out' law) to refer back to this.

In this way a solution of the difficulty is provided, and it is the one which the majority of cricketers with whom we have come into contact feel is the only reasonable one.

There must necessarily be some sentiment in the matter; all cricketers now playing have learned the game under the laws that admit of scoring off 'no-balls' with almost complete immunity of dismissal, and they naturally do not like to see this sporting feature abolished; it is popular alike with players and spectators; it is peculiar to the game, and for that reason alone worthy of retention.

Accordingly we hope that all members of the MCC who are interested in maintaining the old traditions and spirit of the game will find it possible to support Mr A. P. Lucas's amendment at Lord's on 3 May at 6 p.m.

We are, Sir, your obedient servants,
B. J. T. BOSANQUET, J. W. H. T. DOUGLAS,
H. K. FOSTER, C. E. GREEN, A. P. LUCAS,
E. C. MORDAUNT, W. E. ROLLER,
A. W. F. RUTTY, G. J. V. WEIGALL

The amendment was never put because the proposals to alter the law were withdrawn. Instead umpires were reminded that, by the traditions of the game, a batsman could not be stumped off a no-ball.

'GARDENING' THE PITCH

From the Hon. R. H. Lyttelton, 14 August 1924

Sixth of the eight brothers. Respected student and critic of the game and a leading advocate of reform of the lbw law. Regular contributor to *The Times* and an auditor of MCC.

Sir, I have just read your report of the first day's play in the Middlesex and Surrey match at the Oval. In this I find it stated that on a perfect Oval wicket one ball of Peach's startled everybody by getting up straight, with the result that Lee, the batsman, forthwith began the usual hammering or 'gardening' the pitch. Your reporter rightly remarks that something may be said for the view that the bowler who can create a spot may justly claim to use it if he can.

The laws of cricket lay down certain rules as to when the pitch is to be rolled, but 'gardening' the pitch is allowed, and in the Surrey and Notts match I noticed that Hobbs and Sandham beat the wicket down continually, sometimes two or three times an over, not only wasting time, but taking away any advantage an accurate bowler may get by making a spot.

I have long been of the opinion that the rule should be changed and 'gardening' the pitch disallowed. The rule was made when wickets were nothing like so good and run-getting comparatively small; now there are more runs got even on soft wickets which are to the advantage of the bowler than were 40 years ago on fast batsmen's wickets. This 'gardening' of the pitch prevails so much now that the wicket practically gets what amounts to a double rolling, and such a thing was never contemplated by those who drew up the rule.

Of course, this practice of 'gardening' is entirely against the unhappy bowlers; everything is in these days, and if it were disallowed it might be possible that some balls might get up or hang or even keep low and thereby bring out the skill of batsmen and reduce the run-getting, and surely this would be in the best interests of the game.

I am yours obediently,
ROBERT H. LYTTELTON

FOUR STUMPS OR FOUR DAYS?

From Mr H. G. Hutchinson, 21 July 1926

Sir, Why do our cricket authorities talk so much and do so little? They talk, and they write, about the broader or the higher wicket, the narrower bat and the smaller ball, but why do we not see them going to the nets and putting their ideas in practice and trying how they 'work'? And there is yet another alternative which I have not yet seen mentioned – shortening the pitch. Why not 21 yards, or 20? There is nothing sacred about the number 22. I am told: 'It would be horrible for the batsman against fast bowling.' I reply: 'That is just what we want, to make things more horrible for the batsman.' Moreover, the fastest bowling at 20 yards on the wickets of today would be less 'horrible' than the fastest bowling of 50 years ago on the wickets of that day.

Yours, &c.,
HORACE G. HUTCHINSON

See Don Fair's letter on page 26.

From Mr Albert Gray, 22 July 1926

Sir, Of the possible reforms mentioned by 'Free Forester' in your paper of today, the one which seems most acceptable is the widening of the wicket. The two stumps of early days have given place to three: the advance to four would be merely evolution. On the other hand, the reduction of the bat in width or of the ball in size would be revolution: the craft of the batsman and bowler respectively would have to be relearned. The cricket season is short and an extension to four days of first-class matches only would curtail the number of games possible at grounds such as Lord's and the Oval, and be tedious to onlookers.

If the MCC could arrange a test match with good teams and four stumps, during August, it would be of much interest to cricketers, and also productive of a good gate.

Yours, &c.,
ALBERT GRAY

'FOOR STUMPS OR FOOR DAYS?'

From Mr F. Cartwright, 11 August 1926

Sir, Down 'ere we be 'mazed along o' they writer chaps an' the goin's on o' they Testës. Laws be laws, an' rools be rools, an' they as makes 'em should keep 'em. Paarson – they sez as 'ow the rev'rend gentleman played fer the Blues afore 'e was so 'igh – tell'd us: 'Once they arm-chair crickets gets yer into the papers, yer 'ave to be'ave yerself 'cardin'lye. That be the crucks of the matter.' I never learned French lingo, but we agrees along of 'im. So do Joe Rummery, as 'as umpir'd fer us nigh fitty yers.

Laast Saturday we at Firlin' played a side from Lunnon – furrin-ers, they be – an' we 'ad two goes apiece, though I knaws we only played from foor till eight, cuz Farmer Beckley said Eb an' me must finish that ten-acre field first. I was out twice leg-afore, an' it bain't no use sayin' 'wot fer', cuz Joe wunt be druv. 'If it 'its yer leg, yer goes out, sartin sure,' sez Joe, who knaws the rools. Joe 'as the same coppers to count over-balls as when he started, with picturs o' the Good Queen on 'em.

We thinks as 'ow they chaps at Lunnon be narvous, else 'ow should they be allus callin' fer tay as soon as they be done dinner? An' these paper chaps makes 'em wuss, a-tellin' us wot it be about, pilin' up pettigues (Paarson sez 'worries'), till they batters wunt knaw whether they should be ther at all, or som'eres else.

Firlin's played 'ere 'unnerds o' yers, long afore that ther Mary Bone lady started 'er pitch at Lards in Lunnon, though we likes 'er, an' 'opes she'll keep purty blithesome an' not fergit that we be cricketers too. We ain't wantin' foor stumps, as we finds three a plenty, an' we ain't thinkin' that they pros an' such like 'ave read the rools. If they did as Paarson sez his Irish friend did – when yer sees a 'ead, 'it it – ther wouldn't be no cause fer this gurt talk o' foor days.

I am, &c.,

F. CARTWRIGHT

CRICKET REFORM

From Mr J. W. Trumble, 16 October 1926

Victoria and Australia (1883–93). Solicitor. Elder brother of Hugh Trumble, the noted Australian bowler.

Sir, May I, before returning to Australia, avail myself of the medium of your paper to supplement my remarks in my previous letter [30 July] on the subject of cricket reform? I would like also to say that I am pleased to learn, on the announcement of Lord Harris, that the Advisory Committee of the MCC is now giving attention to this matter. There is no doubt that the conditions in which the game is now played unduly favour the batsman as against the bowler, and as a consequence rob the game to a great extent of that attractiveness which was formerly its great charm. Only those of us who had experience of first-class cricket some 40 or 50 years ago and have since kept in touch with the game can fully appreciate this. We know that the groundsman now holds sway over the game, and that he has been encouraged by cricket committees in recent years, largely for financial reasons, to secure a wicket which, mainly by the introduction of binding soils and the use of the heavy roller, is little short of the condition of concrete.

As regards the composition of turf, I may here say that it is possible for the soil expert to produce almost any class of turf, and as indicative of this it may be of interest if I say something of the MCC (Australia) wicket, and its preparation for Test match play. A short time ago the groundsman, at my request, broke open the ground at the wicket, and went down to a depth of over one foot, and, as I suspected from its non-draining condition, I found the soil all the way down similar to what it was at the surface. This represented an accumulation of the heavy black clay top dressing which had been put on yearly over a period of some 40 years. In preparing our wicket, after nursing it for some time, the groundsman, for about 12 days before play, proceeds with its more immediate preparation. He then floods the area, and, when the flooding gradually soaks in, leaving the surface of the consistency of putty, he knows he has the required moisture content to carry the wicket through the period of play, however long that may be. The surface is then worked up daily by the heavy roller, until at last it becomes of the hardness of a marble slab. After the cutter has done its work, an expert scythe-man takes off most of what remains of the grass, and the heavy roller then grinds out the substance of what is left. The final rolling puts a polished face on the wicket, preventing the spin ball from getting a grip of the ground, and the surface of the wicket assumes a coconut matting appearance.

Can one picture a more absurd representation of a turf wicket than this? It might be just as sensible to cut out all this toil of preparation and put down a permanent concrete bed. In the matter of spin on this class of wicket I might instance the bowling of Howell, one of the greatest of Australian medium-pace spin bowlers. The condition of the wicket often beat him in the early stages of a game, but so accurate was his bowling that in time he wore off a patch of the polished face and then succeeded in getting on terms with the batsmen. I question, however, whether on the wickets as now prepared it would be possible for a medium-pace bowler to get in on our wickets as Howell did even at a later stage of play.

This all goes to show to what lengths groundsmen can get in the preparation of present-day wickets. The position in Australia is rapidly becoming farcical, and should have immediate attention. You are interested in this country because you are concerned in Test cricket over there. The first move, however, should be made here. I have given to Sir John Russell, Director of Rothamsted Experimental Station, samples of the Melbourne and Adelaide wickets. He was much surprised at their appearance, and a member of his staff suggested that they resembled a substance with commercial possibilities unearthed in Scotland from which oil was extracted.

It is contended that the ball now used is to a large extent responsible for the non-success of our bowlers. While admitting that bowlers are to some extent handicapped by this ball, I cannot agree that the return to the smaller ball will improve matters very much. The wicket will still beat the bowler. One has only to bring to mind the great medium-pace bowlers of the past, and look for their class now, to realize the change, gradual though it has been, that has come over the game.

Assuredly the secret of what is wrong with cricket lies in the wicket. Let us discard the binding soils and the heavy roller and get back to the old-time natural springy turf, and with batsman and bowler on equal terms matches will end in a reasonable time, and, instead of being tests of patience and endurance, they will bring out those qualities of initiative and resource and the ability to rise superior to surroundings which so characterized the play of many of our great cricketers of the past.

Yours, &c.,
J. W. TRUMBLE

ARE LEG-BYES CRICKET?

From Mr J. C. Binns, 26 August 1972

Sir, The cricket season now drawing to a close, would not this be a good time to finish the stupidity of the leg-bye? Why should a batsman who has made an abortive stroke, because the ball strikes his pads and runs off in odd directions, be allowed to credit runs for his side?

It is unfair to the bowler, who has beaten the bat, and in many cases must have been close to lbw, to see his side so suffer. It is unfair to the wicketkeeper, who may have gallantly and athletically covered all variable balls that have passed the bat, but is frustrated at seeing them deflected from ponderous pads. Even worse, the leg-byes are given when, after playing some feeble effort, the ball bounces forward from the batsman's pad into an empty space and a run is given as a leg-bye.

If there were any justice in this matter, the batting side should be fined a run for every time the ball hits the pads, but failing this let this idiocy be abolished.

Yours truly,
J. C. BINNS

THE LAW OF LEG BEFORE WICKET

The thorniest of all the game's laws. In the 1774 code the batsman was out if he 'puts his leg before the wicket with a design to stop the ball from hitting the wicket'. In 1788 the ball was to be pitched in a straight line to the wicket and the words 'with a design' were omitted. When batsmen began to use their pads as a second line of defence after the bat, the cry grew for reform.

From Sir Charles Oakeley, Bt, 9 April 1901
President of Kent CCC 1876.

Sir, With reference to your remarks on the proposed alteration in the lbw rule, will you allow me to point out that the present rule was itself an alteration from the old law in force for many years, by the introduction of the words 'from it', the effect of which was to make it fair only for the bowler delivering over the wicket? I brought this matter before the general meeting of the MCC so long ago as 1880, Mr William Nicholson being in the chair, arguing how unfair the rule was to a bowler delivering round the wicket, but could not persuade the committee to take action with regard to it. Mr R. A. Mitchell was also unsuccessful in 1884 in endeavouring to get an alteration adopted. The reason of the question being now again forced to the front is no doubt owing to the general consensus of opinion that something must be done to endeavour to diminish the enormous scoring and the number of drawn matches in consequence, which are so ruining the best interests of the game. The proposed alteration in law 24 would have the effect of doing this by giving the leg-break and off-break bowler a chance, and by doing away with the objectionable practice of a batsman being able to defend his wicket with his legs. It would remain quite open to him to place himself in front of his wicket if he thought that the best position for any particular stroke, but if in that position he misses hitting the ball with his bat and his leg prevents it taking the wicket he would be, as he undoubtedly ought to be, out.

Yours faithfully,
CHARLES W. A. OAKELEY

There was strong lobbying from either side throughout April.

From Dr W. G. Grace, 1 May 1901
Gloucestershire, London County and England (1865–1908), each of which he captained. The most famous cricketer of all. His figures – the authorized *Wisden* version – speak for themselves: 54 896 runs and 2876 wickets.

Sir, In yesterday's *Sportsman* Mr C. C. Clarke quoted a paragraph from an article I wrote last February, although it was only published a few days ago. I then said:

'The great evil to be remedied, if possible, is the present large number of drawn matches . . . The changed (lbw) rule would assist the bowler, and so would tend to shorten matches, which would be a great gain; but I do not know that it would improve the game in any other way.'

I was thinking mainly of first-class cricket, and had not realized how unpopular the suggested alteration is among first-class cricketers.

It seems necessary to give my present views.

First, the alteration of the lbw rule would do good to first-class cricket where you have the best umpires; it would lessen the number of drawn matches.

Secondly, in ordinary club and league cricket it would do more harm than good, as local umpires so often give doubtful points in favour of their own side.

Thirdly, may I be allowed to utter a warning? Nearly all first-class cricketers, led by the county captains, are strongly opposed to the change, so strongly, I fear, that the authority of the MCC might be in danger if its members altered the existing law. Surely it would be unwise to make any change, however advisable in itself, if it is against the wishes of a majority of present-day players.

W. G. GRACE

A much longer letter, in the same vein, was published on the same day. The signatories were Lord Hawke (captain and President of Yorkshire) and the captains and/or vice-captains of Essex, Kent, Middlesex and Surrey. The lines were drawn. The reformers won the vote but not the two-thirds majority required to have the law changed. *Wisden* devoted a dozen pages to report the meeting in full.

An experiment with the proposed amendment by the minor counties in 1902 came to nothing and the debate rumbled on . . .

From the Hon. R. H. Lyttelton, 13 June 1923

Sir, The remarks of your Cricket Correspondent in your issue of yesterday on the legs as a second line of defence deserve careful reading and consideration. They repeat what I have contended and pleaded for, for more than twenty years. That the legs are a second line of defence has been acted upon ever since the late Arthur Shrewsbury started it forty years ago, and it was the blot on his otherwise unblemished record. But this pernicious practice has now in a sense received official sanction in the last issue of the *Badminton Library*, on which Mr Pardon rightly comments in the current number of *Wisden's Almanack* in these words:

'One can at least go on protesting against the pestilent doctrine laid down in the new *Badminton* that a batsman, in playing a ball that pitches outside the wicket is entitled to regard two well-padded legs as a second line of defence. Surely nothing could be more flagrantly opposed to the true spirit of cricket.'

Not only does this horrible method of play still go on, as go on it must if coaches are told by the *Badminton Library* to teach their pupils to bat on those principles, but we find your Special Correspondent at Oxford describe the stopping by Mr Jardine of a terrible break-back from Captain Hyndson with his pads as a 'wonderfully good stroke of its kind'.

We hear on all sides complaints about the weakness of the bowling. In former days, to use the legs as a second line of defence was unheard of and would have been regarded as unsportsmanlike. Now, not only does the unfortunate bowler find this detestable practice almost universal, but the wickets get easier every year. No wonder the bowlers are discouraged, but it is not their fault.

ROBERT H. LYTTELTON

and on . . .

From Lord Darling, KC, 28 August 1928

Conservative MP for Deptford 1888–97. Judge in King's Bench Division 1897–1923; Deputy Lord Chief Justice for a period in the Fist World War. Literary wit and versifier (commemorated in *The Times* the deaths of Marshal Foch, Lord Balfour, Lord Birkenhead and others) and writer of letters to *The Times*.

Sir, I make no pretence to a deep knowledge of cricket, yet I have read with much interest the letters of Mr Robert Lyttelton, and your other correspondents, on the best remedy for a prevalent vice in the playing of that manly game.

As I understand, a habit has grown up among batsmen of defending the wicket by intercepting the ball with their legs, rather than with the bat ostensibly designed and provided for that purpose. And I gather that this practice is completely condemned as are some other grave, but hardly criminal, offences – when it is declared that 'it is not cricket'. Moreover, Sir, it would seem that resort to these tactics is more common, and certainly is then more reprehensible, in matches which crowds have paid to see than at those gratuitous exhibitions of rustic prowess which still enliven many of our village greens.

Now, Sir, it sometimes happens that a discovery of value is made by one untrained in the *métier* to which it relates, though not altogether without experience in some other. Thus did Columbus – though not a juggler by profession – prove, at the first attempt, how an ordinary egg may be made to stand firmly on its small end. So, may I be permitted to seek the opinion of Mr Lyttelton, and of others similarly expert, on this my own simple proposal? Wherever at present an umpire, applying the lbw rule, would declare a batsman to be 'out', let him instead order the offender to remove the defensive armour – which at present protects his legs and muffles his conscience – and in that condition to continue to affront the bowling.

Should this my humble suggestion be thought to owe something to the methods used by our chivalric ancestors for punishing any such persons as were suspected of offending against the moral or social code of their day, I still venture to think that it may be none the less worthy of consideration, and possibly of adoption.

I remain, Sir, your obedient servant,

DARLING

and on . . .

From Mr F. G. J. Ford, 25 January 1933

Cambridge University, Middlesex and England (1886–99). Youngest of seven cricketing brothers, he still holds the record for the fastest hundred at Lord's – 55 minutes in 1897. In the 1930s he outdid even Lyttelton with his campaigning through *The Times* for the amending of the lbw law.

Sir, In dealing with the trouble in Australia over this body-line bowling, with its leg-trap attachment, your leading article of the 19th inst, as well as your correspondent Mr T. Faint the day before, has touched the spot – but has not rubbed it in. May I give it a rub? Right at the back of this pother is this leg-play, the *fons et origo mali* whence it has developed, the curse of modern cricket, this canker which has eaten into the very soul of the game and cast a slur upon the moral value of the very word 'cricket'. It is idle, perhaps, now to reflect upon the mishandling of the whole business by the MCC of 40 years ago, when the abuse might have been wiped out by a strong hand at the start. But it is this leg-play which has driven bowlers of all kinds and paces from the off- to the on-side of the wicket, exploiting their clever methods and varieties of pace, swerve, googly, and spin to get rid of the modern batsman as he stands in front of his wicket with his two-eyed stance, behind his mammoth pads, his bat dangled in front for the ball to bump up against, with a snick or a glide or occasional hook as his main method of scoring a run – a boring and distressing sight for cricketers of the 'Roaring

Nineties'. An hour with Tennyson or Crawley, Woolley or Hendren is a great compensation, however.

If the lbw rule were altered in the only sensible way – *i.e.*, applied to the off-side alone – that is the point which Bob Lyttelton missed in his otherwise finely reasoned volume on the subject – the bowling would recover itself from the leg-side to the off-side of the wicket, break-back bowlers would reap their just reward, batsmen would be compelled to take all their scoring chances and play off-side strokes. We might then look forward to the recovery of much of the lost brilliance of the game, together with a proper balance of off- and on-side strokes with bowling of both types in operation. Cricket would sparkle again!

Not that this suggests a remedy for the present crisis. But the crisis might well never have arisen but for this development of pad-play, with its consequent on-side play, nor would the game have become so lopsided and boring to watch.

Yours faithfully,

F. G. J. FORD

Finally came an experiment with the 'Ford amendment' in 1935.

VILLAGE MATCHES AND THE LBW LAW

From Mr Aidan Crawley, 8 August 1935

Sir, While disagreeing with almost all Mr F. G. J. Ford's criticisms of modern cricket there are three points in his letter in your issue of last Tuesday which stand out in particular.

The first is his hope that the MCC will extend the new lbw rule, or a more drastic version of it, to village cricket. I do not know if Mr Ford plays village cricket. If he does he must either be very lucky, or (of which, of course, he is perfectly capable) very brilliant. But as one who plays it pretty regularly may I tell him that the only lbw rule I know is that never, under any circumstances, anywhere, should the batsman allow the ball to hit his body, and that if he does he must expect to be given 'out'? If Mr Ford can improve on that rule he will have at least one new disciple. But otherwise will he not continue to allow us the occasional joy of being given – quite unexpectedly – 'in'?

Mr Ford's other two points are in relation to bowling. If I read him right he deplores the googly and the swerve. As a batsman I hated the googly. (Now, alas, I never meet one.) But I have never been in any doubt that to try to play R. W. V. Robins or Freeman or F. R. Brown on their day was the most thrilling experience in cricket. To judge from the applause earned by X. L. Balaskas in the Test match at Lord's, and that which still greets 'Tich' Freeman on any ground in Kent, the public is of much the same opinion. Lastly, does swerve really impair a bowler's length? Did not F. R. Foster swerve? Have Tate, Larwood, Root (to name an extreme instance), McDonald, O'Reilly, and now Bowes, all been inaccurate bowlers?

As a batsman I am all in favour of handicapping the bowler. Short of the ideal, which would be to take a leaf from the book of 'rounders' and simply order him where to pitch, Mr Ford's half-confessed desire for nothing but orthodox spin-bowlers (with, perhaps, fast bowlers who concentrate only on the middle and off-stumps) would suit very well. But would it improve cricket? There is no doubt that when cavalry rode horses and charged with lances war was a much more picturesque spectacle than it would be today. But is there any doubt, if they came up against the Tank Corps, which would win? Is it not possible that cricket is subject to the same law of progress?

Yours, &c.,

A. M. CRAWLEY

It continued in 1936.

LBW DECISIONS

From Mr H. D. Watson, CIE, CBE, 22 August 1936
Oxford University (1891).

Sir, May an old-fashioned cricketer ask if nothing can be done to stem the flood of 'lbws' which nowadays worries the umpires and disfigures the score-books? Formerly, as a famous player has re-minded me, it used to be considered something of a disgrace to be out in this manner. I doubt if W. G. Grace or F. S. Jackson or A. C. MacLaren throughout the whole of their careers in first-class cricket totalled more 'lbws' than any one of our leading batsmen does today in a single season. And the boys are following the bad example of their elders. I read recently of a public school match in which, I think, there were 12 leg-before-wicket decisions. And I myself witnessed another such match in which no fewer than six boys got out in this way in a single innings.

Such deplorable results cannot all be ascribed to the new leg-before-wicket rule or to the increase of 'swerve' bowling. There is surely something wrong both with precept and practice. I have my own views on the subject, but your readers might be grateful for those of greater experts than myself.

Yours faithfully,
H. D. WATSON

In 1937 it became law. By the 1980 code a batsman is also out if he has made no attempt to play a ball which would have hit the wicket even though it is intercepted outside the line of the off stump.

11
HOW'S THAT?
SOME
CRICKETING
CURIOSITIES

THE FIRST 'CRICKET'

From the Revd C. H. D. Grimes, 7 March 1928

In a document of Edward II, dated 24 April, 1308, confirming certain grants made to the Abbey of Grestain, among the benefactors occurs Sarah, the wife of William Cricket. I wonder whether this is not the earliest recorded use of the word cricket.

C. H. D. GRIMES

The (disputed) earliest reference to cricket, in the Wardrobe accounts of Edward I for 1300, mentions expenditure for Prince Edward to play at 'creag' and other games with his friends.

CRICKET REMINISCENCES

From Mr H. C. Troughton, 18 August 1919

Sir, May I say that I saw George Anderson's famous drive for eight. It was made on Monday, 4 August, 1862, and was, of course, a stupendous hit, but it ought not to have realized eight runs, and would not have done so had not the fieldsman thrown the ball into the middle of my back.

I am, Sir, your obedient servant,
HERBERT C. TROUGHTON

Anderson was playing for North of England against Surrey.

210

CRICKET ON THE ICE

From Mr C. E. Boucher, 8 March 1929

Sir, May I add a reminiscence concerning the winter of 1878–79? At the close of the Term, when many had already gone down, in December, 1878, an attempt was successfully made to arrange a three days' cricket match, Town v. Gown, on the ice of the flooded Grantchester meadows. The veterans Hayward and Carpenter played for the Town, and Charles Pigg, the subject of a memorial notice in *The Times* today, headed 'A Beloved Figure in Cambridge', captained the Gown team. We had a large field of perfect ice kept for us. Scoring was heavy and the game was drawn, though we led easily on the first innings. Fielding was delightful, and the chase of the ball into 'space' when it eluded you most exhilarating. Bowling was our weak point; we could only try lobs, and the umpires were severe on 'no-balls'. The Town took first innings, and Pigg put us all on in succession for two overs apiece to see what we could do. I still recall my delight when I sent up a full toss to Hayward, who, seeing visions of the ball travelling half a mile, over-balanced himself with the effort, with fatal result to his wicket. The *Sportsman* at the time gave some account of the match.

Yours faithfully,
C. E. BOUCHER

The winter of 1878–79 lasted from October until May, although a brief thaw in February put an end to cricket on the ice. *Wisden* records a dozen such matches, including one by moonlight in Windsor Home Park and this one in Cambridge. In 1983 *The Times* recorded cricket on ice in China – and an England XI playing in the desert.

COVER POINT

Because of extreme cold the umpires took the Cambridge University and Essex players off the field at Fenner's.

From Mr J. F. Bailey, 29 April 1981

Sir, Really what are our cricketers coming to – leaving the field just because it is a little cold? (report 25 April). It would not have done for Fred Lillywhite's England team who, in 1859, shrugged off the intervention of a snow storm to go on and beat a whole 22 of the United States and Canada at Rochester, NY, despite having to wear great coats, mufflers and gloves to do so.

No wonder we cannot beat the West Indies when moral fibre is so lacking!

I remain, Sir, disappointedly,

J. F. BAILEY

AVOIDING THE 'MONSOON SEASON'

From the Information Officer, Manchester Corporation, 13 July 1953

Sir, The papers this morning are full of woeful groans about the interruption of the third Test match at Manchester by rain, and some papers have even gone so far as to headline their Test report: 'Why give Manchester a Test in future?' Of course, the idea of omitting Manchester from the Test series will not be taken seriously, but the suggestion that Manchester is an unusually wet city is wholly incorrect.

Manchester does not, perhaps, get as much sunshine as some holiday resorts, but the annual rainfall is less than 30in. – about two-thirds that of many south of England and Welsh coast holiday resorts. The truth of the matter is that Manchester, like India, has a 'monsoon season' in July and August, when the rainfall is sometimes more than double that of other months. The statistics supplied by the Air Ministry meteorological station at Ringway Airport will illustrate my point.

Average rainfall for 10 years, 1942–1951

April	52.1 millimetres
May	66.5 millimetres
June	57 millimetres
July	72.2 millimetres
August	83.8 millimetres
September	68.7 millimetres

Rainfall for the months of June and July, 1949–1952

	June millimetres	July millimetres
1949	23.8	64
1950	64.7	60.9
1951	21.8	82.9
1952	58.2	83.9
1953	60.1	–

The obvious answer is to change the Manchester Test to the month of June, and to put it at the time of the Wimbledon fortnight. This would mean that the second Test would be played in Manchester instead of the third. There is no reason why this change should not be made (except that July and August are probably just as wet in other places) and it would, at least, dispose of the outworn legend that it always rains in Manchester.

Yours truly,
TERENCE F. USHER

OBSTRUCTING THE FIELD

From Mr A. A. Milne, 23 August 1928
A member of the Westminster School XI in 1899 and 1900 with a modest record: 294 runs (average 10.50), highest score 44, and 28 wickets (23.11).

Sir, I must make my contribution to cricket history; the only one I am likely to make. In 1899 I was playing for Westminster v. Charterhouse, the match of the year. Somehow or other the batsman at the other end managed to get out before I did, and the next man came in, all a-tremble with nervousness. He hit his first ball straight up in the air, and called wildly for a run. We all ran – he, I, and the bowler. My partner got underneath the ball first, and in a spasm of excitement jumped up and hit it again as hard as he could. There was no appeal. He burst into tears, so to speak, and hurried back to the pavilion. Whether he would have run away to sea the next day, or gone to Africa and shot big game, we shall never know, for luckily he restored his self-respect a few hours later by bowling Charterhouse out and winning the match for us. But here, for your Cricket Correspondent, is a genuine case of 'Out, obstructing the field.'

Yours, &c.,
A. A. MILNE

The errant batsman was one H. Plaskitt, who won a lawn tennis Blue at Oxford. He must have been practising his smash.

AN UNFORTUNATE EXPERIENCE

From Mr Edward Grayson, 8 June 1953
Barrister and authority on sport and the law.

Sir, The suggestion in your leading article, 'that the bat is provided to hit the ball with and that to miss with it lays you open to all the consequences', may be illustrated by an unfortunate experience to be found in the Badminton *Cricket*, edited in 1920 by Sir Pelham (then P. F.) Warner. For Mr E. R. Wilson tells us at page 95: 'A lob bowler sometimes uses a high dropping full pitch. Mr Simpson-Hayward once dropped this ball on Marshal's head at Worcester, and had him lbw, but it is very hard to bowl it accurately.' No doubt Mr Marshal concurred with this judgment; yet was lbw the correct decision?

Yours, &c.,
EDWARD GRAYSON

No doubt; but Marshal had scored 176.

A CRICKET INCIDENT

From Captain Lord Cornwallis, KCVO, KBE, MC, 29 June 1953
Kent (1919–26), three seasons as captain. Aide-de-camp to Field Marshal Lord Haig in First World War. Lord Lieutenant of Kent 1944–72. President of Kent CCC and MCC committee member, President (1948), Trustee and Life Vice-President.

Sir, I wonder if I am in the unique position of having 'caught and bowled' the batsman off his nose. The incident occurred in a county championship match between Kent and Lancashire at Maidstone. I was bowling to Dick Tyldesley, and he endeavoured to sweep a straight half-volley to leg. The ball struck the top edge of his bat, flew up, struck him on the nose, and came back a high catch to me at the bowler's end. I remember, as the unfortunate batsman collapsed in a pool of blood, the wicket-keeper shouting 'catch it, he's out'. After he had been carried from the field, his cousin James Tyldesley took his place at the crease. Perhaps unnerved by taking his guard in his relative's blood, he also 'took first ball'. I was always a little disappointed that the next Lancastrian prevented my obtaining a hat-trick.

CORNWALLIS

'Took first ball' must be treated with caution, for *Wisden* records that James Tyldesley scored 13.

A TIE WITH THE LAST BALL

From Mr J. A. Hart, 29 July 1932

Sir, In 1924 I was playing for West Harrow v. Wealdstone Wesleyans; and West Harrow, batting first, were all out for 84. On Wealdstone Wesleyans batting, they had 84 on the board for eight wickets. It was my turn with the ball, and I managed to take the last two wickets in that over without addition to the score. Thus the match ended in a tie.

The following season the same two teams met on the same ground. Again West Harrow batted first, and we were all out for 174. Wealdstone Wesleyans then scored 174 for eight wickets. Again it was my turn to bowl, and again I took the last two wickets in that over without addition to the score. Thus that match also ended in a tie, and I think it more than a million to one against the same sequence of events happening again.

Yours faithfully,

J. A. HART

FORCEFUL BATTING

From Mr H. C. Broadrick, 9 August 1949

Sir, The writer of your amusing article on 'Forceful Batting' maintains that no side can hope to better the performance of the Stratford Police eleven. [A 'posse' of eight constables and one cadet, led by an inspector and a sergeant, failed to trouble the scorers.] I can claim, however, that the opponents of a school with which I was connected for many years at Harrow succeeded in making what might be described as a 'minus quantity'. Our opponents, a large South Kensington preparatory school, were dismissed for four runs, and when we went in to bat their opening bowler proceeded to bowl three wides and two no-balls. Thus we won the match without touching the ball with the bat. This, I think, should remain a positive record for many years to come.

Yours faithfully,

H. C. BROADRICK

'Forceful Batting' was written by A. P. (Patrick) Ryan, an assistant editor of *The Times* and one of Sir John Squire's 'Invalids'.

215

FAMILY COUNTY CRICKET

From Major V. F. Ealand, 24 January 1945

Sir, The instance, quoted by Mr H. D. G. Leveson-Gower in your issue of 19 January, of Richard Daft and his son playing together for Notts is uncommon but by no means unique. In and around 1923 W. G. Quaife and his son, B. W., played together in several matches for Warwickshire, and W. Bestwick and his son R. were occasionally together in the Derbyshire team.

At Derby on 3 and 5 June, 1922, the two Bestwicks were opposed by the two Quaifes, and at one period of the match, while the Quaifes were batting, the two Bestwicks were bowling, *Wisden* says this: 'For father and son to be batting against bowlers similarly related was a remarkable incident – regarded as unique in county cricket.'

I am, Sir, your obedient servant,
V. F. EALAND

At the time of the match the Bestwicks were aged 56 and 22, the Quaifes 50 and 22.

CRICKET CURIOSITIES

From C. T., 9 September 1919

Sir, I note in your issue of yesterday a letter from Mr H. J. Ayliffe asking for an authenticated instance of a cricket curiosity ['the prostration of the leg and off stump while the middle one is left standing'].

I feel sure that the following incidents of which I was a witness will interest him. A fast ball delivered round the wicket just grazed the leg-stump with the result that the middle stump alone was left standing with the leg-bail poised on the top of it. The explanation is not difficult. It was clear that both outside stumps were standing very loose; the graze was sufficient to dislodge the leg-stump, jerk the bail across the wicket, and remove the off-stump and bail. It would be a performance difficult to repeat and sounds a tall story. All I can say is that I saw it happen.

Another incident is worth repeating. The middle stump was bowled down, leaving the bails *in situ*. Here, again, the explanation is not too difficult. As most of us know, a pair of bails is often sold as one piece. In this case they had been roughly broken apart, leaving jagged ends sufficient to hold them in poise. I was called upon to decide whether the batsman was out or not, and I had no difficulty in doing so. It seemed to me that if he lost his middle stump he deserved his fate.

I am, Sir, yours obediently,

C.T.

From Major H. C. Dent, 12 September 1919

Sir, The undersigned was on tour through Essex in 1888, playing for Charlton Park CC. In the match against Felsted Long Vacation CC a fast ball was put down to me in the course of the game, which I seemed to lose sight of, but was fortunate enough to put through the slips for two. A dead swallow with broken beak was then found midway down the pitch; the bird had evidently flown head on into the ball. The incident was not noticed by the umpire, and I remember there was a lively discussion in the pavilion after the match as to whether I should have been given out had I been caught or bowled, as, although 'No ball' had not been called, the flight of the ball had obviously been obstructed.

The bird was sent to a taxidermist, and was exhibited in the *Field* office for some little time, and subsequently was on view in the Charlton Park clubhouse for many years. I have known of rabbits and birds killed by golf balls in their flight, but imagine the incident I have recorded quite singular as a 'cricket curiosity'.

I am, Sir, yours faithfully,

HERBERT C. DENT

SPARROWS AT LORD'S

From Mr E. F. Davidson, 7 September 1926

I saw the 1902 incident recalled by Mr F. Mitchell [who was batting at Lord's for MCC against the Australians when Ernest Jones, fielding at mid-off, flicked the ball at a sparrow]. Its amusing side was that the man who went to put the injured sparrow out of its misery was Craig, the 'Surrey poet', who used to sell verses composed by himself in honour of Surrey and other cricketers, and was a very familiar figure, especially at the Oval, in those days. His powers of repartee were great, and very few spectators who tried to chaff him had the better of the argument. Great, therefore, was the delight of the crowd when the sparrow, just as Craig reached it on his errand of mercy, flew away and left him for once at a loss.

E. F. DAVIDSON

'CAUGHT FISH'

From Mr R. Townshend Stephens, 12 July 1934

Sir, Mr Thornton Berry's anecdote [of a half-pound grayling killed by a six-hit] reminds me of a strange incident in far Sohar, where we were wont to peg down a mat on the sea shore and play cricket as an antidote for nostalgia.

The last wicket stand on a memorable afternoon was troublesome indeed, for the temperature was 110 deg., maybe more; and umpiring I found less pleasant than sitting near a well under some palms.

At last a ball was hit for six into the sea; but it fell not into the sea, for it was swallowed by a shark.

I thought of the blessed shade under the palms, and gave the man 'out'.

'c. Fish, b. Birkat Ullah' was duly entered in the score book by a soldier clerk.

I am, Sir, your obedient servant,
R. TOWNSHEND STEPHENS

ARE THE STEELE LAMB CHOPS BENEFITS IN KIND?

From Mr Eric Hall, 15 June 1976

Sir, The admirable David Steele is deservedly to receive lamb chops and steaks from a Northamptonshire butcher and we all hope the quantity will be enormous so that England's Test match prospects will be improved.

From afar one wonders (a) if the cash value of the meat will be regarded as 'benefits in kind' by the Inland Revenue and (b) whether the cost to the butcher will be deductible for tax purposes?

Regrettably Sir Alan Herbert and his friend Albert Haddock are no longer available to present the case for the defence.

Yours truly,

ERIC HALL

Steele, the nation's hero against Australia in 1975 and leading runmaker against West Indies in 1976, was never chosen again for a Test match.

THE TALLEST CRICKETER?

From M. Jahangir Khan, 24 August 1938

Northern India, Cambridge University (1933–36) and India. Bowled a ball which killed a sparrow in flight at Lord's.

Sir, Mr E. A. Hughes, who hails from the West Indies and plays cricket regularly for our club [Indian Gymkhana, Osterley, Middlesex], may well claim the title of 'the tallest cricketer'. His height exceeds 6ft. 7in. His bat has to be specially made, with a handle of such unique length that a person of average height would find it a queer implement to use. Thus armed he smites good-length deliveries with enviable ease over mid-on's head. Is Mr Hughes the tallest cricketer the game has ever known?

Yours truly,

M. JAHANGIR KHAN

From Mr A. C. Austin, 5 September 1938

M. Jahangir Khan's letter on 'the tallest cricketer' gives me an opportunity for blowing my own trumpet. I am 6ft. 7in., perhaps, like Jahangir Khan's friend, a trifle over, and play most of my cricket for the Bluemantles Cricket Club. I have never, however, found it necessary to use anything more formidable than the ordinary full-sized bat, used by all adult cricketers. I am fully aware that my height should give me a considerable advantage, but alas, frail mortal as I am, I all too frequently play back to balls to which far shorter (and more skilled) batsmen would certainly play forward. In the field an inability to stoop as far or as quickly as I should like is offset to some extent by a fairly long reach. As a bowler, I am the target of considerable ridicule, though once again I am aware that, in theory, my height should give me such an advantage that, if I bowled fast, I should be virtually unplayable. Jahangir Khan's letter has, however, given me, as a batsman, new hope. Next season I will play with a bat with a handle of truly phenomenal length, if only to impress and, I hope, disconcert, the opposing side.

A. C. AUSTIN

Joel Garner and Dallas Moir, both 6ft. 8in., were playing county cricket in 1982.

AS LONG AS THEY ARE TALL

From Mrs Patricia Crozier, 1 September 1978

Sir, Today I learned with interest that the average height of our current Test side is 6 feet. Since there are 11 playing members of the team their total length is therefore 66 feet or 22 yards – the length of the wicket.

Is this significant?

Yours faithfully,

P. CROZIER

AN ORIGINAL CRICKETER

From Mr Alec Waugh, 25 May 1949

Prolific novelist and author. Elder brother of Evelyn Waugh. Passionate follower of cricket, he played occasionally for MCC and is immortalized as Bobby Southcott in A. G. Macdonell's *England, Their England*.

Sir, Cricket has, as a spectacle, lost through standardized coaching much of its variety. The majority of modern batsmen are to the spectator indistinguishable from one another. Only the very great develop a personal style. Even in village cricket there is a lamentable lack of eccentricity. Last Saturday, however, my village side encountered a specimen unique in my experience – a right-handed batsman who placed his left hand on the handle below his right. His footwork was orthodox, his bat perpendicular, his chief aggressive stroke – possibly because of the enforced position of his left elbow – was a left-shouldered slash into the covers. He was a cautious player: opening the innings he took 27 minutes, against my bowling,

220

to make seven runs. He was tall, burly, in the middle thirties. He had adopted, he told me, this peculiar method, not because of an accident to a limb in youth, but because 'it came more natural'.

Yours faithfully,
ALEC WAUGH

CRICKETER'S CHOICE

From Mr E. P. Rand, 14 June 1956
Bursar, Milton Abbey School.

Sir, Mr D. F. Jeremy's dilemma, expressed in his letter on 9 June, as to whether to encourage his son to bat left- or right-handed, is capable of the easiest simplification. He should encourage neither, give up the idea and teach his son to row.

I am, Sir, yours faithfully,
EDWARD P. RAND

From Mr R. P. Keigwin, 12 June 1956
Cambridge University, Essex and Gloucestershire (1903–23). England hockey international. Warden of Wills Hall, Bristol University. Authority on Hans Christian Andersen.

Sir, Can it be that Mr Jeremy's 8½-year-old son, referred to in a letter yesterday, is an unconscious pioneer in future batsmanship? Cricket goes on evolving, sometimes happily, sometimes (if I may say so) unhappily; and I have often wondered whether batsmen may not one day learn to bat equally well right- and left-handed. One gathers that the modern umpire does not countenance the left-handed stroke through the slips which a right-handed batsman sometimes used to attempt from a slow ball wide of the off stump. But provided that he gave due notice to the umpire, just as a bowler must do who changes from overarm to underarm, there surely could be no objection to a player batting right-handed to one type of bowling and left-handed to another. (After all, something very similar is done at games like tennis and rackets.)

It is a recognized gambit to send in a left-handed batsman to cope with certain kinds of bowlers, and the ability to bat both right and left would greatly enhance a batsman's value to his side. So I hope Mr Jeremy's young son may be allowed to continue his experiments for the present. He is at just the right age to begin.

Yours faithfully,

R. P. KEIGWIN

Ian Botham and others have played the left-handed sweep in recent years without incurring the umpire's wrath.

LEFT-HANDED

From Mr Jeremy Rayner, 31 July 1975

Sir, In suggesting that Australia's position below the Equator influences the occurrence of left-handedness among the inhabitants Mr Peter MacKarrell might have reached the heart of the problem.

In the Southern Hemisphere the 'Coriolis' forces generated by the Earth's rotation act in the opposite sense from that we experience in the Northern Hemisphere; as a result both ocean tides and cyclonic winds travel in the opposite direction. There is a well-known hypothesis that water flowing out of a bath swirls in the opposite direction due to Coriolis effects. Might this not be extended to include the handedness of cricketers?

Yours faithfully,

JEREMY RAYNER

RIGHT HAND – LEFT HAND

From Mr Tim Hembry, 11 June 1982

Sir, I would be interested to hear from anyone who could explain to me a query I have had for some time now. It is to do with the terms 'right-handed' and 'left-handed' in referring to batsmen in cricket, I myself being a 'left-handed' batsman.

One is called 'left-handed' if one has his front foot (right), shoulder (right), and the top hand, which is supposed to be the one which does the work, is also the right hand.

It only seems sensible to me for a 'left-handed' batsman in fact to be called 'right-handed' and vice-versa. It also seems sensible that if one is right-handed normally for writing, etc, one should be taught to bat 'left-handed' as one's right arm is stronger and would be the 'top hand'.

Therefore if one is 'left-handed' normally one should bat 'right-handed', again for the same reason and surely this would help one to play over the ball and keep it down. As yet no one has been able to explain to me the reason for this phraseology. Is this because there is no logical answer?

Yours sincerely,
TIM HEMBRY

From Professor P. H. Spencer-Silver, 19 June 1982
S. A. Courtauld, Professor of Anatomy, University of London.

Sir, Mr Tim Hembry (11 June) will be pleased to know that there is a certain logic in answer to his concatenation of questions concerning the stance at the wicket of right-handed batpersons. The key to understanding is to be found in the posture of the spinal column.

The position is that in most right-handed people there is a slight asymmetry of the spine as a result of which the left shoulder is held a little higher than the right. When grasping a bat handle the left hand therefore only fits comfortably above the right. At the wicket the raising of the left shoulder is merely brought about by an enhancement of the asymmetry of the spine with which the body is already at ease. Such a starting position feels right, and the movements which flow from it are slick and dextrous.

To grasp the handle with hands reversed (which is required when facing the bowling from the 'wrong' side) requires an elevation of the right shoulder brought about by a twist of the spinal column in an unwonted direction. Such a starting position feels all wrong, and movements based on it cannot flow but instead are clumsy and maladroit.

Let me say about phraseology that by definition right-handed batpersons are those who bat the same way round as most other right-handers (even if they write left-handed). Also the posture of the back and the asymmetry of the shoulders can best be pondered not on the cricket field but on the golf course. French cricket is also worth thinking about.

Yours faithfully,
P. H. SPENCER-SILVER

A STRANGE INNINGS

From Mr Richard Harman, 18 August 1949

Opening the innings for Aylesbury on Whit-Monday in 1922, the curate of the parish church was still not out at the lunch interval. Having to officiate at a marriage service at 1.30 p.m. he hurriedly cycled one and a half miles to the church, donned his robes, and cycled back just in time to resume his innings. Surely this is the only time in the history of cricket that the batsman should have performed, between the start and the end of his innings, a marriage service in church.

RICHARD HARMAN

From Canon Lancelot Smith, 22 August 1949

I had an experience in 1926 very similar to that quoted by your correspondent under the above title, when as a 'not out' at the luncheon interval I left the ground to take a funeral and returned from the cemetery to the batting crease to resume the innings with my pre-lunch partner at the wicket. The match was at Spalding against a team of Indian students which included the Nawab of Pataudi and Nazir Ali.

LANCELOT SMITH

THE OTHER CRICKET MATCH

From Lieutenant-Colonel H. B. T. Wakelam, 9 August 1956

Sporting journalist, author and BBC commentator. Gave first running commentary – England v. Wales at Twickenham 1927 – and first television Test match commentary – England v Australia at Lord's 1938.

Sir, Mr Isaac Foot's report, in his letter of 2 August, of 'Werrington versus St Dominick' recalls to mind the reply given by a village cricketer, when asked, on his return from an 'away' match, how his team had fared. 'First we went in, then they went in and we went in, and they went in, and they won. Then they went in and we went in, and they went in, and we went in, and we won. And then it were tea-time.'

Your obedient servant,

H. B. T. WAKELAM

LAST WICKET STANDS

From Mr B. Medhurst, 25 August 1966

Sir, Lest it should have escaped your notice may I point out that during the recent Test series a quite remarkable feature has emerged.

Can it have happened before that over a complete Test series either country (let alone both countries) should have produced higher average tenth wicket stands than opening partnerships? (West Indies first wicket average, 17.4; tenth wicket, 18.4; and England first wicket average, 20.6, tenth wicket, 26.4.)

Is a new race of batting bowlers appearing, or have we exhausted our supply of competent opening batsmen?

Yours faithfully,

B. MEDHURST

MR A. N. OTHER

From Mr A. N. Other, 28 June 1932
Writing from Harrow.

Sir, I have been very interested in your correspondence about 'Old Cricket Customs' and should be so glad if some of your correspondents who have studied the past could help my memory in a personal matter.

I am now rather a doddering old man, but still able to take a bat in hand on occasion. Could any of your readers give the date I first appeared before the public, my highest score, and if I have ever batted before No. 10, or ever been used as a bowler, instead of being placed at leg in the field, always? I have a score-sheet in front of me, when a close connexion of mine in 1859 batted No. 11 for Harrow School against the Town. On the list he figures as T. H. E. Swell.

I am, Sir,

A. N. OTHER

From Mr J. E. Raven, 1 July 1932

I think the 'rather doddering old man' scarcely does himself justice. I have known him – and his very near relative O. N. E. More – for a large number of years, and my remembrances of both are of the kindliest. As a rule it is a kindly disposition rather than a mastery of the game which brings them into the side, but I have known a case where the former went in first wicket and carried the team on his shoulders. I have also known a case where the latter, who certainly was rather a late selection, was barred from bowling by his opponents. Anyhow, I claim them both as very decent fellows and most acceptable to 'a skipper', even if they only save him from the humiliation of describing his team as one short. May this cheer him up in his old age.

JOHN E. RAVEN

From Ditto, 1 July 1932
Writing from Edinburgh.

Sir, I am in a position to recall to 'Mr A. N. Other's' recollection an experience in his past career which apparently he has forgotten. Can he not remember that match at Porth on 11 August, 1866, when he played for the Gentlemen of Scotland against the Oxford and Cambridge Universities' Rovers? According to my record of the match, Mr A. N. Other went in one wicket down and scored 67 runs. He was put on to bowl and took seven wickets, to which was mainly attributable the victory of his side. Apparently when not bowling he kept wicket, for one of the three wickets for which he was not responsible as a bowler appears as 'st. A. N. Other, b. Balfour.'

I am, &c.,

DITTO

A LAWN OF TEST TURF

From Mr C. R. Yeomans, 10 February 1972
Chairman, Council of Cricket Societies; Hon. Secretary, Northern Cricket Society.

Sir, It is interesting to read Mr Dodsworth's letter (29 January) about cricket lovers cherishing a piece of the Lord's pitch now that it is to be relaid over the next four years.

Some 15 years or more ago, I made my own lawn from 23 pieces of the major first-class cricket grounds of this country, including all the Test match playing grounds. About 23 different grounds were represented.

By prior arrangement with the groundsman, or an official of the club concerned, I collected a piece of turf, some two-feet square, and carried it home, by train, in a hessian sack and then laid it. With due ceremony, of course.

I made a 'map' so that I could tell where each ground was represented.

Fenner's, I remember, produced the best piece of turf, and the Oval, I'm afraid, quite the worst. It was so thin, it almost crumbled away. No wonder Lock and Laker got all those wickets.

Yours sincerely,
RON YEOMANS

CAUGHT AT MID-WICKET

From Wing Commander E. Bentley Beauman, 15 August 1980

Sir, During practically every cricket match watched on television, one frequently sees the two batsmen meeting in the middle of the pitch for a two or three-minute chat.

It would be interesting to know what they discuss on these occasions. Perhaps they compare notes on the best way of bringing down inflation, or the advantages or otherwise of a new Middle Party, or some such urgent topic?

Yours etc.,
E. BENTLEY BEAUMAN

From Dr J. L. Crosby, 19 August 1980

Sir, Over 40 years ago there appeared in *Punch* a small drawing by Fougasse of two conferring batsmen. The caption read 'It seems that the one in pink is their wicketkeeper's sister'.

Yours faithfully,
JACK CROSBY

From the Captain, Poet's and Peasants' CC, 2 September 1980

Sir, Not all mid-wicket conferences concern matters of import. Last season, I once came to the wicket when the score was 12 for five. The other batsman, who had been there from the outset, solemnly beckoned me to mid-wicket to give, I assumed, some useful advice as to what I should do. 'I'm sorry to trouble you', he said, 'but I've just lost a fly-button. Would you mind keeping a look-out for it?'

Unfortunately, I did not remain long enough to assist him in the search.

Yours faithfully,
DAVID A. PEARL

DOWN THE CHIMNEY

From the Headmaster of Wallasey Grammar School, 24 June 1955

Sir, Cricket balls in flight do strange things. Their impact has ignited boxes of matches in umpires' coats. And there was the sparrow killed by a ball bowled at Lord's, the heroic bird thereby attaining the immortality of a glass case in the Long Room of the pavilion. But is there precedent for what happened here yesterday? A boy playing in a junior match mightily smote a towering hit high above this two-storey building. The ball, descending with the steep trajectory of a howitzer shell, fell clean into the mouth of a chimney pot whence by devious ways it issued soot-stained in a downstairs classroom.

The pity of it is that this happened just after school was over. Had it been half an hour earlier when the room was occupied the boys would have had the enjoyment of this uniquely dramatic interruption of a lesson. And in future years what a splendidly improbable tale they could have told of a sudden rattle in the chimney and the startling emergence of a high-velocity missile which, however suspicious it may have looked to the master, was in fact a cricket ball legitimately going about its lawful business.

I am, Sir, your obedient servant,
F. L. ALLAN

BURIED BALL

From Mr W. M. L. Escombe, 28 July 1958

Sir, With reference to a report on 18 July of an urchin's ball being rolled into the pitch at Southampton, this reminds me of a story told me many years ago by a friend of mine, about a match which I believe took place on the Gloucester ground.

One of the batsmen drove a ball towards the boundary, before reaching which it was rolled into the ground by the heavy roller, which was being moved round on the outskirts of the ground. The fieldsman was unable to dig it out with his fingers and at last in desperation ran back to the wicket and fetched a stump, with which he eventually succeeded in gouging it out, by which time the batsmen, who had been on the run since the stroke was made, were completely overcome with exhaustion and laughter.

Yours, &c.,

W. M. L. ESCOMBE

From Mr Hugh Merrick, 1 August 1958

Sir, In the celebrated case where the ball lodged in a rabbit-run, near the boundary, at exact finger-tip length from the fielder lying on the ground trying in vain to retrieve it at the length of his outstretched arm the umpire ruled that, since the ball could be plainly seen and everyone present knew precisely where it was, the 'Lost Ball' provision could not apply.

The 26 runs, necessary at the time for the home side's victory, which were run before it was eventually recovered were therefore allowed to stand as legitimate.

Yours truly,

HUGH MERRICK

YORKED

From the Master in charge of cricket, Sherborne School, Dorset, 20 December 1975

Sir, Kindly inform the compiler of *The Times* Crossword Puzzle, No 14,178, that a yorker is not a bouncer – far from it.

Yours faithfully,

D. J. W. BRIDGE

CRICKET INSURANCE

From Mr M. F. W. Booker, 24 May 1975

Sir, With the start of the 1975 cricket season, the inadequacy needs to be stressed of the public liability insurance arranged for most amateur (and probably professional) cricket clubs.

It appears that most club secretaries take out a standard form of third party policy with one insurance company for a comparatively low fee, but the limitation of cover afforded may not be generally known – as I am now forced to realize.

My cottage is 60 yards from the village pitch and during a match last September a ball shattered a double glazed window damaging a porcelain figure at the back of the room. The club admitted liability and as on previous occasions when roof tiles have been broken, the bill for repairs, including the replacement value of the figure, was sent to their insurance company.

To my surprise, after much lengthy deliberation and the seeking of counsel's opinion, my claim of some £100 was refused, quoting the precedent of Bolton v Stone (1951) that when a cricket ball leaves the ground, the club is not liable for the damage it causes.

I am therefore apparently left with the alternative of either going to my own insurers or obtaining the money from the cricket club. In the first place I don't feel that my house policy should be called upon to pay for an action accountable to someone else, and in the second, an awful lot of unpleasantness must result from my efforts with the club whose finances naturally do not cater for this supposedly insured risk.

It is therefore advisable for everyone living within range of a cricket pitch – and probably a football ground or other venue too – to campaign the owners or organizers of matches and events to effect proper insurance so that compensation is payable in the event of personal injuries or damage to property for spectators, passers-by or adjacent householders alike.

Yours faithfully,
M. F. W. BOOKER

From Mr S. D. Freer, 29 May 1975

Sir, According to the precedent of Bolton v Stone, Mr Booker cannot recover damages from the cricket club or its insurers. He may yet have a case against the batsman.

Yours faithfully,

S. D. FREER

From Mr Henry Blyth, 4 June 1975

Sir, In this village [Rottingdean, Sussex], where some rather odd things seem to happen from time to time, the cricket and football clubs occupy adjoining pitches. The RCC insure against a cricket ball damaging cars, etc. The RFC insure against a football doing similar damage. I remember an occasion when a football was kicked onto the cricket pitch and an irate cover point kicked it back with such vigour that it went through the windscreen of a car. Under which insurance policy, if either, could a claim have been made?

Yours faithfully,

HENRY BLYTH

LEWIS CARROLL

From Mr E. V. Lucas, CH, 9 January 1932

Essayist, satirist and man of letters. A frequent contributor to *The Times* and author of books on cricket. A member of Sir James Barrie's team, the Allahakbarries; Barrie said of his playing ability: 'had (unfortunately) a style'.

Sir, Lewis Carroll's description of his one and only experience of active cricket is good fun. Having been put on to bowl, he delivered, he said, a single ball, 'which, I was told, had it gone far enough, would have been a wide'.

I might add that one of the syllogisms in the Revd C. L. Dodgson's *Symbolic Logic* proves that 'no hedgehog reads *The Times*'.

I am yours, &c.,

E. V. LUCAS

12

BLUES
AND BOATERS

UNIVERSITY CRICKET AND THE FOLLOW-ON

Oxford were five runs short of avoiding the follow-on, which was then compulsory and required a deficit of only 80 runs, when their last pair decided to give the wicket away. This would enable Oxford to bat again while the pitch was still good. However, the bowler, C. M. Wells, frustrated Oxford by deliberately giving away eight runs in wides and no-balls. Cambridge eventually won by 266 runs.

From Sir Courtenay Boyle, KCB, 10 July 1893

Oxford University (1865–67). Permanent Secretary of the Board of Trade. Author, as 'An Old Blue', of articles on cricket reform entitled 'High Scores and Drawn Matches' which were published in *The Times* in 1899 and drew considerable response.

Sir, I left a busy office early on Monday afternoon to see my old University play an uphill cricket match against Cambridge at Lord's. The sight was painful. Apparently the popular method at Oxford of playing a short-pitched ball to the off is to cover the wicket with the legs and keep the bat out of the way; the popular method of playing a half-volley on the leg stump is to plunge a little way out and make it a yorker, and of playing a full-pitch is to see how near the crease the ball can be made to stop.

Bowling has certainly improved greatly since my time; but there appears to be no sufficient justification for a tight wrist and tied shoulder style of play, which is as unpleasant to watch as it is barren of result; and the sooner a little more vigour can be infused into

Oxford batting, the better for cricket and the worse for lawn tennis and other competing pastimes.

But my object in writing was less to criticize play than to suggest for consideration and discussion a change in the law of 'follow-on'. The rule that the second side follows its innings if 80 behind was reasonable when grounds were rough and scores short. It is not reasonable when scores of over 300 are frequent. There is no such difference between 310 and 390 as justifies the disadvantage imposed on the leading side by the necessity of fielding again. I submit that the minority necessitating a follow-on should be proportioned and not absolute. And I suggest for consideration and discussion that when the second side are 40 per cent behind they should have the option of following on, and that when they are 50 per cent behind their adversaries should have the option of making them follow on.

Your obedient servant,
COURTENAY BOYLE

After much controversy the deficit was increased to 120 runs from the 1895 season; but that this was inadequate was shown up the following year when the Cambridge captain, Frank Mitchell, instructed E. B. Shine to give away 12 runs in byes and no-balls to prevent another Oxford follow-on. (This time Cambridge collapsed and Oxford scored 330 to win.) Angry voices were raised in the Lord's pavilion as Cambridge left the field – and in *The Times*.

THE OXFORD AND CAMBRIDGE MATCH

From Lord Cobham, 7 July 1896

Cambridge University (1861–64) as the Hon. C. G. Lyttelton, Liberal MP for East Worcestershire 1868–74. Lord Commissioner 1881–89. Railway Commissioner 1891–1905.

Sir, I wholly differ from the view taken by your cricket correspondent of the 'no-ball' incident in the Oxford and Cambridge match. He accuses the Cambridge captain of overriding one of the first principles of the game. The first and only principle of the game is that the players should do their best to win it, subject to a strict adherence to the letter and, if you will, to the spirit of the rules.

What rule has been infringed either in letter or in spirit, and what pretence is there for making the odious charge that there has been a 'breaking of the bounds of honourable play'?

In 1893 the Cambridge captain, in a perfectly open and above-board way, asserted his right to act precisely as his successor acted on Friday. This position has never been receded from; it constituted a distinct notice of the view of the matter taken by Cambridge, and indeed, if your correspondent's reference to the 1893 incident is correct, by Oxford as well, and this view the MCC has deliberately refrained from condemning.

Cricket in these days excites too deep an interest and too keen a partisanship to admit of its being regulated by vague traditions and understandings, or otherwise than by strict law. Even, however, if it were not so, I utterly deny that there ever has been or can have been an understanding, or whatever else you might call it, against a side purposely throwing away runs or wickets, and I say to attempt to establish such an understanding would be disastrous in the extreme. You can never be sure that a batsman has purposely allowed himself to be bowled out or that a bowler is purposely not bowling his best. But whenever at the critical moment the last wicket or two may have opportunely fallen, or a wicketkeeper may have let a boundary bye, angry imputations of unfair play would inevitably be made, discreditable exhibitions of feeling, as on Friday, would become frequent, and the good humour which has hitherto characterized our keenest games would become a thing of the past.

I so far agree with your correspondent that I think the rules of the game should not encourage any tampering with its natural course, especially when they operate in a one-sided manner. At present the in-side cannot prevent the out-side depriving them of the advantage (when it is one) of following on, and I do not see why this advantage should be conferred upon the side winning the toss in addition to the many which they already enjoy. I would suggest, as one way out of the difficulty, that the in-side at any time before the follow-on has been saved should have the option of closing their innings. The closure rule was passed to prevent intentional knocking down of wickets and such like practices, and it gives an enormous advantage to the closuring side – *e.g.,* the Eton and Harrow match last year. Why not counterbalance this to some extent by giving the other side a similar privilege?

I write in the hope that there will be sober discussion followed by well-considered legislation on this difficult subject, and that we shall have no more offensive and unjust aspersions cast upon men who have done nothing to deserve them.

Yours obediently,

COBHAM

From Revd the Hon. E. Lyttelton, 7 July 1896
Younger brother of the foregoing.

Sir, The best way to test the quality of the Cambridge tactics last Friday is to suppose such play to be allowed, and freely practised. What would be the result?

As the critical time drew near, the bowlers would begin to bowl wides, and the batsman in retaliation would knock down his wicket, or would call his companion to run, and both would remain standing out of their ground when the ball was returned. The MCC committee would then have to determine whether a batsman was out for 'hit wicket' when the ball was out of his reach. Failing in this, the batsman might, conceivably, stop the wide ball with his hands and throw down his own wicket. I suppose he would be out. But is it not perfectly legitimate if once you admit the principle that a captain must play to win, and that to this object all traditions of the game must be sacrificed?

The public come in their thousands to Lord's to see the great game played as well as it can be by two picked elevens. If Mr Mitchell's ideas of winning a match are to prevail, the public will have to look on at the game being played as badly as it can be by these elevens. And, moreover, granted sufficient eagerness on each side, the farce might be protracted for some time. But, though the question of these tactics being 'sportsmanlike' or not seems to me hardly a matter for dispute, that is no reason why the law should be altered.

The rule allowing 'follow-on' ceased to have any distinct reason for existence as soon as the closing of the innings was allowed. Let it therefore be abolished altogether. This will be found simpler and better than making it optional.

Yours obediently,

E. LYTTELTON

Reform of the law, though demanded immediately, was postponed until 1900, when the follow-on was made optional and the margin for a three-day match became 150 runs.

AN UNMERITED REPRIMAND

Two unrelated incidents involving the universities brought reprimands from the MCC for bending the laws as applied to the first-class game. At Oxford G. T. S. Stevens was invited to continue batting against Somerset after being mistakenly given out lbw; at Cambridge a university player was allowed to bat as substitute for a Free Foresters player (J. N. Buchanan, incidentally an MCC committee member) who was ill and went on to make top score.

From Mr S. H. Day, 30 June 1922

Kent and captain of Cambridge University (1897–1919). England football international.

Sir, The MCC has now seen fit publicly to reprimand both Universities for perpetrating offences contrary to the laws of the game of cricket.

Fortunately there is a deep-rooted belief on the part of all sections of the British public that the Universities are beyond suspicion in the matter of sportsmanship and fair play. So, probably, no great harm has been done. I should have thought, however, that the MCC Committee would have been the first, and not the last, body to realize how important a plank this belief is in the somewhat curiously constructed fabric of our social edifice.

But, in any case, why go out of the way to insult both Universities? I use the word insult deliberately, as I hope to prove that reprimands have been given on false arguments.

I have searched the 'Laws of Cricket' and I can find there nothing to condemn the action of Cambridge, or their opponents, in allowing a substitute to bat. Mr Lacey adds that it is 'contrary to the practice observed in first-class cricket'. Surely he is confusing first-class cricket with county cricket, and there is a good deal of the latter nowadays that can hardly be described as first-class, although the MCC refuse to take any steps to remedy it. The match Cambridge University v. Free Foresters is not played for points; surely, therefore, courtesies may be allowed which it is not customary to offer in a county match for fear of annoying the public in their lust for 'points'. I cannot see how this can in any way be fairly described as 'a disregard of the laws of cricket'.

Similarly in regard to the incident for which Oxford are reproved. Mr Lacey takes pains to point out that an umpire is entitled to alter his decision, should he realize that he has made a mistake. Will Mr Lacey deny that a fielding side is entitled to withdraw its appeal on realization of a mistake? In this case no decision is required of the umpire, who is there for the convenience of the players and for no other purpose whatever.

If then, as I maintain, both Universities have been reprimanded for incidents in which they have acted not only in accordance with the spirit of the laws, as would be expected of them, but also within the letter of the same, some steps should be taken to demand a public apology. It is probably too much to suggest that each University should require this apology before consenting to play the University match at Lord's, but I would ask the respective captains to give this matter their earnest consideration, although I realize that Mr Stevens is much handicapped by being so closely connected with headquarters.

I should like to get an ex-captain of Oxford to act as co-signer of this letter, but I hesitate to ask anyone to share the unpopularity in official circles which it must necessarily entail. Yet I consider it a public duty to protest at any cost when the governing body publicly condemns actions on the cricket field which are all on the side of common sense and fair play and are calculated to set a good example of the true spirit of the game, as is only to be expected from sides representing the Universities of Oxford and Cambridge.

I should like to end with a word of warning. I have frequently heard club cricketers complain that all cricket legislation is conducted by the MCC solely on behalf of county cricket, and that the club cricketer and his requirements are never considered. When I try to recall where I have previously heard similar mutterings, I remember the split in the football world and the formation of the Amateur Football Association. *Verb. sap.*

Yours faithfully,
S. H. DAY

LAWS OF CRICKET

From the President of MCC, 5 July 1922

Viscount Chelmsford, formerly the Hon. F. J. N. Thesiger (Oxford University 1888 and captain 1890). Governor-General of Queensland, 1905–09, and New South Wales, 1909–13. Viceroy of India, 1916–21. First Lord of the Admiralty, 1924. Warden of All Souls College, Oxford, 1932–33.

Sir, You have been receiving correspondence on the subject of the late decisions by the MCC Committee.

I am not writing to discuss the questions raised by your correspondents, but to make one matter clear. These decisions were made by the Committee and not, as I have heard it suggested, by Mr F. E. Lacey, the secretary of the club.

Mr F. E. Lacey signed the decisions which were communicated as secretary, and his share in the matter began and ended there.

Yours faithfully,

CHELMSFORD

THE DEBT ON FENNER'S

Having rented Fenner's since 1848, Cambridge University CC bought the ground in 1896 with a 30-year mortgage.

From Mr H. G. Comber, DSO, 11 July 1923

Fellow and Treasurer of Pembroke College, Cambridge. Treasurer of the Cambridge University Cricket, Rugby Football and Hockey Clubs. President of the rugby and lawn tennis clubs.

Sir, The presence of the Cambridge University Eleven at Lord's seems an opportune moment at which to draw the attention of Cambridge men who are members of the MCC to the financial position of the University Cricket Club. Constant appeals have been made in recent years to enable the club to wipe out the debt of over £3000 which is still outstanding for the purchase of Fenner's.

But why should Cambridge men be asked to subscribe money for this purpose when such large sums are taken each year by the MCC at the inter-University match? The gross receipts, excluding proceeds from sale of match cards, charge for tents, and sale of refreshments, amounted I understand, in 1921 to something like £4000, and in 1922 to £5500, whilst the expenses were roughly £500 in each year. In addition there were annual donations of £500 to Oxford and £500 to Cambridge.

If the gross expenses for the two years 1921 and 1922 – £3,000 – are deducted from the gross receipts – £9500 – the share of these two matches taken by the MCC amounted to some £6500, a truly remarkable charge for the use of Lord's for six days, if these figures are correct. [MCC records give the receipts as £2273 8s for 1921 and £3105 2s for 1922.] It would further be interesting and enlightening to know how many complimentary tickets are issued to members of the MCC and how many to the two clubs that provide the match.

There may, of course, have been additional expenses of which the writer is unaware, but these could not account for more than a small portion of the £6500 which the MCC reserved for itself. Surely a more equitable method of division would be to deduct the gross expenses from the gross receipts, and then to divide the balance in equal shares between the MCC, Oxford, and Cambridge, the Oxford and Cambridge Clubs also receiving some consideration for the complimentary tickets issued to members of the MCC.

I am, Sir, your obedient servant,

H. G. COMBER

The mortgage was paid off in 1926.

THE UNIVERSITY MATCH

From Mr W. B. de Winton, CIE, 10 July 1930

Sir, I share your Cricket Correspondent's surprise at the poor attendances at the University match. I have seen many of them, from Cobden's triumph in 1870 to the present day, and cannot remember seeing so many empty seats. And it would be difficult to imagine a more interesting day's cricket than we saw on Monday, with its rapid vicissitudes of fortune. Indeed, I think these matches of cricketers in the making are always more interesting than those of maturer men.

But all is not quite as it should be. The standard of batting and bowling has been well maintained through the years. I wish I could say the same of the fielding, which is neither so smart nor so sure as in the days of the Studds, to name a period which has left a vivid impression on my memory, and in one particular, the throw-in, it has sadly deteriorated. In the days of my youth the ball came to the top of the wicket, either as a full pitch or long hop, like a shot from a gun, and the wicketkeeper had not to move an inch. Now both speed and direction are often lacking, and the wicketkeeper has to run many yards to gather the ball. Good fielding is the finest sight at cricket, and schools would quickly mend matters if they concentrated on it and on throwing in hard and straight. As a fag at school, if I misfielded a ball I was put at the wicket and bowled at with no bat to protect me, and woe betide me if I shirked the ordeal. A little of this discipline might do good now.

Your obedient servant,

W. B. DE WINTON

From Mr J. C. Craigie and others, 13 July 1933

Sir, Having witnessed the first day's play in the Oxford and Cambridge match at Lord's, we agree entirely with your Correspondent when he describes the cricket as 'Dull, deadly dull, it was; with never a ball that could hit the stumps'; and again, 'To relieve this dismal story, which in fact was felt by every one at Lord's, we can rejoice in the beauty of Cambridge's fielding.' Surely we do not expect to read reports of this nature in regard to this great match. We regret that the tactics employed on Monday seem to us to savour of those employed in the late Test series.

We do hope very sincerely that when Eton and Harrow meet at the end of the week their respective captains will not find it necessary to resort to these methods, which, in our opinion, destroy the whole charm, spirit and enjoyment of the game.

Yours faithfully,
JOHN C. CRAIGIE, GEOFFREY PALMER,
E. P. LUCAS, GUY A. I. DURY, SUFFIELD,
J. S. HUGHES, HOME GORDON

From Mr Cortlandt MacMahon, 26 July 1937

Governor of St Bartholomew's Hospital from 1940. Author of medical textbooks.

Sir, I am writing to plead strongly that the University cricket match should begin on Saturday. So many people, who have to work, see hardly anything of the match. I arrived after 5.30 p.m. on the Monday, and several others arrived with me. On Tuesday, late in the afternoon, one saw a little more of the game, and on Wednesday none at all. Think what a whole day of the match on a Saturday would mean to thousands of old members of the universities, who, with their wives and children, could enjoy a full day's cricket.

I am told that tradition is against the change in the days in which the match is played. What utter nonsense this is! The country parsons are the only persons to be seriously considered. A few might have to miss the Saturday's play, but they would have Monday and Tuesday. The gate money which would be taken on a Saturday would be a large sum and both University cricket finances would be greatly helped.

By the University match finishing on the Tuesday Eton and

Harrow could start on Thursday and so play out their matches properly, instead of having many draws or being hurried into declarations which may end disastrously.

Yours obediently,
CORTLANDT MacMAHON

The match started on Saturday in 1938 but *only* 6372 paid for admission.

From Mr J. H. C. Leach, 12 July 1967

Sir, As I write this, the University cricket match is being played at Lord's before a 'crowd' which even on a warm Saturday was tiny, and today will doubtless be smaller still.

Is it not high time that this outworn tradition was given up and interest restored to the match by playing it in alternate years at Oxford and Cambridge towards the end of the Trinity term?

Yours, etc.,
J. H. C. LEACH

In 1983 the University match was played at Lord's for the 134th time, despite suggestions from many quarters, including one reporter for *The Times*, that it be moved elsewhere. Bletchley was one of the more interesting propositions.

BATSMEN'S WEAR

From Mr Rockley Wilson, 14 July 1947

Cambridge University, Yorkshire and England (1899–1923), captaining Cambridge. Master and outstanding cricket coach at Winchester.

Sir, In the recent university match many members of both universities gazed with surprise at the caps of the Cambridge opening batsmen. The captain wore the Quidnunc and his partner the Crusader. For a parallel we must go back 40 years. In 1907 R. A. Young, who wore glasses, had to bat in a drizzle, and preferred a Crusader cap to his 'Blue' cap because it had a bigger peak. This instance apart, these caps, honourable as they are, have, I think, never previously been worn on this occasion except by substitutes. If the batsmen plead want of coupons, I am certain other members of the side would have lent them 'Blue' caps for batting, for surely in the university match the 'Blue' is the only wear? It is no time for motley.

Yours sincerely,
E. R. WILSON

UNIVERSITY CRICKETERS

From the Revd J. C. Cuningham, 27 May 1958

Sir, It is not really surprising that university cricket today is not so attractive as in the past. The modern undergraduate has to think more of success in examinations than was the case in former years. And there is little prospect for the university cricketer to continue long in first-class cricket unless he decides to become a professional or secures a post as secretary to a county club.

It does seem ridiculous that the university matches with counties still rank as first class. Either the county treats the game as an opportunity to have some early season practice in the middle or they field a team below their normal strength. The amateur is rapidly disappearing from first-class cricket. In 1939 there were 108 playing in county cricket while last year the number was 54.

I do not think, like Mr Churcher, whose letter you published on 24 May, that cricket is losing its appeal in the whole country. But for those who cannot play full time cricket golf is a game that can be played at any time and does not require 22 players.

Yours faithfully,
JOHN C. CUNINGHAM

In 1982 there were more than 20 Blues playing county cricket, five of them for England, and another captained the Pakistan touring team.

INCOGNITO AT LORD'S

From the Revd J. W. Cole, 15 July 1971

Sir, May I correct your correspondent's statement that at Lord's on Monday, 'there was not a clergyman present'? He should have written, 'there was not a clerical collar'.

Sydney Barnes, for whom my father sometimes 'kept' and whose hand I touched with awe as a small boy, gave a veteran's benison from the wall of the Long Room and I a cleric's from my seat, to Ward, our fellow 'Staffordshire pot' as he saved the Oxford innings.

Yours faithfully,

JOHN W. COLE

FENNER'S PAVILION

From Mr E. Armitage, 27 June 1973

Director, Sixth Form Centre, City of Ely College.

Sir, The appositeness of the photographs (*The Times*, 21 June) of the old and new cricket pavilions at Fenner's to the recent correspondence on the proposal that architects should sign their buildings as painters their pictures should not pass without comment. It is indeed a melancholy sign of our times and of the pseudo-progress that is such a feature of them that a building of the grace and elegance of the old pavilion should be pulled down to be replaced by the graceless erection that looks as though it had been knocked up by the Royal Engineers in a hurry.

Yours faithfully,

E. ARMITAGE

The new pavilion was designed by Colin Stansfield Smith, Cambridge fast bowler 1954–57.

COACHING AT SCHOOLS AND UNIVERSITIES

From Mr S. H. Day, 20 July 1935

Sir, To all lovers of cricket, except to the blindest partisans, the recent 'Varsity match must have proved extremely disappointing. I am not speaking of the Oxford collapse on Wednesday, as that I did not see, but of the general standard of cricket, played on the Tuesday.

It was my good fortune to play in 'Varsity matches where such great stroke players as H. C. Pilkington, R. E. Foster, T. L. Taylor, L. J. Moon, and E. M. Dowson, to mention only a few, all made runs. It did not matter from what schools they came, they were

243

capable of making cricket strokes in the right way and with comparative certainty. I do not blame the present 'Varsity cricketer for not being able to make strokes, as it appeared quite obvious that he has never been taught how to do so, and the same weakness was apparent, on one side at any rate, in the Eton v. Harrow match. The Eton cricket results as published in the recent edition of the *Eton Chronicle* make dismal reading. Played 11, drawn 10, lost one. Surely this wants looking into?

I suggest, Sir, that there is only one thing to save or revive English cricket, and that is a complete alteration in our methods of coaching. I suggest that the MCC should issue instructions, or even an order, that boys must be taught by coaches to hit the ball, and make the strokes in the correct manner, before they are taught defence. For this purpose, I suggest that a text-book be issued by some good writer who is skilled in the theory as well as in the practice of the game (the name of C. B. Fry leaps to my mind, but no doubt there are many others available), and that coaches be instructed to follow this text-book.

The fact that de Saram played as good an innings as one could wish to see in this recent 'Varsity match is evidence for rather than against my views. He was not, I believe, educated in an English school. Some of the English cricketers now getting past their prime are still stroke-players. Need I quote Woolley? We have also had Cameron, Bradman, Headley, and many others to show us that it can be done, and in the orthodox manner. Can we not learn the lesson?

Yours, &c.,

S. H. DAY

ETON AND HARROW MATCH

From Mr Philip Guedalla, 17 July 1926

Historian and political biographer.

Sir, I observe that Sir Home Gordon, in his impressive history of the Eton v. Harrow match, reproduces as its *fons et origo* the Harrow challenge of 1805, although the suggestion of an earlier match in 1804 finds admission to the text. It may be opportune to state that there is evidence of a challenge by Eton so early as 1796. This is contained in a letter of 29 May, 1796, from the small Lord Palmerston, then at Harrow, to his mother, cited inaccurately by the Marquis of Lorne in his volume on Palmerston in *The Queen's Prime Ministers*, and preserved among the Broadlands Papers. The relevant passage is as follows:–

> 'I wish you would send me two pairs of stumps for cricket and a good bat. Some of the boys say that we have accepted the challenge sent us by the Eton boys, who have challenged us to fight, not with cannons and balls, but with bats and balls in the Holydays, 18 of our best players against 18 of theirs.'

Perhaps you will permit me to add that it is some satisfaction to a Rugbeian to repair this evident gap in Etonian and Harrovian knowledge.

Your obedient servant,
PHILIP GUEDALLA

From the Vicar of Pinhoe, Devon, 18 July 1928

The Revd Oliver Puckridge

Sir, Your leading article and the poem on the cricket of last week are worthy. The spirit of a hundred years ago still survives. The following may be unknown to some readers. At the close of another Eton victory the following verse was sent:–

> 'Ye silly boys of Harrow School, Of cricket ye've no knowledge,
> It was not cricket, but the fool, Ye played with Eton College.'

The reply came clear and true from the pen of George Gordon, afterwards Lord Byron:-

> 'If as you say we played the fool, No wonder we were beaten;
> For at that game no other School Could e'er compete with Eton.'

I am, &c.,
VICAR OF PINHOE

A MEMORY OF WISDEN

From Mr C. H. Weekes, 7 March 1929

Sir, Your account of *Wisden's Almanack* in yesterday's issue of *The Times* reminds me of an odd occurrence in the cricket field at Harrow. Wisden was, in or about 1854, the highly valued coach of the school eleven. During a pause in some match, in which he was umpiring, one of the Old Harrow eleven, who was captain in 1852, a very tall and very athletic Old Harrovian, who was fielding behind Wisden, who was short, took a run and jumped clean over Wisden's head. I remember the occurrence because Wisden was so very angry. He said that he should not have minded so much if Marillier had not got spikes in his cricket shoes – which made the *feat* more dangerous. Marillier was the son of the dear old mathematical master, of whom all the then Harrovians were very fond. Some four or five of my old schoolfellows may perhaps still be left and may remember the occasion.

Yours faithfully,

C. H. WEEKES

While Wisden was 'cricket tutor' at Harrow they were never beaten by Eton.

ETON v. HARROW, 1863

From Mr William Toynbee, 16 July 1929

Sir, I went to Harrow in April, 1863 and saw for the first time the match with Eton in July of that year. The charge for admission was 6d., and, according to my recollection, there were no stands, ropes or regular boundaries; the seating accommodation consisted of small green wooden benches, scantily distributed, and a large proportion of the spectators sat on the ground; equestrians disported themselves freely among the pedestrians, whose perambulations were thereby rendered somewhat precarious. The 'chaffing' was stridently incessant throughout the game, every ball being greeted with a tornado of 'bubba-bubba-bowled'. A year or two later the headmasters of the respective schools joined in the entreaty for the discontinuance of what they euphemistically described as 'ironical cheering', an appeal that was to some extent successful.

In the Harrow eleven there were two players who later acquired great renown in the cricket world: I. D. Walker and C. F. Buller. I. D. Walker was captain, and his somewhat mature appearance – he was adorned with side-whiskers – prompted rumours in Etonian circles that he had re-entered Harrow for the occasion. The ease and finish of C. F. Buller's play won great admiration, as did his strikingly good looks. His brilliant career, unhappily somewhat clouded towards its close, was in many respects exceptional. At Harrow his popularity and prestige were immense; with masters, boys, and townspeople alike; in cricket, football, athletics, boxing, fencing he was pre-eminent, and, when he so chose, he could turn out a set of elegiacs with the best.

I am, Sir, your obedient servant,

WILLIAM TOYNBEE

Noisy crowd behaviour in the preceding years contributed to the match being reduced in 1982 from two days to one.

HARROW CRICKET

Eton had beaten Harrow for the fifth year in succession.

From an Old Harrovian, 14 July 1914

Sir, As a member of perhaps one of the strongest elevens that ever played for Harrow, I venture to submit some impressions left upon me by the Eton v. Harrow matches of the last few years.

I think it will be generally agreed – at any rate the opinion was expressed on all sides in the pavilion during the recent match – that the failure of the majority of the Harrow batsmen was due to their apparent inability to play with a straight bat. With the exception of Wilson, de Uphaugh, and Renton, no member of this year's Harrow team appeared to have any idea of defence. Nor, again, was there a single batsman in the eleven who could deal with a ball on the leg. It must have occurred to every intelligent observer of the match that, had the Harrow batsmen punished even a moderate proportion of the loose balls on the leg side presented to them by the Eton bowlers during the second innings, the Harrow total must have been nearer 244 than 144. These defects have been equally in evidence during the past few years.

One cannot help thinking that what is needed to remedy this state of things is the engagement of some really first-class professional. In making this observation I have no wish in any way to detract from the valuable services rendered to Harrow cricket by the gentlemen who give up so much of their time to coaching the Harrovians. Their services have been of inestimable benefit to the school cricket, and we one and all owe them a deep debt of gratitude for all they have done in this direction. It must, however, be admitted that their efforts are sadly hampered by the absence of any first-class professional. One can imagine the incalculable assistance which a George Hirst, for example, could give in detecting and correcting the defects of promising batsmen. The lesson afforded by the remarkable revival of Winchester cricket since the engagement of Haigh as professional to the college is very striking.

I venture, therefore, to suggest that, should the school not be in a position to defray the expenses of engaging a first-class professional, application for subscriptions for this purpose should be made to Old Harrovians. I am confident that I am only one of many thousands who would be happy to subscribe for such an object.

I am, Sir,
OLD HARROVIAN

From Forty Years On, 17 July 1914

Sir, If the general feeling of the boys themselves can be trusted, the explanation of the series of Harrow defeats at Lord's in the last few years is extremely simple. It is staleness. The mistake on the part of the cricket authorities is *trop de zèle*, and the boys get thoroughly tired of cricket before the match. The captain this year, being on the verge of a breakdown, was sent away for a few days' rest, and as a consequence played magnificently. The rest were partly stale, partly brow-beaten.

Let their devoted instructors next year try the effect of knocking off cricket for a few days before Lord's and see the result.

Yours, &c.,
FORTY YEARS ON

Harrow's next victory over Eton was in 1939, when 8000 delirious supporters invaded the field.

BETWEEN WICKETS

From Mr John Galsworthy, 5 July 1926

Novelist and dramatist. Received the Order of Merit in 1929 and the Nobel Prize for Literature in 1932. A noted athlete at Harrow (captain of football), he played village cricket for Bury, Sussex.

Sir, The Eton and Harrow match is again at hand. May an imponderable quantity, who with countless other such, has suffered from four consecutive draws, venture a suggestion?

Whatever the rule, could it not be the practice in this match for the ingoing batsman always to leave the pavilion gate for the wicket as the outgoing batsman reaches the pavilion gate? Considering that there are 30 to 40 intervals on the fall of wickets, during each of which at least a minute (on the average) is lost, more than half an hour would be saved. Last year's match would have been finished and not impossibly that of the year before. In fact, one has seen several draws in this match which another half-hour would have converted into a win.

This definite practice would have one other advantage : it would automatically save whichever side was tempted in that direction from lingering to the legal limit between wickets to avert defeat. Good sportsmanship, as a rule, takes care of that, but one remembers hearing shouts of 'Hurry up!' The reasons against this saving of time no doubt will now be given to him, for they are with difficulty imagined by

Your faithful servant,
JOHN GALSWORTHY

Under the 1980 code of laws a tenth mode of dismissal was introduced, *timed out*, applicable if an incoming batsman wilfully takes more than two minutes – from the fall of the wicket to the time he steps on to the field – to come in. A note to law 31 says that captains must ensure that the ingoing batsman passes the outgoing before the latter leaves the field.

CRICKET REMINISCENCES

From An Old Eton Boy, 4 June 1919

Sir, In connexion with your correspondent's lively allusions to hard hitting in past years, may I add one incident which will be of interest to *The Times*? In the course of an innings in which he scored over 100 for the Eton Eleven in 1865, Mr A. F. Walter made so many strong and hard drives and smart cuts that the 'fields' had to be extended in all directions, and the captain called out to a long cover-point to go still farther back 'to save *four*'. But the very next stroke was a sharp cut which went beyond him for five, much to the delight of the batsman and his Etonian applauders and the admiring disgust of the opponents on the other side. He was indeed a brave and formidable hitter when patience allowed him time to get his eye in.

Your obedient servant,
AN OLD ETON BOY

Arthur Fraser Walter, who took six wickets – but made a pair – for Oxford in the University match of 1869, was Manager and Chief Proprietor of *The Times* and Chairman of the Times Publishing Company at his death in 1910.

ETON v. WINCHESTER

From Mr R. G. Hargreaves, 2 July 1919

Hampshire player (1875–85) and later a Vice-President of the club.

Sir, I can add a curious fact to your article on the Eton and Winchester matches. My brother-in-law, W. E. Bryan, played for Winchester in 1860 with two arms and in 1861 and 1862 with only one, his left arm having been amputated above the elbow in the autumn of 1860. He took seven wickets for 59 in the first innings in 1860, including those of Mitchell and Lyttelton, and five for 30 in 1861. In later years he made a hundred in a minor match. I imagine he is the only boy who ever played in a school eleven with one arm.

Yours faithfully,
REGINALD G. HARGREAVES

In 1981 a boy from South Wales, who was born with only one complete arm, joined the MCC staff of young professionals.

LORD'S SCHOOLS

From Sors Tertia, 18 July 1950

Sir, I am sure your invitation to Winchester to return to Lord's is kindly meant; so I will not charge you with committing a bad notion. Most of my Wykehamist friends, however, agree with me that Dr Moberly, who insisted on our declining the invitation in 1858, better interpreted the ethos of our society. We regard Eton with affection and Harrow with respect, but their ways are not ours. We have dwelt where our wise founder placed us nearly 600 years ago, far from the madding crowd's ignoble strife, withdrawn among the ambient streams of Itchen. We lift up our eyes unto Hills, not unto the grandstand. We do not, like younger schools, hold speech days, or other public demonstrations. We think that from our seclusion has come our power to serve the commonwealth in our perhaps peculiar way.

We love to entertain our Etonian friends in our own beautiful fields, and to enjoy their hospitality on Agar's Plough. Here we believe we preserve more of the *Amicabilis Concordia*, which we signed with them in 1444 and have kept inviolate ever since, than could survive the harsher rivalry of the metropolitan arena. Please, Sir, allow us still, like the Shunammite woman who might have been commended for the king or the captain of the host, to dwell among our own people. Believe me, Sir, I write with no disrespect for great schools of a different tradition. It was an Old Harrovian head master – happily still with us in his eighty-ninth year – who taught me the essence of the Wykehamist spirit in the phrase 'We do not advertise.'

I am, Sir, your obedient servant,

SORS TERTIA

Until the 1850s Eton, Harrow and Winchester met each other in the Triangular Week at Lord's. The Headmaster of Winchester doubted the benefits of the Festival on his boys.

RUGBY v. MARLBOROUGH

From Mr R. H. Spooner and Sir Pelham Warner, 25 July 1955

R. H. Spooner: Lancashire and England (1899–1923). England rugby international.

Sir, On 27 and 28 July Rugby and Marlborough play their annual match at Lord's. This year is a special, indeed a unique, occasion for it celebrates the centenary of this fixture. May we, Sir, invite the all-pervading aid of *The Times* in making known an event which will surely appeal to old boys of two famous schools? For many years all those who have watched these matches, apart from their partisan interest, have been delighted by the zest and keenness of the play as well as by the high standard of the elevens engaged.

In these days when first-class cricket has, perhaps, become both serial and serious it may be refreshing even to those not specially in the two schools to watch a game in which the will to win predominates the players on both sides and a large percentage of the spectators. A feature of this match is that one of the teams, Rugby, will be wearing light blue shirts, a custom which has been in vogue for over a century. At every school the XI play for their colours, but few, if any, carry them into action on their backs.

Yours faithfully,

R. H. SPOONER (Marlborough)

PELHAM WARNER (Rugby)

Because of relaying the square the match, first played at Lord's in 1855 and in most years subsequently, was removed from the ground in 1973.

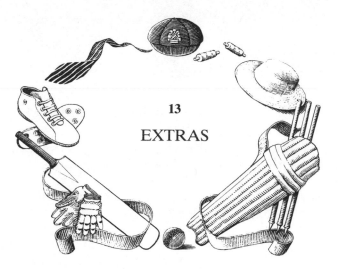

13
EXTRAS

THE BIRTHPLACE OF CRICKET

From the Revd H. A. Floud, 19 February 1908

Hon. Secretary, Hambledon CC,

Sir, Will you allow me through your columns to publish a statement which will be of interest to all cricketers, and probably to other Englishmen? Hambledon, in Hampshire, claims to be the birthplace of cricket. The old records show that cricket was played on Broad-Halfpenny Down, the Hambledon ground, at least as early as 1750; and in 1777 a Hambledon eleven played a famous match against the Rest of England, and won a single innings victory. It is proposed to revive the match this summer, when the Hambledon team will probably be captained by Mr C. B. Fry (a Hampshire man). It has also been arranged to erect a memorial at the corner of the field, to mark the site where the cricketing heroes of old fought out their battles. Subscriptions to this memorial, limited to one guinea, will be received by

Yours obediently,
HAROLD A. FLOUD

Fry led Hambledon to victory over England by five wickets.

PLAY IN THE 'FORTIES

From Mr Frederic Harrison, 20 May 1919

Writer, political theorist and traveller. Special correspondent for *The Times* in Paris 1876 and a frequent contributor to the newspaper. Honorary Freeman of Bath 1921.

Sir, As I am one of the few living men who have played a ball from W. Lillywhite, the 'Non-pareil Bowler', the practical author of round-arm bowling, you may care for a few things I recall. In the forties the London schools were free of Lord's, both for practice and matches and I was playing there from 1846 to 1849. Old Lilly, the First, would occasionally give us boys a ball or two for fun, as we left the ground. He was very short, wiry, and artful, slow and tricky. Fuller Pilch at the wicket was a wonder, and George Parr would often lift the ball clean over the tennis court into the road outside. Tom Box kept wicket in a stiff tall white hat, but he had a long stop even to Lilly. The great Alfred Mynn, with his tremendous fast balls, upset all calculations, and was the W. G. of the forties. It was a joy to see his huge person as active as a boy, both as bowler and with the bat. The event of my schoolboy days was the single-wicket match between Felix and Mynn. Mynn sent back a hot return over the bowler's head, which Felix leapt up and caught in his right hand. Then Mynn sent down rattlers hour after hour, which Felix played, but which he could not drive before the wicket, and so he lost the match. We used to study 'Felix on the Bat', and worked hard at 'the cut', which we understood him to have devised. Then William Clarke, of Nottingham, with his 'lobs', again revolutionized the game. On some wickets he was unplayable.

Cricket in the forties was not so scientific, but it was far more amusing to the mere public – far less maiden overs, far less 'leg' play, quicker scoring, rattling 'skyers', and long-field catches. Lord's was much smaller, much rougher and the crowd was not so far off the wicket. As long as I ever played cricket – and I bowled in the school eleven, 1847–49, and in the college eleven, 1850–52 – a ball delivered above the shoulder was a no-ball. 'Sneaks' would often beat good men. Umpires wore ordinary clothes. I remember in the forties as the finest figure in the whole field Sir Frederick Bathurst, third baronet, a magnificent cricketer all round.

FREDERIC HARRISON

ENGLAND'S TEAM IN 1859

From Mr A. W. Arnold, 12 July 1938

Sir, Many and many a time as a child in the sixties I have seen the very same photograph that appears in your issue to-day of the England team of 1859 [the United England XI] in a barber's shop at Dorking. The barber's name was Caffyn, and he was a cousin of the English captain, Caffyn, who lived at Reigate. I remember some members of the team were in the Surrey County Club, and how they came down to play 22 of Dorking. Among them were Caffyn, Lockyer, and Stephenson, and, as it happened, two famous Dorking players, Harry Jupp and Tom Humphrey. Jupp made many a run by what was called a 'draw', a stroke one never sees now. Later on these two usually went in first for Surrey.

In those days Caffyn had, as most barbers had, wax busts in his shop, and old Caffyn, who had a rare sense of fun, told me that on one very hot summer day, in his haste, when he was going to play at Reigate with his famous cousin, he forgot to pull down the blinds of his shop, and, to his horror, when he returned found that a blazing sun had caused Queen Victoria to lean forward with the Duke of Wellington leaning on her shoulders; while the King of Prussia was so badly melted that he had fallen right into a corner.

I am, &c.,

A. W. ARNOLD

BASEBALL

From Grandmother, 13 August 1874

Sir, Some American athletes are trying to introduce to us their game of baseball, as if it were a novelty; whereas the fact is that it is an ancient English game, long ago discarded in favour of cricket.

In a letter of the celebrated Mary Lepel, Lady Hervey, written in 1748, the family of Frederick, Prince of Wales, are described as 'diverting themselves with base-ball, a play all who are or have been schoolboys are well acquainted with.'

Your obedient servant,

GRANDMOTHER

Not everyone was so scathing. *Wisden* devoted four pages full of compliments to the one-month tour by the two leading American baseball teams.

At Lord's they played cricket (Eleven Gentlemen of MCC v Eighteen Gentlemen of America) as well as baseball, 3580 paying a shilling to watch on the first day. The Americans had their doubts. In 1881 the *New York Times* said:

'Our experience with the national game of baseball has been sufficiently thorough to convince us that it was in the beginning a sport unworthy of men, and that it is now, in its fully developed state, unworthy of gentlemen. Cricket will probably become as popular here in the course of a few years as it is in England . . .'

BASEBALL AND CRICKET

From Mr W. C. J. Garrard, 19 October 1956

Of Dunwoody, Georgia, USA.

Is it not a remarkable coincidence that within the short space of a few months, unique, unprecedented and similar bowling and pitching feats have been performed? Mr Jim Laker's feat of taking all 10 Australian wickets in the fourth Test match has recently been matched by Mr Don Larson's feat of pitching a perfect game in the fifth game of the World Series. The exact cricket equivalent of pitching a perfect baseball game is, I suppose, taking all 10 wickets for no runs. However, this feat is probably beyond the capability even of Mr Laker.

W. C. J. GARRARD

Hedley Verity took 10 wickets for 10 runs for Yorkshire against Nottinghamshire in 1932.

CRICKET

From the Revd R. I. Woodhouse, 1 June 1883

Writing from Kensington Branch of Young Men's Friendly Society.

Sir, Every one must allow that the game of cricket is more popular now among the working men of London than it was say five or ten years ago. Then, on Saturday afternoons such a thing as an artisan in flannels was never to be seen; now there is not a more common sight. I am venturing to trouble you on his behalf with the following suggestion. The question is often asked where can he play? Every year the population increases 50,000, consequently green fields are further and further from the scene of his labours, and the expenses of reaching the place of recreation, together with the increase of the value of land and competition for suitable grounds, all tend to hinder rather than to further his love of our national game.

It has occurred to me that some suitable fields in all parts of the suburbs of the City should be secured at once, either by the aid of the State under the strong plea of needful recreation for the masses, or better still by the representative club of the country, the Marylebone, and should be let to the working-men's clubs at a fair rental. If four such grounds were secured, each large enough for three wickets, they would do more for the game of cricket than can be estimated. It is well known that lawn tennis is injuring this game among the upper class. If we would hold our own against our colonies we must make the love of it even more national than it is at present. I understand that the MCC committee have paid off the whole debt on their most perfect ground, so that they are free to set the example in a manner becoming to their prestige, and I have no doubt that many clubs and private members would ably second any scheme they might propose, and I feel confident generations of future cricketers 'would rise up and call them blessed'.

I must ask you, Sir, to excuse this trespass upon your space during the session of Parliament, but I am emboldened by the desire in everything to bridge over the gulf that separates the east and west, the lower and the upper class, and by the assurance that both Lords and Commons have the people's welfare both bodily and spiritually at heart, and will unite in furthering this charitable, desirable, and practical scheme.

Yours,
R. I. WOODHOUSE

SUGGESTION FOR A TEST MATCH

From Sir Home Gordon, Bt, 31 October 1908

Sir, As the arrangements for the tour of the Australians in this country next summer are now being concluded, may I be permitted to suggest another ground for the first Test match, the subsequent ones (Lord's, Oval, Manchester, and Leeds) being all adequate? So far there seems to have been no alternative to Birmingham but Nottingham. Those who have witnessed the comparatively limited and listless attendance on both grounds at these great encounters will endorse my proposal that next summer the first Test match should be played at Leicester. The ground will accommodate 17,000, whilst an additional stand to seat 2,000 could be erected on the score board side. The turf is excellent, the local support to cricket is increasing, and the position of Leicester is central and is only an hour and three quarters by train from London. I have not the least connexion with the county, and my proposition is made solely with the view to benefiting cricket generally. The stimulus afforded locally would be obviously invaluable, and the Australians themselves are not likely to object to the prospect of a larger attendance than has been averaged at Trent-bridge or Birmingham.

Yours faithfully,

HOME GORDON

Leicester was eventually awarded an international fixture – an England v. Australia one-day match of June 1981 – only for it to be transferred to Birmingham, whose larger capacity offered the prospect of larger gate receipts. From 1901 to 1939 Leicestershire played at Aylestone Road; since 1946 their home has been Grace Road.

PLEA BY A MINOR COUNTY

From Sir Kenneth Kemp, Bt, 14 September 1910

Twelfth Baronet of Gissing. Norfolk player (1877–84) and Hon. Secretary (until 1889).

Sir, In your review of the cricket season today you make a suggestion that there should be three matches of Gentlemen and Players – one at Lord's and the other two in other parts of the country. May I humbly make a further suggestion that these should take place in the North, South, East, and West of England alternately?

Norfolk has earned the position as champion of Minor Counties for 1910. What a magificent reward it would be, and what a stimulus it would give to cricket, if one of these matches were played here!

We small and minor counties have very hard work in keeping a county team up. If we have a promising professional he is enticed away by higher pay than we can give – yet it is only by having a fair number of professionals that we can get gates or enthuse our country districts.

We have over 100,000 population, a ground we are proud of; and we could produce a crowd in that event that would in appreciation equal one on any other ground in England.

Yours faithfully,
KENNETH KEMP

Norfolk men enticed away over the years include: Fuller Pilch; Bill, John and several other Edriches; and Peter Parfitt. One 'star' stayed loyal – Michael Falcon, an all-rounder considered good enough to have represented England, played for Norfolk from 1907 to 1946, captaining them from 1912 until his retirement.

BAD LIGHT AND INTERRUPTED MATCHES

From Lord Harris, 7 August 1913

Sir, Some short time back, at the annual meeting of the Cricketers' Fund Friendly Society, I deprecated the modern practice of drawing for light, and stated that I could not remember any case of such a thing in the 20 years, 1870–1890, when I was actively engaged in first-class cricket.

A correspondent of the *Sporting Life*, signing himself 'Long Leg', challenges the accuracy of my statement in a recent issue. I have therefore referred to Dr W. G. Grace, Mr A. N. Hornby, and Mr A. P. Lucas, who all confirm the absolute accuracy of my statement. Dr Grace adds:-

'We never dreamt of appealing for bad light. I have played at the Oval when the gas lamps have been lighted.'

I know well that it is very little use appealing to the umpires to display more independence; but surely the captains need not be so timorous. I quoted at the above meeting two recent cases – Eton v. Winchester and Kent v. Surrey. In the former, by staying at the wickets in a really abominable light, the Eton batsmen made their position practically safe; in the latter the Surrey batsmen, when well in, appealed for light when it was nothing like so bad as that at Eton and pehaps lost the match in consequence.

Faithfully yours,
HARRIS

P.S. By the way, at the same meeting I told a most charming story of my dear friend and old time comrade, Alfred Lyttelton, which the reporters, for reasons best known to themselves, chose to omit all reference to.

In a Middlesex v. Lancashire match at Lord's Lyttelton was magnificently stumped by Pilling off Crossland's fastest ball breaking back between bat and leg. When the innings was over Lyttelton unostentatiously met Pilling at the players' entrance and slipped a sovereign into his hand as a token of a brother wicketkeeper's appreciation of a splendid bit of work.

THE SPIN OF A COIN

From Sir Jeremiah Colman, Bt, 12 January 1925

Vice-President of Surrey CCC (President 1916–23). Cricket devotee with superb collection of pictures, catalogued in *The Noble Game of Cricket.* Chairman of J. and J. Colman Ltd., Chairman of Commercial Union Assurance. Master of Stationers' Company.

Do not present-day conditions point to our having reached a time when a change should be made in the custom governing the toss for choice of innings? It is recognized that choice of innings is an important factor, and it seems deplorable that each side should not, as far as possible, be given equal advantages. To the glorious uncertainty of cricket it is surely unnecessary to add the gamble of the spin of a coin. A simple course would be for each side to be given choice alternatively. Teams travel thousands of miles to meet friendly rivals, and it must be unsatisfactory to winners and losers alike to feel that it is common belief that success or failure are due to the toss – a belief which the winners would probably welcome an opportunity of dispelling.

JEREMIAH COLMAN

England had just lost two tosses – and two Test matches – in Australia. The series ended 4-1, England's only victory coming, by an innings, when they won the toss.

LONDON CLUB CRICKET

From Lord Harris and others, 21 December 1925

Four England captains and an England cap. Leveson Gower: captain of Oxford University and Surrey (1893–1920); MCC committee; President of Surrey; Chairman of Test selectors; knighted for services to cricket 1953. Christopherson: Kent and England (1883–90); President of MCC. 1939–46; important figure in the City and ultimately chairman of the Midland Bank.

Gilligan: Cambridge University and Surrey and captain of Sussex and England (1919–32); Test selector; President and Patron of Sussex CCC; President of MCC 1967.

Sir, It has become a matter of grave concern to those who recognize the important part which London club cricket plays in the national game to observe the straits to which some of the clubs are reduced in order to retain their grounds.

Economic conditions in some cases have increased site value to such an extent that the landlord feels obliged to sell and the club has either to buy or to seek a new home. The Hampstead Cricket Club finding itself in this position has with great energy set about raising a fund of over £20,000 to buy its ground.

The Wimbledon Cricket Club is faced with a difficulty of a less reasonable and to our minds unnecessary kind. The Club, which has been in existence over 70 years and is already the freeholder of its beautiful ground, is threatened with the compulsory acquisition of it by the Wimbledon Borough Council for use as a sports and pleasure ground. While we have every sympathy with the desire of local authorities to provide sports grounds for all classes, we do think that this action shows little discrimination on the part of the local authority inasmuch as it already owns a large extent of suitable but undeveloped ground.

Knowing as we do the Wimbledon Ground and the high traditions of the Club, we have no hesitation in saying that anything that is done to disturb its development on former lines will be deeply regretted by all sportsmen.

We are, yours faithfully,

HARRIS, H. D. G. LEVESON GOWER, P. F. WARNER, STANLEY CHRISTOPHERSON, ARTHUR E. R. GILLIGAN

An agreement was reached in Wimbledon 'satisfactory to both parties'.

AUTOGRAPH HUNTING

From Mr W. B. Franklin, 21 June 1928

Sir, Autograph hunting has in the last few years increased to such an extent that it is fast becoming a real nuisance and inconvenience to those who are 'hunted'. I am referring more particularly to the practice at cricket matches, where it is often impossible to venture outside the comparative safety of the pavilion to go for a walk round the ground, for fear of encountering every few yards the persistent cry of 'May I have your autograph?'

Whilst in no way wishing to discourage the enthusiasm of schoolboys and others, who admire the skill of those whose signature they want, I would suggest that, adopting the principle that something obtained for nothing is less valuable to the owner than something for which he has had to pay, touring teams such as the Australians and West Indians should announce on their arrival that they will only give autographs upon payment of some small charge, such as a penny or twopence a signature or a shilling for the whole team, the proceeds of which could be devoted to Earl Haig's Fund at the end of the tour. I discussed this suggestion with the present captain of the West Indian XI yesterday and he expressed himself as being in complete agreement with me. If the scheme were adopted widely by counties and others, not only would a considerable sum be collected for charity, but many unnecessary requests for autographs would cease and the time and trouble of the players be saved.

I am, Sir, yours faithfully,

WALTER B. FRANKLIN

MODERN WICKETS

From Mr H. J. G. Hines, 14 August 1928

Assistant in chemical department at Rothamsted Experimental Station. Later lecturer in soil chemistry at the University of Queensland.

Sir, The recent spell of dry weather, coupled with its crop of drawn matches, has produced an outcry against the modern wicket. The use of marl and 'liquid manure' is said to have produced a wicket so true that it is impossible to get good batting sides out in time to ensure a definite result to matches. A plea has been raised for a return to the 'natural' wickets of a past era. What is a natural wicket? Before any definite measures can be taken to limit the amount of preparation of the pitch it is surely necessary to get more exact information on this point. It is desired, I take it, that pitches should be prepared which, while being plumb and level, should, under average climatic conditions, take the spin of the ball easily and quickly, and give every encouragement to the spin bowler keeping a good length, rather than to the mere 'bumper'.

This characteristic of the wicket may be affected by two causes:

first, the nature of the soil; secondly, the nature of the vegetation on that soil. Of these the soil is by far the most important. There surely must be wickets in the country which have the desired characteristics described above. If these could be found and the physical characteristics of their surfaces examined by a competent soil authority, surely some more exact standard could be aimed at than the present loose definitions of a 'natural' wicket. For it is evident that a wicket pitched on sandy soil would differ considerably from one pitched on clay. If, having arrived at a satisfactory standard, both from the physical and botanical point of view, a complete survey of the principal grounds of the country were made, it would assist considerably in the further doctoring of our wickets to suit the bowler rather than the batsman, if such be possible.

I am, Sir, yours truly,
H. J. G. HINES

CRICKET ON THE GREEN

From Mr S. P. B. Mais, 10 May 1932

Journalist, broadcaster and voluminous author. Later Professor of English, RAF Cadet College. FRSA.

Sir, The sad sight of a village green on a sunny Saturday afternoon in May as empty of children as the streets of Hamelin after the Pied Piper's departure impels me to solicit your readers' sympathy and advice.

In 1902 the local council bought the Southwick village green for £25. Until this summer games, with due regard to the weather, have been freely permitted. A few weeks ago the cricket club, who have played on a carefully nurtured pitch in the middle of the green for many years, were informed that in future cricket was to be limited to one regulated game only, confined to children under 14. A referendum was taken showing an overwhelming majority in favour of the continuance of cricket on the green. The council ignored it. A protest game was played in order to find out the limits of the council's legal rights in the matter. The council ignored it. I have myself offered to buy the green back again for twenty times what the council gave for it, and to present it to the village for ever on the sole condition that cricket should for ever be permitted on it. The council ignored my offer. It is hoped that a more amenable council will rescind the present council's decision, as the ban on cricket was only carried by the chairman's casting vote, but what I am concerned about is the summer of 1932.

This village lies in a very congested area, and that the demand for public playgrounds and cricket pitches in this neighbourhood far exceeds the supply is proved by the fact that our own new recreation ground, acquired and laid out at a colossal cost, already resembles a town park on Saturdays. If the village green, for so many years the focus of our communal life, is now to be compelled to stand, swept, garnished, and derelict to satisfy the whim of those who object to seeing children at liberty to play as they like, it means the death-knell of the place. No sportsman, no parent, and no lover of liberty who can possibly help it will continue to live in a place where such restrictions are enforced. I suggest that the Playing Fields Association make it their business to find out why two glorious cricket pitches are to lie unused (except by stray dogs) throughout the whole of this summer in an area where hundreds of keen adult cricketers and thousands of children cannot find grounds to play on.

I am, Sir, your obedient servant,

S. P. B. MAIS

Cricket was being played on Southwick village green in 1983.

QUEER NAMES IN CRICKET

From Mr C. S. Kent, 12 August 1937

Manager of *The Times*.

Remembering that a former Nottinghamshire wicketkeeper was named Oates, I notice with interest that the present occupant of the position is Wheat. It recalls my youthful glee to find Root following Beet on the Derbyshire card years ago, and, more recently, that the Surrey team long included both Hobbs and Fender.

C. S. KENT

A PLAYING FIELD WAR?

From Lord Crewe, KG, 30 July 1940

Lord Privy Seal 1908 and 1912–15; Secretary of State for the Colonies 1908–10; Secretary of State for India 1910–15; HM Ambassador to Paris

1922–28; Secretary of State for War 1931; leader of the Liberals in the House of Lords.

Sir, At our annual meeting of the London and Greater London Playing Fields Association on Monday, 22 July, the annual report was presented, in which it was stated that on the outskirts of London, as of other great cities, it has often been found that playing fields and other open spaces are the best, and sometimes the only, sites available for search-light and anti-aircraft stations, but that the Departments concerned had shown great consideration in preserving as much room as possible for their customary use and enjoyment.

It is pleasant to hear that the Wednesday issue of the [Berliner] *Lokal Anzeiger* appeared with a flaring headline:– 'Revolt in England against the ploughing up of cricket pitches. A violent struggle is proceeding between the two factions, and the whole country is in a state of ferment almost amounting to civil war'! Apparently it is thus that an important German newspaper tries to console its stupider readers for any local hardships they have to suffer.

Your obedient servant,

CREWE

CRICKETERS' INITIALS

From Mr J. C. H. Hadfield, 8 July 1950

Novelist and figure in publishing. Author of *A Wisden Century, 1850–1950.*

Sir, No amount of over-familiar allusions to 'Len', 'Bill' or 'Roley' in the descriptive prose of cricket reports can make up for insensitive treatment of the score sheet, which is, after all, the true poetry of the game. The popular Press today (*The Times* is an honourable exception) grants initials indiscriminately to amateurs and professionals alike, but has apparently decided that a ration of only one initial a player can be allowed. How can Mr N. W. D. Yardley, who was so richly endowed by his godparents, maintain his moral authority as England's captain when the penny papers either 'Norman' him or write him down in the score sheet as a mere 'N. Yardley'? Meanwhile his team-mate, Wardle, is allotted a wholly superfluous initial 'J.', though he was blessed at birth with a surname which, without adornment, expresses the quintessence of Yorkshire slow left-arm spin and guile.

I do not wish to appear undemocratic or a mere *laudator temporis acti*, but I admit some nostalgia for the Arcadian days when the score of the recent leaders in the county championship (though they were then lowlier placed) glowed with the lyrical simplicity of such names as Quaife or Lilley, or glittered with the baroque splendour of the Honourable F. S. G. Calthorpe (who possessed even more initials than that, I believe, but modestly discarded some of them on the cricket field). At a time when London has a superb exhibition of the literature of cricket [presented by the National Book League with the co-operation of MCC] it is surely fitting to make a plea for a higher aesthetic approach to the nomenclature of players.

Yours faithfully,

J. C. H. HADFIELD

FAILURE TO SCORE

England had scored 128 runs off 114 overs on the third day of the second Test match against West Indies.

From Captain C. B. Fry, 15 February 1954

Surrey, Hampshire and captain of Oxford University, Sussex and England (1891–1921). Great scholar and all-round athlete. England football international and holder of world long jump record. Test selector. Writer and reporter on cricket. Served at the League of Nations and for 42 years was director of the training ship *Mercury*, for which service he was made an honorary captain of the Royal Naval Reserve.

Sir, In regard to criticism of recent events in the West Indies it may be of interest to recall that Mr J. A. Spender, the eminent editor of the old *Westminster Gazette*, caused a boldly lettered notice to be posted in his sports department, saying: 'The failure of a first-class batsman to score is not to be represented as an instance of extreme moral obliquity.' [*sic*]

Yours, &c.,

C. B. FRY

From Sir Pelham Warner, 17 February 1954

Sir, May I be allowed to supplement Captain C. B. Fry's letter in your issue of today? Will our sterner critics read *Tom Brown's Schooldays* and note in the description of the famous match in the Close, at Rugby, between Rugby and the MCC, in June, 1841, these words: 'But cricket is full of glorious chances and the goddess who presides over it loves to bring down the most skilful players.'

Compton, who a few years ago was the darling of the gods and filled Lord's and every other cricket ground on which he played, and is still a great batsman, now finds but few to do him reverence. Ingratitude indeed more base than traitors' arms! Cricket is a very difficult game, probably the most difficult of all, and you cannot make runs to order. Every great batsman, from W. G. and Ranjitsinhji to Fender, Hammond, and Hutton – Sir Donald Bradman is the only exception so far as I know – has had to meet triumph and disaster, and therefore I would plead with those stern critics to be a little kinder and more mellow.

One final word. Their strictures do not help to give confidence to a team, and has not every great general, from Caesar to Field-Marshals Montgomery and Alexander, always made it a cardinal point in his strategy to encourage his troops to remember their former prowess?

Yours, &c.,

P. F. WARNER

From Field-Marshal Viscount Montgomery of Alamein, KG, GCB, DSO, 22 February 1954

Honorary life member of MCC. Captain of rugby at St Paul's School and a member of the cricket and swimming teams. In 1905 he scored 60 not out in a last-wicket stand of over 100 when defeat for the school was impending.

Sir, In his letter to you published in *The Times* of 17 February Sir Pelham Warner mentions my name. But I am not clear as to the point of his reasoning, whether it is applied to Caesar or to any British commander. A commander-in-chief will certainly encourage the troops under his command. But he cannot count on public opinion in the home country, or in the Press, to help him in giving confidence to his armies; he would like such help, but as to whether he gets it will depend on himself and on no one else. The greatest single factor making for success in war is morale; and the surest road to high morale is success in battle.

A general is meant to win battles. And if he does so with a minimum loss of life he will have the complete confidence of his soldiers and also of the public in the home country. But once a general begins to lose his battles he must expect to be replaced in command. It is of no avail to plead bad luck, or inefficient subordinates, or bad weather, or that events were too much for him. He is given the best possible resources; if he succeeds he gets the credit and the honour; if he fails he probably gets another chance; if he continues to fail he goes. This may be hard; but it is what happens in life and I reckon it is about right. Do not the same principles apply in cricket, in political life, and in fact in every sphere where leadership is required?

When all is said and done the true leader must be able to dominate, and finally master, the events that surround him. Once he lets events get the better of him those under him, and the public, will lose confidence and he will cease to be of value as a leader. If you are Captain of England you must win your battles; if you do not you must expect criticism, and will most certainly get it. The team you lead must be good and disciplined. It must also have that infectious optimism and offensive eagerness that comes from physical well-being. It is then up to you, the leader.

In the end no leader can long continue unless he wins victories. The supreme example of a British leader who was always able to dominate, and finally master, the events that surrounded him, is Sir Winston Churchill – and he is still doing so, thank God.

I am sure that my friend 'Plum' Warner will not mind my suggesting to him that the principles outlined above are equally applicable in cricket.

Yours sincerely,
MONTGOMERY OF ALAMEIN

MERELY PLAYERS

From Mr M. E. Simons, 13 June 1980

Sir, Is our national economic predicament ascribable to cricket?

The game involves one pro-active batsman backed up by a mate, and one bowler supported by 10 reactive fielders, whilst nine members of the batting team sit in the pavilion with their feet up. Periodically everyone has a drink.

Yours truly,
MARTIN E. SIMONS

From Mr Frank Stewart, 16 June 1980

Sir, As a life-long cricket lover one must recoil from any inference by Mr M. E. Simons (13 June) that the game is actually responsible for our national performance. But, alas, it certainly displays the same symptoms. If one compares the recent match at Trent Bridge with the Australian Test there in 1938 the following 'productivity' statistics emerge:

	Now	Then
Days of play	4+	4
Overs bowled	363	503
Runs scored	1032	1496
Centuries	—	7
Extras as a percentage of runs scored	10.7%	4.9%

Yours faithfully,
FRANK E. STEWART

From Mr Paul Watkins, 17 June 1980

Sir, Mr M. E. Simons (13 June) does well to draw attention to the probable connection between the game of cricket and our economic problems. However, I am surprised that he makes no mention of that sinister pair of white-coated figures who appear to be at least nominally in control of the whole business but who actually do nothing except transfer coins from their left to their right pocket and back again, while periodically making extravagant gestures.

Yours truly,
PAUL WATKINS

From Mr John E. C. Tupman, 27 June 1980

Sir, Mr Francis W. Cundy's suggestion (letters, 24 June) for an appropriate remedy for a disgruntled batsman is inspiring. Unfortunately the industrial tribunal does not have jurisdiction to entertain applications for 'wrongful dismissal' which is the domain of the civil courts. Even given an application for 'unfair dismissal' over which the industrial tribunal does have jurisdiction, I regret to say that the aggrieved batsman would have to have been at the crease for a period of at least 52 weeks and he would then be entitled to receive written reasons for dismissl from the umpire.

Yours faithfully,
JOHN E. C. TUPMAN

THE MOTHER OF THE GRACES

From Mr Stanhope Kennedy, 31 July 1929

Sir, Probably the only woman of the Victorian age (possibly of this age, too) who understood cricket technically was Mrs Grace, mother of 'The Three Graces'. Richard Daft, who knew her, spoke of her knowledge of the game in his book, and he said that George Parr often spoke, in after years, of a letter he had received from Mrs Grace in connexion with her son, 'E. M.', going to Australia with Parr's 1862 team; but the great interest of this letter was that Mrs Grace said that she had a much younger son who showed great promise, particularly on account of the strength of his back play. This was 'W. G.', then 14, who fulfilled his mother's prophecy to the letter, for nobody ever saw him use an ordinary forward stroke to any bowling: he never went farther than 'half-cock' in defence. The uncanny ease with which he played back to Jones's very fast bowling in the first 1899 Test match at Trent Bridge remains vivid.

STANHOPE KENNEDY

Mrs Martha Grace remains the only woman to have been recorded in *Wisden*'s 'Births and Deaths of Cricketers'.

A CRICKETER'S WIFE

From Mr Wallis Myers, CBE, 28 April 1938

For over 30 years lawn tennis correspondent of *The Daily Telegraph* and one of the greatest authorities on the game.

Sir, 'The Splendid Mrs Small', mentioned by your Cricket Correspondent in his appealing article, surely had a counterpart in New

Zealand in Mrs Wilding, wife of Frederick Wilding, KC, and mother of Anthony Wilding, four times lawn tennis champion at Wimbledon.

When Frederick Wilding, one of the best all-round athletes Herefordshire had produced since the days of Tom Spring, migrated to New Zealand in the eighties, he fulfilled his promise as a great cricketer when bowling for Eighteen of Canterbury in 1888, by taking eight wickets for 21 against Shrewsbury's team. Among his victims were George Lohmann and Johnny Briggs.

Mrs Wilding not only watched every ball bowled in her husband's matches; she kept a complete score together with an analysis of the bowling. So accurate was she that the official scorer often consulted her before checking up his sheet. She was, indeed, a devoted student of games. Her cuttings-books, with several volumes relating to her son's exploits on the courts all over the world, all carefully indexed, were probably unique for their comprehensiveness. When Anthony Wilding fell in Flanders she dispatched one of his lawn tennis prizes to each of his intimate friends, of whom Lord Balfour was the oldest.

Faithfully yours,
A. WALLIS MYERS

WOMEN IN CRICKET

From Sir John Squire, 16 April 1938

Editor, poet and man of letters. Founder and captain of the Invalids CC, for which the only qualification for membership was to be a friend of the captain. Between the wars an eleven took the field every Saturday, containing leading figures from the literary world. Their activities are immortalized in the cricket match in A. G. Macdonell's *England, Their England*, Sir John being the model for Mr Hodge.

Sir, It is pleasant to see your Cricket Correspondent sticking to his guns about women's cricket. He has put his thumb on the right spot in saying that the scoffs about the women's Test matches last year have come from those who 'weren't there'.

I, too, saw the Oval Test match. I was as surprised at it as your Correspondent; but when the surprise was over, like him, I admitted the facts. Immediately thereafter, and throughout the winter, I have heard the sort of comments which he himself seems to have heard. I have remarked that those two teams fielded better than some first-class county sides and produced a lovely variety of strokes from straighter bats than are now common, and had bowlers who kept a length, both slow and (by any standard) very nearly fast, and have been informed by diehards who 'weren't there'

(a) politely, either 'You are exaggerating' or 'You must be romantic about women' or (b) impolitely, 'They are only fit to cope with men playing left-handed with broom-sticks' or 'You are talking through your hat.'

The crowds, those days, steadily increased; the astonishing rumour ran round that women could not merely bat but *throw*, thereby upsetting the age-long legend that 'girls can't chuck' – an operation not natural, I think, even to boys. Those 'girls' at the Oval picked up and threw in from the boundary with an accuracy which would have done credit to a University side, and the knowledgeable Oval crowd duly recognized it. They were 'on their toes' all the time, and some of the catches were miraculous: there was one Australian 'girl', with an extremely Australian hat, who took a somersault catch from the bat's point which I have never seen bettered at Lord's. There were shots through the covers and fizzing square-cuts for 4 which reminded one of former days.

They played with a ball slightly smaller than 'men's size'. That is reasonable; on the average their hands are smaller than ours, though averages are not everything, and there was at least one pair of hands on the field which looked like hip-baths in comparison with my own. They hit, I think, no 6; they had obviously been trained to keep the ball on the ground; they had not the size or 'beef' of Mr Percy Fender; there were one or two hits that might have got a 6 by the tavern at Lord's; but the Oval is a very large ground, as anybody (like myself) who has had to walk from wicket to the pavilion after making a duck in a humble holiday match well knows.

I still stick to my view that, given the women's-size ball, either of those teams might have beaten some of our county sides. Not our best; brawn counts. Cricket is coming into line with the other games. Mlle Suzanne Lenglen was not better than some men, but she was better than most men. Miss Joyce Wethered (though she is a moot point on her day) might not have been able to beat, on level terms, some of the male golfers of her time, but she could have taken on most of them, and I am sure that your Golf Correspondent will bear me out.

In lawn tennis and golf they have men's singles, women's singles, and mixed foursomes; a similar process will operate in cricket and in billiards.

Otherwise the men will not be allowed to play at all, which would be hard.

Yours faithfully,
J. C. SQUIRE

From Captain C. B. Fry, 21 August 1953

Sir, Apropos of Dame Meriel Talbot's letter of 18 August about women and cricket may I say that no man with real knowledge of the game has ever denied the female potential. We all know, who know at all, that a slim girl, if she swings properly and times her stroke precisely, can hit a ball from the centre of Lord's on to the top of the pavilion. Cricket is not a game of strength but of poise and skill.

Yours, &c.,
C. B. FRY

PAVILION FOR MEN

From Miss Margaret Morris, 14 June 1972

Sir, Being interested in cricket I decided this year to join a county club, thinking that I would gain knowledge of the sport by watching it in the company of experts. Unfortunately I did not think to take sex into account. The club pavilion is naturally the meeting place of members: it is there that the game is discussed, there that the club notice board is housed. I find however, that as a mere lady member, I am denied access to the pavilion until after the close of play – is this cricket?

Yours faithfully,
MARGARET MORRIS

The county club is Middlesex; the pavilion is at Lord's, one of the last bastions of male exclusiveness.

A MATCH FOR NAUSICAA

From Miss Jessica Jacobson, 24 June 1981

Sir, I was very angry to see a degrading reference to girls' catching in Mr John Woodcock's cricket report (Saturday, 20 June): 'with catching that would have put a girls' school to shame . . .'

I go to North London Collegiate School, a girls' school, where there is absolutely no lack of good catchers – and neither do I see why there should be a lack.

One particular catch, made by a classmate of mine in a game of rounders, comes to my mind immediately. It was a one-handed catch, taken while the girl was running at full tilt, and I am sure even Geoff Boycott would have been proud of it.

Yours sincerely,
JESSICA JACOBSON

From Major W. N. F. Carter, 27 June 1981

Sir, Miss Jacobson's letter about girls' catching (24 June) reminds me of a match I saw in Canterbury recently where Bob Woolmer hit a low trajectory, stinging six into the crowd.

Amid the warning shouts and ducking of heads, a white-haired lady calmly and cleanly caught the ball and tossed it coolly to the nearest fielder, who graciously invited her to join in the game.

England could do with her.

Yours, etc.,
W. N. F. CARTER

CLOTHES FOR CRICKET

From Mr A. C. Sutcliffe, 22 August 1953

Sir, The new television camera lens which enables us to enjoy a close-up view of the Test matches also reveals how many of the players are constantly fidgeting with their clothes. They seem to be constantly hitching up their trousers, tugging at their belts, tucking-in their shirts, or rolling up their sleeves. Is there any reason why a comfortable garment should not be adopted? Tennis players have progressed steadily in recent years and most men wear shorts and shirts with short sleeves.

It would be too drastic a revolution to expect cricketers to wear shorts, but perhaps a one-piece garment hanging from the shoulders would meet the need. If this were made in cream flannel possibly the effect might be something like the long woollen combinations worn in winter by the Victorians and this would be deplorable, but one of your readers may be able to design a garment that would be acceptable to sportsmen, both playing and watching the game.

Yours faithfully,
ALAN C. SUTCLIFFE

From Mrs B. S. Hogg, 28 August 1953

Sir, May a great-grandmother, who played cricket on the sands with A. C. MacLaren, suggest that 'fidgeting with their clothes' may assist a cricketer's play? I remember that Hilton, of golfing fame, tossed off his cloth cap at the follow-through of every drive.

Yours faithfully,
B. S. HOGG

FLANNELLED FOOLS

A correspondent suggested that long flannel trousers reduced a fast bowler's speed.

From the Headmaster of Winchester, 4 May 1967

Sir, The headline in the paper of my neighbour in the train yesterday, 'Snow Stops Play', is perhaps as apt a comment as any on the correspondence in your columns about the foolishness of flannel.

I am, yours sincerely,
DESMOND LEE

LONG HAIR AT CRICKET

From Senex, 21 August 1937

Sir, One detail of the recent schoolboys' matches aroused a good deal of criticism in the pavilion at Lord's, but I think it escaped comment in the Press. I refer to the handicap imposed by their very long hair on some of the boys who played without caps.

Batting, every such boy had to brush back his hair before each stroke. During the stroke the obscuring mat fell forward again and had once more to be smoothed back, and thus an appreciable fraction of time was lost in calling for a run. Bowling, a similar procedure had to be followed: Smoothe back the hair, run and deliver the ball, and then smoothe back again. More, some boys who took a long run had to unblind themselves when half-way to the bowling crease. All this handicapped the bowler in fielding a straight drive or in effecting a caught-and-bowled.

It occurred to us critics that, assuming there to be a compelling objection to shorter hair, the trouble could be prevented by the boys being taught not to discard their caps. Of course we realized that in criticizing we laid ourselves open to remarks about the fox who lost his tail or hints that we at any rate would have no difficulty in going bald-headed for the bowling.

But is long hair which at the least exertion falls like a curtain before the eyes really desirable in young athletes? And, if it is, could not their coaches touch delicately on the fate of Absolom and insist on the retention of the cap?

I am, Sir, your obedient servant,

SENEX

UNCAPPED

From Dom Gregory Murray, 12 July 1974

Of Downside Abbey.

Sir, It was unfortunate that Mankad lost his wicket in the recent Test match when his cap fell off and dislodged a bail. But, surely, the lesson is obvious. The traditional cricket cap is not suited to the current long hair fashion, being designed to sit firmly on the head, not to balance precariously on a shifting mass of hair. Perhaps our cricketers will now abandon either the trendy flowing locks or the cap – unless, of course, they prefer to wear hat-pins.

Yours, etc,

A. GREGORY MURRAY

HAT TRICK

From Mr Bernard Ineichen, 3 June 1978

Sir, Are we about to witness in this cricket season the award to players of their county helmet?

Yours faithfully,
BERNARD INEICHEN

BATSMAN'S ARMOUR

From Mr F. B. Singleton, 20 August 1975

Tony Greig, the England captain, adopted batting gloves which appeared to owe their origins to the boxing ring.

Sir, I wonder if the voluminous batting gloves which quite properly arouse Mr Kenneth Gregory's scepticism (letters, 14 August) have much at all to do with protection? Are they not simply part of the tendency, diligently fostered by commercial interests, in the last decade or so to introduce more and more sophisticated gear into sports and outdoor pursuits? Climbing is perhaps the outstanding example and now it is cluttering up the cricket fields.

Mr Gregory writes of batsmen in the twenties who wore only one glove. Even in the late thirties many a No. 10 or No. 11 showed as little concern for his shins as for his knuckles and sported only one pad. I never saw Tom Mitchell, the old England bowler, quite totally equipped. Old hands at Chesterfield and Buxton used to say that his single pad, which he buckled up so imperfectly that it invariably fell off during his brief outing to the wicket, was the result of a detested compromise with the Derbyshire committee and that his real preference was for bicycle clips.

My own impression was that any sort of attachment to his legs got in the way of his very effective scoop, the high point of his reputation as a batsman. It was a deceptively simple shot played from an almost kneeling position. In essence the blade of the bat was placed horizontal on the pitch and lifted briskly as the ball came into line with it; rather as one tosses a pancake. The object of course was to propel the ball sufficiently far in the direction of the sky as to allow Mitchell and his partner (more often than not a single-padded Copson) to cross at least three times before its collection on the downward flight by the nearest of the 11 men keenly following its progress.

Pads, gloves, wrist bands, finger stalls, toecaps, chewing gum; none of these were essential adjuncts of this splendid man's stroke play.

Yours faithfully,

F. B. SINGLETON

TONY GREIG'S EPILEPSY

From Mr C. G. R. Plowman, 16 September 1978

Sir, During the last few decades many major diseases such as cancer, tuberculosis and diabetes have come under public discussion, to the great benefit of their victims: epilepsy, however, is a significant exception. It has remained the object of widespread prejudice and until now has been a subject which both the sufferer and the general public have preferred to avoid.

As an epileptic it was with great satisfaction, therefore, that I read Richard Streeton's article (11 September) on the accomplishments of Tony Greig despite his handicap.

One of the foremost authorities on the subject, Professor W. G. Lennox, has said in his book *Epilepsy and Related Disorders*: 'We must ask what, in a word, is the epileptic's most serious and implacable handicap. It is of his own choosing, secrecy.'

Let us hope that Tony Greig is not going to be the only eminent person at present suffering from this disease to speak out and acknowledge the fact. Were more professional people who suffer with epilepsy, particularly those who have achieved fame, more willing to discuss openly a disability, which in many cases, with the aid of modern medicines, can be controlled, this unwarranted secrecy could be abolished once and for all.

Yours faithfully,

C. G. R. PLOWMAN

'THE DULLEST GAME'

From Sir Pelham Warner, 1 June 1946

Sir, Your Correspondent at Ottawa reports that our new Ambassador to the United States, Lord Inverchapel, went out of his way, at his first interview in the New World, to emphasize that he found cricket 'the dullest game ever invented'. Lord Inverchapel is of course entitled to his own opinion, but, as his country's representative, I find it regrettable that he should see fit to make a *pronunciamento* so at variance with the feelings of the majority of his countrymen. For cricket today, throughout the Empire, at all levels, surely enjoys as great, if not a greater, popularity as it ever did, in spite of all the difficulties we have to face after six years of war.

I would like to recall to Lord Inverchapel the words of another Scot, Andrew Lang, who wrote: 'Cricket is simply the most catholic and diffused, the most innocent, kindly, and manly of popular pleasures, while it has been the delight of statesmen and the relaxation of learning. Heaven might doubtless have devised a better diversion, but as certainly no better has been invented than that which grew up on the village greens of England.'

I am, Sir,

P. F. WARNER

THE LATEST SCORE

From Mr T. L. Geddes, 1 May 1948

Sir, Being a Scotsman, I have no interest in cricket. But at this season when all my mad English friends constantly ask me: 'Have you heard the latest score?' – to which question, obviously, I have neither the knowledge nor the desire to give an intelligent answer – I venture to suggest that the General Post Office might turn one of its golden-voiced girls on to the job of providing a cricketing service for telephone subscribers. At the usual charge of 1d. per call, my friends would then be able to dial CRI and obtain the score at any time of night or day.

The implementation of this suggestion would greatly increase my peace of mind, and that of all my compatriots similarly condemned to eke out a miserable, if somewhat more lucrative, existence among the extraordinary people who inhabit the southern portion of this island.

Yours faithfully,

T. L. GEDDES

The Post Office recorded score service began for the Lord's Test of 1956 when about 1 million calls – records are incomplete because the counting equipment was overloaded – were made to WEB 8811 (after Roy Webber, leading statistician of the day). The service, now available from plain 16, 154 or 160, has been extended to all major matches and in 1982 received 20.5 million calls. Several Scots, incidentally, have played Test cricket.

CRICKETERS OR JOURNALISTS?

Reports by Rockley Wilson and Percy Fender, to the *Daily Express* and *Daily News* respectively, contained criticism of the umpiring in Australia, and Wilson's comments in particular caused offence.

From the Hon. Treasurer, Lancashire CCC, 25 January 1921

Sir, I believe that most people interested in cricket will feel that a great mistake has been made in permitting cricketers who have been selected to represent the Mother-Country in these important games to write reports and criticisms of the matches in the newspapers. I am convinced that the Marylebone Cricket Club will be well advised in taking steps to prevent any recurrence of the practice. It certainly is not the province of the player to report and criticize the play of his colleagues, either individually or collectively, and such action in my view is very undesirable, for obvious reasons – and more especially so in the big matches.

I feel most strongly that men selected for Test match cricket ought to be strictly debarred from writing accounts of such matches. It is not their job, and if we are to avoid a feeling of resentment being caused, these players' Press reports ought undoubtedly to be stopped.

Yours faithfully,

EDWIN F. STOCKTON

At MCC's annual general meeting a motion was passed deprecating the reporting of matches by the players. Most tour contracts since have forbidden the practice and in 1983 Ian Botham was fined on tour, also for comments about Australian umpires, which were attributed to him in *The Sun*.

MEREDITH AT MELBOURNE

From Mr Charles Morgan, 8 January 1947

Novelist, essayist and literary critic. Principal Dramatic Critic of *The Times* 1926–39.

Sir, May a faithful reader of cricket reports be allowed to thank you and your Special Correspondent at Melbourne for the best he has read these 40 years? Who shall dare to say now that George Meredith is forgotten?

'Naturally the English players were now men uplifted: mercury bubbled in the blood . . . The issue was here a very ache of intensity; the arms of the deities above were stretching far beyond their reach as Miller went out of his ground to Wright . . .'

And might not this be a fitting end to *The Tragic Comedians*: 'A great match, even if much greater than the players in it'?

Your obedient servant,
CHARLES MORGAN

THE MEANDERING ARMY

From Mr Harry Marland, 16 January 1947

Sir, In your Special Correspondent's report of the third Test match, dated Melbourne, 7 January, appears the following sentence: 'But the army of clouds, not far distant for long, seemed to wander and vacillate and never find real contact with the main forces, like Napoleon's meandering army at Waterloo.'

This, like his other reports, was a joy to read, not only for its sportsmanship but for its very delightful literary style, which is unique; but was it not Grouchy's army which meandered at Waterloo?

Yours faithfully,
HARRY MARLAND

The Special Correspondent was Neville Cardus, for whose services *The Times* paid £500 to the *Manchester Guardian*. Cardus lived in Australia from 1939–48.

WRITING ALL ROUND THE WICKET

Yorkshire dismissed Johnny Wardle, their England slow left-arm bowler, who wrote a series of articles for the *Daily Mail* criticizing the running of the county.

From the General Secretary, National Union of Journalists,
12 August 1958

Sir, In your timely leading article yesterday on the public washing of dirty linen by cricket-writers (ghosted and otherwise) you rightly say the MCC will have 'the backing of players and spectators if it denounces a growing and pernicious habit in no uncertain terms.' It will also have the backing of the great majority of organized journalists.

The exploitation by agents and some sections of the Press of so-called 'big names' and notoriety in sport lowers standards in both cricket and journalism. This is due not only to the deplorable revelations of some sportsmen but to the fact that the professional sports journalist, temporarily supplanted or thrust into the background by a player-writer, is tempted to write more sensationally or scandalously to keep his place in the newspaper. Many professional journalists resist this temptation, but it is at the risk of seeing their functions increasingly usurped by the non-journalist sports-writer.

Surely it is time the MCC and county executives followed the example of the Rugby Union and Lawn Tennis Association and placed restraints on player-writers. I believe that many editors and some newspaper proprietors, who at present feel themselves forced by competition into publishing these effusions, will welcome a truce.

I do know that a growing number of working journalists are saying that if their employers and the governing bodies of sport will do nothing then they themselves will have to consider if the time has come when they will refuse to handle the often offensive (but highly rewarded) outpourings of player- and ex-player-writers.

Yours faithfully,

H. J. BRADLEY

Wardle's invitation to tour Australia that winter was withdrawn by MCC; but he went to Australia – to comment on the tour for the *Daily Mail*. In 1959 county players were ordered to submit for official approval all writing intended for publication on pain of banishment from English first-class cricket.

HOBBS AND HIS GHOST

From Mr Alan Ross, 11 September 1978

Editor of the *London Magazine*. Cricket correspondent of *The Observer* 1954–72 and writer on cricket for *The Times* since 1980.

Sir, Ion Trewin's reference to Jack Hobbs and his ghost(s) (7 September) reminds me what a pleasure it was to sit next to them in the press box during a Test match. During play Jack kept up a running commentary on the technical deficiencies of various batsmen which his ghost would dutifully transcribe. But Jack was a kind man and when the typescript was given back to him to check he used to screw it up and say to his ghost 'Oh, just write that X batted well and looks very promising'. I once invited the novelist Henry Green into the press box at Headingley and he was much taken at the idea of being sat next to Hobbs's 'ghost'.

Yours faithfully,
ALAN ROSS

BUT NOT THE TEST MATCH

From Mr A. G. Stevenson, 7 December 1932

I fear it must be left to the Mad Hatter for a suitable explanation, but it bewilders me to find a British station broadcasting a running commentary on American football, while it is left to a French station to carry on the same service for those who want to hear an 'all-British' Test match. I suppose there must be a reason which would be above the heads of ordinary listeners.

A. G. STEVENSON

Radio Paris *and* Poste Parisien covered the Bodyline series from the start. The BBC did not start until the second Test match.

I'LL SING YOU NINE, OH

From the Revd John Tatum, 14 July 1960

Sir, Is it really necessary for the BBC to employ nine strapping men to comment on the Test matches against South Africa?

Yours faithfully,
JOHN TATUM

CRICKET COMMENTARY

From Mrs René MacColl, 4 May 1971

Her husband, an outstanding journalist, played in one first-class match for Oxford University in 1924.

Sir, If no one more important is defending the BBC cricket commentators I must, humbly, do so.

Your correspondents who see all and know everything without help from the commentary are fortunate: I find that, either from vagaries of eyesight or TV reception, I cannot always even see the ball, and am glad to be told which way it turned, and other subtleties.

To me, and I have found to many others, one of the great pleasures of watching cricket 'live' is the accompaniment of murmured words from the wise men in the row behind. The TV commentators, I think, replace this murmur very nicely.

Perhaps Mr Marston (28 April) – who can see the scoreboard between overs – while admittedly sacrificing the music of bat on ball, could just turn down the sound.

Yours faithfully,
HERMIONE MacCOLL

CRICKET ON THE THIRD

From Mr Chaim Raphael, CBE, 15 June 1972

Historian, one-time doyen of Whitehall information officers and, under the pseudonym Jocelyn Davey, crime writer.

Sir, Third programme music lovers shouldn't push their luck. So far they have lost out to cricket commentaries only on Test match days: it might be worse. The appeal of the cricket commentary, as all folklorists know, has almost nothing to do with the occasion itself. It is an abstract art form built around the telling of tales in prescribed form, the audience knowing it all but still hanging on every word. Any action referred to is only symbolic. The drama lies not in seeing the villain slain but in the long build-up, the apparent banalities, the repetitions, the pregnant silences, a tingling sense of doom, as if Father Arlott's words were a dialogue by Ivy Compton Burnett re-written by Harold Pinter. The 'story' is as unimportant as the plot of an opera: the actual 'occasion' is no more relevant than – say – the occasion for which a Bach cantata was first composed. Those to whom this art form speaks (and we are told that they are very numerous) would surely enjoy hearing recordings of great perform- ances played over and over again, day and night, in season and out, as music lovers do. Indeed I wonder sometimes if what we hear now doesn't come out of the BBC's great record library.

Yours faithfully,
CHAIM RAPHAEL

Conflict is avoided now by broadcasting the cricket on medium wave and the music on VHF. In some parts of the country, however, Radio 3 medium wave has all the qualities of a fading echo in a drainpipe.

WHILE RAIN STOPPED PLAY

From Mr Dudley Jones, 4 August 1973

Sir, On Sunday, 22 July, rain having prevented play in the match to be televised from Nottingham, John Arlott filled in with an enchant- ing talk on the history of cricket and the photographs in the Pavilion, apparently without script or rehearsal.

In the eight days since then I have seen no mention of this in the press and I should like to pay tribute to the most astonishing display of professionalism in broadcasting since the days of Richard Dimbleby in election-night programmes.

Yours faithfully,
DUDLEY JONES

AN INVITATION TO DINNER

The Times had published a short story, 'A Last Innings: The Brigadier's Exit'.

From Sir James Barrie, OM, 30 April 1930

Playwright and novelist, best remembered for *Peter Pan*. President of the Society of Authors, 1928–37. Chancellor of Edinburgh University 1930–37. Wrote the Christmas story, 'Farewell, Miss Julie Logan', exclusively for *The Times* in 1931. Founder of the Allahakbarries CC (a corruption of *Allahakbaris*, God Help Us).

Sir, Now that May and the Australians are upon us is it permissible, for just this once, to make use of *The Times* as a means of inviting an attractive man to dinner? I don't know him but he is a Brigadier and he says in *The Times* of today that he realizes his cricketing days are over; surely this is a combination that will melt even your stubborn heart. In this hope I ask you to forward my invitation to him, and to take note that I leave it open as a guarantee of good faith.

Dear Brigadier, Though I don't know you I wish I did, and that is the only excuse I can offer for my presumption in begging you to dine with me at any time or place that is seemly to you. I have already known one brigadier, which makes me the more desirous to know another, but it is today's confession in *The Times* about your last cricket exploit that makes me long to see you sitting opposite me at a table for two. This, however, can create no similar craving in you, and so I hasten to offer you my credentials.

Though I am not a brigadier (through no fault of my own) I, too, can look back upon days when I led my men into the tented field; and to the last match of all when I performed so differently from you that ordinary civility prevents my stating at this early period of our acquaintance what I did, though it may come out at our little dinner. As cricket teaches most things and being a brigadier must teach the rest, you will, I am sure, pardon me for pointing out that on the great occasion you made a regrettable mistake in going in last. I gather indeed (reluctantly) that it was your practice to be tenth man or so, for the same reason that always made me go in first. Modesty, of course, was at the root of it in both cases but I had evidently thought the matter out more elaborately than you. You were no doubt influenced by the reflection that with a little luck you might carry out your bat, though you should have known (I say it with all deference) that when the ninth wicket falls there are always four more balls to that over. Furthermore, you were playing for the glory of the moment when you should have been thinking of posterity. No one seeing you go in last, or hearing that you go in last, or noticing in *The Times* that you went in last, will ever credit you with being a batsman, not even if you get into double figures. Now, having thought the matter out profoundly, I always as captain went in first. This did not deceive the onlookers, and still less my side, as to my prowess, but I was intentionally playing a waiting game. Readers of the local weekly seeing that I opened the innings, same as Hobbs does, took for granted that I was an accomplished bat who on this occasion happened to be 'unfortunate'. I never got into *The Times*, but I became vaguely known to its readers as a man who went in first and all the rest followed. If I had been you in your last match, instead of going in last I would have gone in first. The result of the match would have been the same, but very likely the reporters (hoodwinked) would have said it was owing to my not making my usual stand.

The things we can talk about if you will only come to dinner! The Australians, for instance, I must admit that I have a leaning to them, being such a young side and having, all the time they are batting or holding out their hands for a catch, to remember the 67 rules they have sworn not to break about wives and autographs. This puts me into an awkward position, which I shall ask your opinion of at dinner, and is briefly this. I daresay when you were a captain (I mean a real captain, not a military one) you had my experience about tossing? The opposing captain, after looking me over, always told me to toss, and he called 'The Bird', and then, whether the coin came down head or tail, he said, 'The Bird it is: we shall go in'. I often felt there was something wrong about this, but could never quite see what it was. Now do you think that, as the Australians are such a young side and have so many things to remember, I would be justified in dropping a line to Mr Woodfull, saying that the toss is very important, and putting him up to calling 'The Bird'?

Another thing, ought I to give him or Mr Hornibrook a tip about slow left-hand bowling? Mr Hornibrook I understand is their only slow left-hand bowler, and I am a slow left-hand bowler myself. I was elated to read of Mr J. C. White's success in Australia, and as soon as he came back I hurried to Lord's to see him. To my horror I discovered that he did not know what slow left-hand bowling is. I would have called it (and did so) fast left-hand bowling. You say nothing of bowling in *The Times* except that you were out first ball, so that perhaps you find all bowling alike and inclined to be fast. Now my left-hand bowling is so slow that it exasperates the batsman, who has gone through all his flourishes by the time the ball reaches the middle of the pitch. My bowling does not so much take the wickets as lie against them. If I think I have sent down a bad delivery I can pursue the ball, recapture it, and send it down again. Ought I to tell Mr Hornibrook about this, or would it be more patriotic to tell Mr White, or should they be left to go on in the old way?

Do you feel a special interest in the very young Australians? I do, especially in Master McCabe, who is so young that his schoolmaster has had to sign 34 rules not to appear on the field and take him back to school. There are also Mr Jackson and Mr Bradman. I know something that is going to happen to all three of them, besides centuries. At some period in a Test match they will be found in a dressing-room, each one drooping on a seat and murmuring in anguish: 'Oh gosh, oh gosh, why did I play forward to that ball!' Ought I to prepare them for this, or leave them looking happy with 97 on the board?

Perhaps wisest to give them no tips. A side that can leave out Macartney needs them not or is mad. Did you ever see a swallow with a sense of humour chased by dogs? It would come down close to them to tempt them, then soar, then down again and then soar again, and so round and round the lawn. That was Macartney with his bowlers. They say Jackson is such another. How splendid! I mean, Oh, dear! Such a talk we shall have if you will dine with me.

J. M. BARRIE

EPILOGUE

Because of a solar eclipse the second day of the Golden Jubilee Test match in Bombay between India and England was declared the rest day. The cricket authorities, it was reported, would not be held responsible for stopping the crowd from looking skywards and damaging their eyes.

From Mr Nicholas Butt, 21 February 1980

Sir, It seems a fitting epilogue to the memory of the British Empire that a cricket match, held to commemorate the great days of yore when the sun never set over our Sovereign's lands, should be halted by the sun suddenly vanishing from the sky.

Yours faithfully,
NICHOLAS D. BUTT

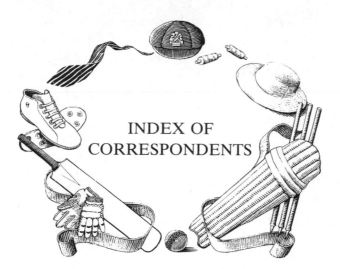

INDEX OF
CORRESPONDENTS